Glossary
of
Antique Terms

DISCOVERING ANTIQUES

THE STORY OF WORLD ANTIQUES

GREYSTONE PRESS/NEW YORK · TORONTO · LONDON

HOW TO USE THIS GLOSSARY OF ANTIQUE TERMS
This glossary incorporates several features that make it
especially useful. The italicized cross references that immediately follow many of the glossary entries direct the
reader to additional entries in volumes 19 and 20.

Below the glossary term you will find, whenever applicable, a small open box followed by the words "ALSO
SEE" and page number. This page number(s) refers to
material contained within the first 18 volumes of
DISCOVERING ANTIQUES. (Italicized numbers denote
illustrations.)

A chart is provided showing the pages contained in
each of the 18 volumes.

ART NOUVEAU POSTERS

Colored lithograph posters were first produced in France in the 1870's, but very few posters were produced in the Low Countries before the middle of the 1890's. The Belgian artist Fernand Toussaint designed this alluring Art Nouveau poster for the Café Jacquemotte about 1896. The poster was printed by the Brussels lithographer O. de Rycker, whose work was much praised for its subtlety, and who was himself the author of a book on printmaking. *For further reading see* Volume 2, pages 235-39; and Volume 19, page 2263.

BAROQUE CABINET

During the first half of the 17th century, the Flemish city of Antwerp was famous for producing luxurious cabinets mounted on stands, and pieces such as this were exported to many European countries. This cabinet's typical features include drawer fronts covered with a tortoiseshell veneer and decorated, as are the inside panels, with painted scenes from classical mythology. *For further reading see* Volume 16, pages 1948-52; and Volume 19, page 2270.

BOULTON CLOCK

Matthew Boulton (1728-1809) designed a vast number of ormolu-mounted vases and ornaments for his fashionable patrons. Fitted with a horizontal watch movement, this marble-and-ormolu piece made in 1771 represents Venus and Cupid weeping at the tomb of Adonis. It was the prototype of many allegorical timepieces produced at Boulton's London factory. *For further reading see* Volume 7, pages 860-64; and Volume 19, page 2283.

BRACKET CLOCK FACE

London was the center of English clockmaking, and the production of bracket clocks expanded rapidly there during the 17th century. The bracket clock, so called because it was originally set on a matching wall bracket, was spring-driven. These clocks made up in convenience what they lacked in accuracy—they could be easily carried from room to room by the handles on their domed tops. Illustrated is the face of a bracket clock attributed to John Martin. *For further reading see* Volume 5, pages 518-22; and Volume 19, page 2284.

CHINESE JADE

For thousands of years, Chinese craftsmen have been shaping jade into useful and ornamental objects. Today jade is still cherished as being more valuable than gold or jewels. The carp, fabled king of the fishes, and capable of turning into a dragon, represents vigor and endurance. These leaping carp, symbols of advancement, were carved in the 19th century. *For further reading see* Volume 3, pages 296-300.

COLONIAL AMERICAN SPOUT CUP

There were no silversmiths listed among the Pilgrims who sailed to Plymouth, Massachusetts in *The Mayflower*. But the men and women who made that voyage were soon followed by many others—farmers, laborers, artisans, and merchants —who helped establish new settlements that shortly grew into towns and cities very much like those they had left. Early American silver is understandably rare, confined mainly to essential pieces such as spoons, porringers, drinking vessels, and church plate. About 1700, William Cowell (1682-1736) made this spout cup, which was probably used by invalids. *For further reading see* Volume 1, pages 34-38; and Volume 19, page 2313.

COLONIAL AMERICAN SUGAR BOWL

The New World silversmith generally patterned his work after English styles, indulging in the extravagances of elaborate baroque designs at the turn of the 18th century. By 1720, the modifications of baroque elements had been introduced into American silver and were beginning to form themselves into a style distinctly their own. With an emphasis on contour, plain surfaces, and rhythmic curves, objects became basically circular with little decoration other than engraving as seen in this sugar bowl by Simeon Soumain (1685-1750). *For further reading see* Volume 1, pages 61-64; and Volume 19, page 2313.

ELIZABETHAN HELMET

The history of English armor in the 16th century is dominated by the figure of Henry VIII, who was a Renaissance monarch in the grand manner. Henry set up an armor workshop in Greenwich in 1515. The Greenwich workshop continued to flourish during the reign of Elizabeth I, because the tournament became, as never before, a court game forming part of the elaborate theatrical performances in which the aristocracy participated. Illustrated is the helmet of Sir Philip Sidney (1554-1586), the English Renaissance ideal of the perfect gentleman. *For further reading see* Volume 4, pages 430-34; and Volume 19, page 2339.

EMBOSSED TANKARD

There was a great rivalry among the lesser German princes during the 17th and 18th centuries. Nothing was more suitable for the ostentatious display they desired than silver, and because obvious splendor was what mattered, most of the silver plate produced was partly or totally gilded. This silver-gilt tankard made by Daniel Mylius in about 1700 is embossed with a banquet scene. Embossed designs were produced by hammering, stamping, or molding. *For further reading see* Volume 14, pages 1677-81; and Volume 19, page 2339.

EMBROIDERED SAMPLER

Lovingly created or dutifully executed embroideries were used in the 16th and 17th centuries primarily as a means of recording a repertoire of stitches. It was only in the late 17th and early 18th centuries that learning to read and write became of prime importance—hence the use of the alphabet and of moral verse. This embroidered sampler was made by Hannah Taylor of Newport, Rhode Island in 1774. *For further reading see* Volume 1, pages 101-103; Volume 19, page 2340; and Volume 20, page 2465.

EMPIRE BED

During the Empire period in France the bedroom furnishings were dominated by the bed. Shown here is a design for a canopied bed on a dais. The headboard and facing side have a profusion of gilt-bronze mounts on the uncarved wood, and the canopy is surmounted by a winged figure. During Napoleon's reign, swans were used in decoration in deference to the Empress Josephine. Embellishments are to be found on all furniture of the period and include such shapes as wreaths, laurel branches, ribbons, palmettes, stars, and thunderbolts, all taken directly from Greek or Roman sculpture. *For further reading see* Volume 13, pages 1528-32; and Volume 19, page 2340.

FLINT-LOCK PISTOLS

In an age of lawlessness, travelers and householders protected themselves from highwaymen and ruffians with pistols of many kinds. By the 18th century the flint-lock was in use all over the world. One advantage of the flint-lock was the simplicity of its internal mechanism; another was that there was no limit to its size. This handsome pair of flint-lock pistols was made by Wilson of London in 1668. *For further reading see* Volume 6, pages 687-90; and Volume 19, page 2350.

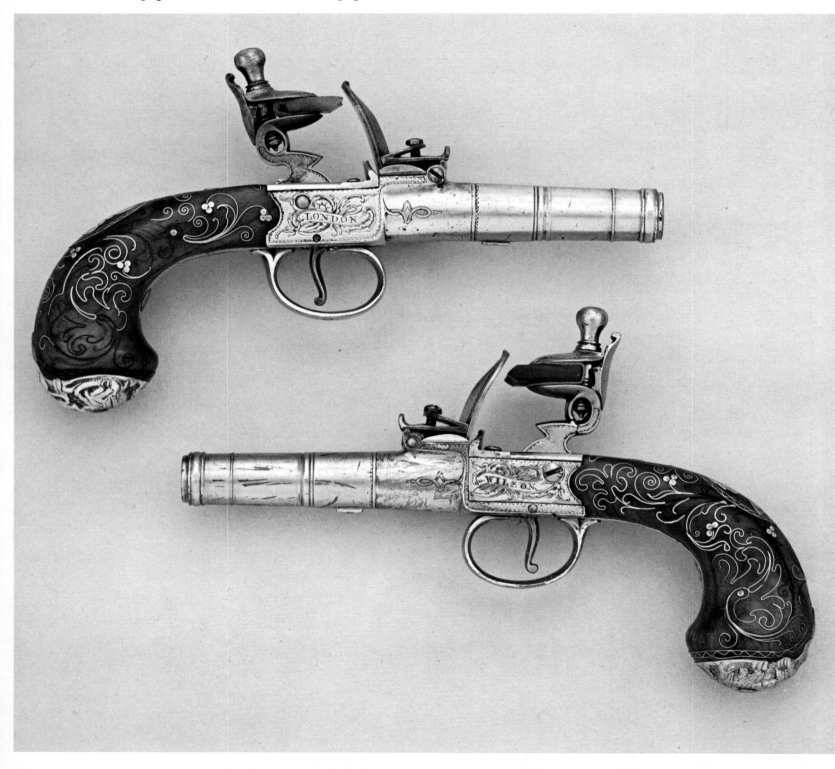

GEORGIAN BABY HOUSE

Dolls' houses were nursery toys for children, and the first houses designed specifically as toys were built near the end of the 18th century. Baby houses, on the other hand, were strictly for the amusement of adults and were in fashion from about 1700 to 1790. The baby house was furnished with miniature silver, porcelain, and furniture—all made by skilled craftsmen such as Thomas Chippendale. This baby house, made in Dorset in 1760, is modeled on an 18th-century English country house. *For further reading see* Volume 8, pages 892-96; and Volume 19, page 2359.

ICON

The great period of Russian icon painting began when Christianity reached Kiev in the 10th century, and continued to the 16th century. Early icon painters never sought originality or personal fame. They were monks content to serve within an ancient tradition. After the fall of Constantinople in 1453, a gradual change began to take place: the icons became more individualized. This can be seen in the sweetness and naivete of the *Scene from the Life of St. Nicholas* below. The St. Nicholas series is from the first half of the 16th century, and was possibly painted by an artist of the Rostov School. *For further reading see* Volume 17, pages 2027-31; and Volume 19, page 2374.

HOW TO USE THIS GLOSSARY OF ANTIQUE TERMS
This glossary incorporates several features that make it especially useful. The italicized cross references that immediately follow many of the glossary entries direct the reader to additional entries in volumes 19 and 20.

Below the glossary term you will find, whenever applicable, a small open box followed by the words "ALSO SEE" and page number. This page number(s) refers to material contained within the first 18 volumes of DISCOVERING ANTIQUES. (Italicized numbers denote illustrations.)

A chart is provided showing the pages contained in each of the 18 volumes.

Glossary of Antique Terms

ABATTANT. The French term for a "drop lid" or "fall front," as in "secrétaire à abattant" (a drop-leaf secretary). A Chippendale design is illustrated.

ACACIA. A figured wood that varies from light brown to shades of red and green, and is similar to the American locust tree. It was used as a veneering wood in France and England during the 18th century.

ACAJOU. The French word for *Mahogany.*

ACAJOU MOUCHETÉ. A fine-quality mahogany with wavelike markings and small dark spots in the grain. The wood was popular in the late Louis XVI period, and was used for tables and commodes.

ACANTHUS (AKANTHOS) LEAF. A carved or painted ornament that resembles the foliage or leaves of the acanthus. A classic design used by the Greeks and Romans, it appears in Gothic art and architecture, and was revived in the Renaissance. The acanthus leaf appears in the Corinthian and Composite capitals. The Greek design has pointed leaf edges, but the Roman version is rounder and broader with more vigorous curves. In Byzantine and Romanesque decoration, the acanthus is stiffer and less delicate. It becomes rounder and more bulbous in the early Gothic period, then becomes bizarre with long thistle-like foliage in the late Gothic. With the Renaissance, the acanthus and tendril motif reaches its highest degree of refinement and elegance.

ACCOTOIR. The French word for "arm stump." It is the wood stile that extends from the frame of the chair seat up to, and supporting, the arm of the chair. Illustrated is a 17th-century Flemish Renaissance chair. See *Arm Stump.*

ACORN. A turning that resembles the acorn (fruit of the oak tree). It was used as a finial, drop pendant, or furniture foot in the Jacobean furniture of the early 17th century in England.

ACORN CHAIR. A 17th-century Jacobean oak chair with acorn-shaped pendants decorating the cross rail of the back.

ACROTERIA. Greek for "summit" or "extremity" (acroterion is the singular form). In classic architecture, the blocks or flat pedestals at the apex and the lowest ends of a pediment. They were often used to hold carved ornaments or statues. The term is sometimes applied to the carved ornament itself, which resembled a stylized palmette leaf. See *Akroter.*

In English and American 18th-century furniture, the acroteria refers to the end blocks of the pediment top of a secretary or bookcase, or the central block in a broken pediment which might hold an urn, vase, finial, or other ornament.

ABATTANT

ROMAN   GREEK

ACANTHUS

RENAISSANCE

ROMANESQUE

ACCOTOIR

ACORN

ACROTERIA

ACROTERIA

ACT OF PARLIAMENT CLOCK. A mid-18th- to early-19th-century English hanging clock with a short trunk and a large wooden dial, without a glass cover. The clock usually was painted black and accented with gold numerals. The trunk design was varied: oblong and paneled, bulbous or fiddle-shaped. The overall measurement of these clocks varied from 3'9" to 5' tall.

ADAM BROTHERS, John (1721–1792); Robert (1728–1792); James (1730–1794); William (1739–1822). Four Scottish architect-designers who greatly influenced English interiors and furniture design during the middle and latter half of the 18th century. Robert and James were the most famous, and they designed many important buildings and interiors in a restrained, classic manner. They were very much influenced by the discoveries at Pompeii and Herculaneum, and these classic motifs appear frequently in their work: honeysuckle, swags, husks, oval paterae, flutings, wreaths of flowers festooned between rams' heads. The classic urn appears as a decoration and it was also used as a cutlery container and wine cooler. Amorini, sphinxes, and arabesques were painted on Adam furniture by such artists as Pergolesi, Zucchi, and Angelica Kauffman. The Adams also used Wedgwood medallions, which were frequently designed by John Flaxman, for inserts, and composition ornaments for bas relief ceilings and friezes. See *Adelphi* and *Composition Ornament.*

ADAM

ADAM

☐ ALSO SEE 133, 555, 610-11, 636, 638, 642, 664, 701-02, 705, 731, 752, 776-79, 784-85, 786, 825, 851-52, 854, 875, 941-42, 1389, 1451, 1898, 2074, *2089*

Carpets *608-11*
Designs *610-11, 778, 788-90, 851, 854*
Furniture *703, 705, 786-87, 799*
Houses & Interiors *582, 585, 637, 692, 775-76, 778-79, 873, 2071*

ADELPHI. Greek for "brothers." The trademark name of the Adam Brothers of England, in the latter part of the 18th century. They were architects and designers of interiors and furniture. See *Adam Brothers.*

ADELPHI

AESTHETIC MOVEMENT. A diverse 19th-century English movement on the part of artists and craftsmen, having the general purpose of reasserting aesthetic standards that were threatened by rapid industrial expansion and the spread of mass production. See *Art Nouveau; Beardsley, Aubrey; Burne-Jones, Edward; Morgan, William de; Morris, William; Pre-Raphaelite Brotherhood;* and *Webb, Philip Speakman.*

☐ ALSO SEE 1244

AFFLECK, THOMAS. One of the Philadelphia school of cabinet-makers of the mid-18th century in America. He was known for his highboys and lowboys, and chairs which were executed in the Georgian and early Chippendale styles.

☐ ALSO SEE 128

AGATA GLASS. Art glassware produced by Joseph Locke of the New England Glass Company, beginning in 1887. It is characterized by random patterns composed of brownish and purplish stains.

☐ ALSO SEE *179,* 181

AGATE WARE. Originally an 18th-century pottery produced by Wedgwood and others in England. The finish was made to resemble agate or quartz.

☐ ALSO SEE 783, 923

AGE OF MAHOGANY. The period of interior and furniture design in England lasting from approximately 1710 to 1765. Mahogany was favored by designers and clients as well, and much of the Georgian and Chippendale type of furniture was produced in this wood. Illustrated is a Chippendale mahogany sideboard table of about 1760.

AGE OF MAHOGANY

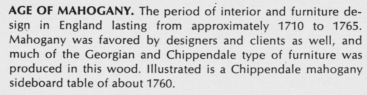

AGE OF OAK

AGE OF OAK. The period of the English Renaissance (about 1500–1660) when oak was prominently used for furniture and interior paneling, wainscoting, etc. It encompasses the Tudor, Elizabethan, Jacobean, and Cromwellian periods. Illustrated is a carved oak Elizabethan bedstead of the late 16th century.

AGE OF REVIVALS. The 19th century was essentially a time of revivals of periods and styles of the past. The Classic, Renaissance, Rococo and Gothic revivals followed and overlapped one another. See *Victorian* for the various furniture style revivals. The Conservative Club in London, here shown, was built in the early 19th century and reflected the Renaissance revival.

AGE OF SATINWOOD

AGE OF SATINWOOD. The elegant period in England from about 1765 to 1800, when the cabinetmakers and designers favored the light, delicate-toned satinwood for furniture. The Adam brothers used it extensively in their work as did Hepplewhite, Shearer, and Sheraton whose corner washstand of the late 18th century is illustrated. See *Satinwood*.

AGE OF WALNUT. The Restoration, Stuart, William and Mary, and Queen Anne periods in England, which ran from about 1660 to 1714. Walnut was the popular furniture and interior show wood of this time. A William and Mary walnut secretary is illustrated.

AGE OF WALNUT

AIGRETTE

AIGRETTE. French for "egret," a beautifully plumed bird. The term also refers to a decorative feather or plume.

AJOURÉ. A design produced by piercing holes in a definite set pattern in ceramics, wood, metal, etc. It is decoratively used today on dark parchment lampshades, the pierced design having a brilliant, jewel-like effect when the lamp is lit. See *Pierced Work*.

AKANTHOS

AKANTHOS. See *Acanthus Leaf*.

AKROTER. An ornamental finish for the apex of a gable. On ancient Greek and Roman structures, the akroter, which decorated the top angle of the pediment, was usually a variation of the palmette ornament, though griffins, figures, and other sculptured devices were used. See *Acroteria*.

AKROTER

ALABASTER. A fine-textured, compact variety of sulfate of lime or gypsum. A milky white or semitranslucent marble-like material used for ornaments and sculpture.

ALBARELLO. An Italian term for a tall, narrow-waisted majolica vessel used for the storage of drugs.

☐ ALSO SEE 1213, 1807-09, 1863, 1945, 2124-25

ALCAZAR

ALBERTOLLI, GIOCENDO (1742–1839). An Italian Neoclassic designer of ornaments who was greatly responsible for the rise and spread of the Neoclassic style in Italy.

ALCAZAR. A magnificent castle built in Seville, Spain, in the middle of the 14th century. It is noteworthy for its blend of Gothic and Moorish motifs.
☐ ALSO SEE 2116

ALCORA POTTERY. The tin-glazed earthenware produced in Spain between about 1726 and 1780 by a factory in Alcora, Valencia. The early products are deep reddish pink. Lustered pottery was produced there from 1749 and hard-paste porcelain from about 1774.
☐ ALSO SEE 2145-48

ALCOVE. A recess in a room, or a small room attached to a larger one and often designed to accommodate a bed, piano, etc. A niche for a statue, a seat. Originally a Spanish concept; a private area separated from the main room by an estrade or partition of columns. Illustrated is an Elizabethan interior of the late 16th century. An alcove is created in effect by the oriel window. The window-seat arrangement makes it a secluded area away from the main activity of the room.

ALCOVE

ALCOVE CUPBOARD. An 18th-century English corner cupboard which was often part of the paneling of the room.

ALDER, RED. An American hardwood which has a maple-like figure but can be stained to imitate mahogany or walnut. Because of its strength it is often used for plywood cores. In 18th-century England, the alder wood was used for country or provincial furniture.

ALENÇON LACE

ALENÇON LACE. A decorative fabric with a solid design outlined in cord on a sheer net ground.

ALEXANDRE. A 17th-century French painter of historical scenes who worked in the Gobelins factory during the period of Louis XIV.

ALHAMBRA. A citadel and palace, which is a masterpiece of 13th-century Spanish-Moslem art, near Granada in Spain. It was begun in 1248 and enlarged in 1279 and 1306. Much of the decoration is in tile and stamped plaster with exquisite geometric patterns, intricate arabesques, and Arabic characters intertwined. Some of the noteworthy parts of Alhambra are: Gate of Justice, Court of Alberia, Court of Lions, Hall of Ambassadors, Tower of Canaries, Court of Myrtles, Hall of Justice, and the many gardens, fountains, and panoramas. See *Stalactite* for the unusual ceiling treatment in the Wall of the Abencerrages. See also *Mauresque*.
☐ ALSO SEE *1001*, 2125

ALHAMBRA

ALHAMBRA VASES. Tall, amphora-shaped vases of luster earthenware done in the Hispano-Mauresque style. These vases were made in Valencia in about the 11th century, and were usually decorated with arabesques and Arabic inscriptions.
☐ ALSO SEE 2124

ALMERY. Originally a cupboard set into the thickness of a wall of a medieval structure. Later the almery was a cupboard which contained the portion of food set aside for the servants and pensioners. See *Ambry*.

ALMIRAH. An Anglo-Indian term for a mobile wardrobe or cupboard.

ALTO-RILIEVO. A high-relief sculpture. The carved area projects well out beyond the main surface of the panel, and appears almost full round. An early French Renaissance carved medallion is shown. See *High Relief*.

ALTO-RILIEVO

AMARANTH. A wine-red or dark violet mahogany of Central and South America, especially Brazil and the Guianas. Its brilliant, exotic coloring is apt to fade when exposed to light. Amaranth is a hard strong wood and is also called violet wood, purpleheart and bois violet. It was popular during the latter part of the 18th century in France for veneering and marquetry.

AMBERINA. American art glass patented by Joseph Locke in 1883. The pieces shade from an amber color at the base to a deep red at the top.
☐ ALSO SEE 179-80, 181

AMBOYNA. A rich golden brown to orange wood, highly mottled and marked with a "bird's-eye" figure. Adam and Hepplewhite used amboyna as a furniture veneer in the second half of the 18th century in England.

AMBRY

AMBRY. From the Latin for "chest" or "cupboard." In ecclesiastic work, the ambry or aumbry was a small cupboard used to hold the sacred vessels, books, and altar linens. It was referred to as an almery.

AMBULANTES. A French term for small, portable serving tables, tea tables, etc. This type of furniture became popular in the Louis XV period in France. See *Rafraîchissoir* and *Serviteur Fidèle*.

AMELUNG, JOHN FREDERICK. A German glassmaker who established the New Bremen Glassware Factory in Maryland in 1784. His presentation pieces are considered the finest glass produced in America in the 18th century.
☐ ALSO SEE 71, 112-14

AMERICAN EAGLE PERIOD. The early part of the Federal period in America, immediately after the Revolutionary War (late 18th, early 19th century), when the eagle was a popular motif on mirrors, and was carved on the bases of couches or other furniture. The eagle also appeared on finials, standards, and the exteriors of public buildings.

AMERICAN EMPIRE MIRROR. See *Constitution Mirror*.

AMERICAN EMPIRE PERIOD. The style of furnishing and design popular in the United States from about 1820 to 1840. It was basically the French Empire style and the later Sheraton designs interpreted in crotch-grain mahogany veneers, cherry-wood, curly maple, and maple. Duncan Phyfe was the leading designer of the period, and acanthus leaves, pineapples, cornucopias, and stencil gilding were important decorative motifs and techniques of the period.

AMORINO. The Italian word for "little love." A small cupid or cherub used as a carved or painted decoration in the Italian Renaissance period, and again in Louis XV ornament. The Adam brothers used the amorino in wall panel designs and ceiling decorations, and these elements were often painted by artists like Pergolesi and Zucchi. See *Adam Brothers.*

AMORINO

AMPHORA

AMPHORA. A large, two-handled earthenware vase of ancient Greece. It had a narrow neck and an ovoid body.

AMSTELHOEK POTTERY. The Dutch Art Nouveau ceramics produced by the Amstelhoek workshops. The decoration is neo-Greek, with designs cut out of the clay and filled in with clay of another color.
☐ ALSO SEE 241-44

ANAGLYPH

ANAGLYPHA

ANAGLYPH. A type of relief sculpture or ornament which has more depth than a bas-relief, but is not as deep as a high relief. See *Mezzo-Rilievo.*

ANAGLYPHA. A metal urn, vase, or vessel which has raised or relief ornamentation.

ANAGLYPTA. The Greek word for "raised ornament." Raised ornaments have been made in gesso and plaster compounds. They are now being produced of rag stock which is liquefied, then poured into a form and molded. The molded pieces are then applied to walls and ceilings to simulate a carved, bas-relief effect. It is, in effect, similar to the Adam brothers' 18th-century technique of "composition ornament" or "carton-pierre." Illustrated is an Adam design for a ceiling and cornice to be executed in carton-pierre for the Duke of Richmond's home Goodwood. See *Composition Ornament.*

ANAGLYPTA

ANDIRONS

ANDIRONS. A pair of upright metal supports with a transverse rod which holds the logs for burning on an open hearth. The French word for andirons is "chenets."
☐ ALSO SEE *635, 638, 666, 1079, 1359,* 1361-62, *1680, 1699*

ANDROUET, JACQUES. See *Du Cerceau.*

ANGEL BED. An 18th-century French bed with a canopy that usually extends only partially over the bed. There are no front pillars, and the canopy is supported by back pillars or posts. The side draperies continue down to the floor and are pulled back at either side of the bed. See *Lit d'Ange.*

ANIMAL COUCHANT FOOT

ANGUIER, GUILLAUME (1628–1708). One of the French painters employed by Le Brun at the Gobelins Factory. He created many painted interior decorations, and was also an architect. His brothers, François and Michel, were famous sculptors of the period.

ANIMAL COUCHANT FOOT. An antique furniture leg or support sculptured to resemble an animal lying down. This motif is found in ancient Egyptian, Greek, and Roman furniture, and was successfully revived in the Empire period in the early 19th century.

ANTHEMION. Greek for "flower." A classic Greek and Roman decoration; a conventionalized honeysuckle or palm leaf ornament which appears to radiate from a single point. It was used to enhance cyma recta moldings. It was a popular motif during the French Empire period in the early 19th century.

ANTHEMION

ANTIMACASSAR. A mid-19th-century favorite; a crocheted or knitted doily placed over the upholstered backs of chairs and sofas to prevent them from being soiled by the macassar hair dressing used by men of the Victorian era. It became a symbol of gentility and elegance, and some are still used today. Matching doilies were often used on the arm rests.

ANTIQUE. According to U.S. Customs, a work of art dating from before 1840. Antique furniture is also dated from before 1840. Carpets and rugs must have been made before 1700 to be considered antique.

ANTIQUE FINISH. A furniture-finishing technique used on wood to give it an aged look, an artificially created patina. A darker shade of paint or stain may be applied over a lighter tone, and then rubbed off; or a lighter tone may be used over the darker wood. Wood can also be "antiqued" by artificial weathering, distressing, gouging, or nicking.
☐ ALSO SEE 371-72

APPLIED MOLDING

APPLIED MOLDING. A geometric-shaped molding applied to the face of furniture to create a paneled effect. It was also called Jacobean ornament and was popular in the late-17th-century English cabinet and cupboard designs.

APPLIQUE. A French word for a wall bracket, sconce, or candelabrum applied to a wall. See *Girandole* and *Sconce.*

APPLIQUÉ. A French term for a design or motif which is cut out and sewed or pasted onto the surface of another material as a decorative trim.
☐ ALSO SEE 1930

APPLIQUE

APRON

APRON. The structural part of a table directly beneath and at right angles to the top, connecting with the legs. It is often shaped, carved, or ornamented. On a chair, it is the surface below and perpendicular to the seat. The apron, frieze, or skirt on case furniture is the perpendicular face below the lowest drawer. In architecture, the protective covering over the joint where the roof and a chimney, or a dormer, meet. It is usually made of lead or zinc.

AQUARELLE. A true watercolor painting produced by using transparent colors and water. The painting surface reflects through the applied paint, and affects the tonal quality of the painting. Water colors dry very rapidly, and the technique calls for speed and dexterity.

AQUATINT. A form of intaglio etching which produces tones. It renders a transparent effect similar to that of a watercolor. It was first used by Paul Sandby, but Goya (late 18th, early 19th century) is considered the greatest aquatinter. See *Engraving*.

☐ ALSO SEE 815-16, 992, 1139, *1140*, *1469*, 1581-83, *1582*, *1584*, 1779, *1781*, 2157-60

ARABESQUE (Arabian). The complicated ornamental designs based on plant growth fancifully intertwined with lines and geometric patterns used by the Moors, who were prohibited by their religion from representing animal forms.

In Greek, Roman, and Renaissance art, the arabesques are used in carvings, paintings, and inlaid work, combining plant and animal forms in complicated intertwining vertical patterns. Mohammedan arabesques are geometrical, and may go in any direction.

ARABESQUE

ARCA

ARCA. A Spanish term for a storage chest of the early Renaissance period.

ARCADED BACK. A furniture back with an arcade effect between the top rail and the seat. A Louis XVI motif, it was also used by Sheraton in the late 18th century in England.

ARCADED BACK

ARCADED BACK

ARCADED PANEL

ARCADED BACK

ARCADED PANEL. A popular motif in early English Renaissance woodwork. The field or face of a panel is ornamented with small piers supporting an arch form. It was also used as a decorative device on chests in the French Renaissance period. Illustrated is an old Jacobean carved chest with a guilloche band trim (17th century). Also see *Bedstead* for Jacobean headboard with arcaded panel.

ARCHAIC. Ancient, antiquated, or primitive. Some pieces of ancient Greek furniture are illustrated.

ARCHAIC

ARCHEBANE-COUCHETTE

ARCHEBANE-COUCHETTE. A 16th-century Renaissance combination coffer and bench. The slight upward projections of the sides of the chest are similar to armrests, or a headrest, should one wish to lie down.

ARCHED MOLDING. A simple, undecorated, half-round convex molding. It is sometimes used in pairs.

ARCHED MOLDING

ARCHED STRETCHER

ARCHED STRETCHER. An arc-shaped or hooped stretcher used between the legs of tables, chairs, or case furniture in the English Restoration period. It was introduced into England from Spain, where it was popular in the 17th century. See *Rising Stretchers*.

ARCHITECT'S TABLE

ARCHITECTS' PERIOD. The furniture and decoration of the 18th century in England was dominated by architects like Christopher Wren, James Gibbs, William Kent, Isaac Ware, and the Adam brothers. Their work was characterized by the use of architectural motifs and concepts in the furniture and the interior design. Marble was a popular material, and the classic orders appear over and over again. Illustrated is an Adam tripod and candleholder.

ARCHITECT'S TABLE. A combination drawing table and desk with an adjustable lid that lifted up to make an inclined surface. It was an 18th-century English innovation.

ARCUATE. Arched or archlike. Illustrated is a late-17th-century English chest. Note the arched base arrangements.

ARDABIL CARPET. The largest surviving Persian carpet of the 16th century. Its central medallion is so delicately designed that it is reminiscent of a stained-glass window.
☐ ALSO SEE 2006, *2008*

ARDISH. An East Indian form of decoration. Bits of colored glass were embedded in the ceiling or wall plaster to create a sparkling effect.

ARFE OR ARPHE. 15th- and 16th-century German silversmiths whose work influenced the Plateresco architectural ornament in Spain. See *Plateresco*.

ARCHITECTS' PERIOD

ARCUATE

ARFE

ARGAND LAMP. A lamp invented in 1783 by a Swiss named Argand. The lamp had a round wick with provisions for introducing air into and around the outside of the wick. This increased the draft, and the wick produced a much brighter flame.

ARITA WARE. The Japanese porcelain produced after the discovery of porcelaneous clay in Arita in 1616. Imari and Kakiemon are the two well-known types of decoration.
☐ ALSO SEE 322-24, 351, 375

ARKWRIGHT. A late Gothic term for a "cabinetmaker," and his products which were usually more like carpentry than cabinetry. Illustrated is a late Gothic trestle table.

ARMADIO. Italian for *Armoire*.
☐ ALSO SEE 1800-01, 1854

ARMCHAIR. A chair with armrests or arm supports as distinguished from an armless side or pull-up chair. Armchairs as we know them today were introduced into popular use in the late 17th century. See *Cacqueteuse*.

ARM PADS. The partial upholstery on the arms of a chair. They serve as padded armrests on the wood arm supports of a chair. In French they are called "manchettes."

ARKWRIGHT

ARMCHAIR

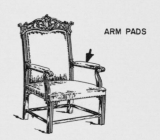

ARM PADS

ARM STUMP

ARM STUMP. The vertical element which supports the front part of a chair arm. It may be a turning, a carved device, or a shaped piece of wood. In French it is called *Accotoir*.

ARMARIUM. A bookcase or cupboard. Originally the armarium was a bookcase near the entrance to a church in the cloister of a monastery.

ARMOIRE. A French word for a large, movable clothes wardrobe or closet which was originally used to store armor. It is usually an important case piece of furniture. An 18th-century French Renaissance Régence armoire is illustrated. See *Lebrun, Charles,* for an illustration of a Louis XIV armoire. See *Garderobe.*
☐ ALSO SEE 1238, 1445

ARMOIRE

ARMOIRE À DEUX CORPS. A Renaissance cupboard of two parts. The lower part, which was formerly only a supporting base, now became enclosed and functioned as a larger cupboard, with a smaller cupboard set on top. Illustrated is a 16th-century Dutch piece. See *Beaufait.*

ARMOIRE À DEUX CORPS

ARMURE. A raised satin (nonreversible) pattern on a fabric with a rep background. The pattern usually consists of small, isolated, conventional motifs arranged to form an all-over design. Originally it was a fabric woven with a small interlaced design of chain armor, and was used during the crusades (11th and 12th centuries).

ARRAS

ARQUETA. A Spanish term for a small chest, usually to hold jewels, which was kept on a table. The box was often highly ornamented.

ARRAS. Handwoven tapestry. Woven Gothic hanging, usually with figures as part of the design, and produced in Arras, France, in the 14th and 15th centuries. They had a particular texture and often had precious metals woven into the design. Illustrated is a 15th-century French interior with arras on the wall.

ARRICCIATO. An Italian term for the second coat of plaster applied to a wall which will eventually have a fresco decoration. See *Fresco.*

ARROW. A slender shaft with a triangular pointed tip at one end and a "feathered" end at the back. It had been used as a decorative motif in the classic revival periods starting with Louis XVI and continuing through the Directoire, Empire, and Biedermeier periods.

ARROW

ARROW SPINDLE. A decorative flattened spindle with an arrow tip used in Sheraton chair backs and also in American Federal furniture. It also appeared in some American Windsor chairs.

ARROW SPINDLE

ART GLASS. In America, the decorative glassware in the Victorian style, produced between 1875 and 1900, and characterized by ornate design and technical sophistication. Art glass is also the term for Austrian and French Art Nouveau glass.
☐ ALSO SEE 178-82, 1590-93, 1731-35, *2090, 2091*

ART NOUVEAU

ART MODERNE. The "modern" concept in furniture and decoration prevalent in America during the 1920's. It was not a truly contemporary style, so much as an affectation of one.

ART NOUVEAU. The "new art" that took hold in Europe and America in the 1890's. It was a style of architecture and decoration which used flat patterns of twisting, tortured plant forms based on a naturalistic concept. It was strongly influenced by Japanese and Gothic art forms. Aubrey Beardsley, the illustrator, William Morris, the designer, and James Ensor, the Belgian painter, were prime forces in this movement. Horta and Van de Velde were outstanding names in the architecture and interiors done in this style as were Charles Rennie Mackintosh in Scotland, Hector Guimard in France, and Antonio Gaudi in Spain. See *Horta, Victor.*

☐ ALSO SEE American 193, 204-07, 210-14, 222
　　Austrian 1728
　　Belgian 225-48
　　Dutch/Netherlandish 1988
　　English 1078, 1087
　　French 1579, 1585-1610, 1612, *1613*, 1616
　　Russian 2069
　　Scottish 2099-2102

ARTESONADO

ARTISAN

ARTE POVERA (poor man's art). An 18th-century form of decorating furniture similar to the French "découpage." Engraved prints were hand-colored and applied to wooden furniture in imitation of the fine painted embellishments of the court furniture of the period. See *Découpage.*

☐ ALSO SEE 1857-58

ARTESONADO. Moorish woodwork or joinery usually made of Spanish cedar. The wood used for paneling, ceilings, and doors was often left in its natural state, but painted or gilded in important public buildings. Illustrated is a painted balustrade in the Spanish Gothic tower of Santo Domingo. It is very Moorish in design.

ARTIFACT. An article of great antiquity made by man, such as prehistoric carvings or clay objects.

ARTIFACTS

ARTISAN. A skilled craftsman in an art or a trade; a silversmith, cabinetmaker, weaver, etc. Illustrated is a silver gilt jug by a master craftsman, Johann Heinrich Mannlich, who worked in Augsburg, Germany, till 1718.

ARTS AND CRAFTS MOVEMENT. A movement that flourished in England during the latter half of the 19th century. Its goal was to bring art into the daily life of all social classes. The major figure and guiding force of the movement was William Morris, whose ideas exerted a profound and continuing effect on the development of popular taste. See *Morris, William; Pre-Raphaelite Brotherhood;* and *Webb, Philip Speakman.*

☐ ALSO SEE 210, 215-19, 244, 1075-93, 1120, 1172, 1728, 2099-2100

ARUNDEL MARBLES

ARUNDEL MARBLES. A collection of Greek and Roman statues and fragments that belonged to the Earl of Arundel in England during the reign of Charles I (first half of the 17th century). Arundel was a great patron of art, and brought the symmetrical planning of the Renaissance architecture into England. Illustrated is an artist's conception of the gallery of Arundel Marbles in the Arundel mansion which was destroyed in 1678.

☐ ALSO SEE 415, 416, 417

ARYBALLOS. A rounded or globe-shaped ancient Greek wine jar. See *Lagynos* and *Oinochoe*.

ARYBALLOS

ASH, ENGLISH. A native English wood sometimes called olive burl. It has an unusual lateral grain known as "fiddleback" or "ram's horn." It was used for country-made or provincial furniture in 18th-century England. See *Olive Wood*.

ASHBEE, CHARLES ROBERT (1863–1942). An English craftsman-designer and a disciple of William Morris and the Arts and Crafts movement. He was a "medievalist" in his preferences, and in 1888 founded the Guild and School of Handicraft. His belief was that "the constructive and decorative arts are the real backbone" of any artistic culture.
☐ ALSO SEE 1078-79, 1087-89, *1164*, 1165, *1167*, 1176, 1728

ASPIDISTRA STAND. A late-19th-century jardiniere or plant stand. It was usually a tripod made of bamboo, three to four feet in height, and reinforced near the bottom with bamboo stretchers. The open top of the stand was made to receive a flowerpot, usually containing an aspidistra plant.

ASTER CARVING. A decorative carving of three flowers which appeared on the central panel of Connecticut chests made in New England during the 17th and 18th centuries. Sunflower carvings also appeared on these chests.

ASTRAGAL

ASTRAGAL. In architecture, a small torus molding which is semicircular in section. When it is decorated with beads or olive or laurel berries, it is called a barquette, chaplet, or bed molding. In furniture, the small convex molding used on the edge of an overlapping door of a cabinet, chest, secretary, etc., to keep dust out.

ASTRAL LAMP. An early-19th-century oil lamp with the burner set on a swinging tubular arm, and positioned lower than the fuel reservoir. The lamps were made of brass, cast iron, silver plate, or china, and sometimes adorned with prisms. They were usually equipped with an Argand burner. See *Argand Lamp*.

ASYMMETRICAL. The opposite of symmetrical. Unequal. Not evenly proportioned or balanced. A favorite decorative line device of the Rococo period. See *Symmetrical*.

ASYMMETRICAL

ATAUJIA. A Spanish term for a form of Moorish inlay work somewhat like boulle work. Gold, silver, other metals, or colored enamels were set into a metal surface. See *Boulle Work*.

ATELIER. French word for a studio or workshop, usually of a designer, artist, or artisan. Illustrated is a mid-18th-century furniture atelier.

ATELIER

ATHÉNIENNE

ATLANTES

ATHÉNIENNE. A small tripod table of the Louis XVI and Empire periods. It was sometimes used as a basin stand.

ATLANTES. Full or half male figures used in place of columns to support an entablature; or in place of furniture legs to support chests, tabletops, etc. The Atlantes are male versions of the caryatids and were popular in Renaissance architecture and interior design. See *Caryatids*.

AUBUSSON. A rug with no pile. It is woven like a tapestry and the motifs are usually French floral and scroll designs. The name originally referred to a famous French tapestry works located in the town of Aubusson, dating back to the 15th century.
☐ ALSO SEE Carpets *1348*, 1350-51
   Tapestries *1306*, 1307-10, 1320

AUDRAN, CLAUDE II (1639–1686). A French painter and relief carver in bronze, gold, and silver. He painted historical murals and was employed at the Gobelins works during the reign of Louis XIV.

AUDRAN, CLAUDE III (1658–1734). A French painter, decorator, and designer who created wall murals and tapestries. He made the decorations for the Luxembourg Palace in the period of the French Régence and was a teacher of Watteau.
☐ ALSO SEE 1217, *1218*, 1222, 1377

AUDRAN, GÉRARD (1640–1703). A celebrated engraver. The third son of Claude Audran I (1597–1675).

AUDUBON, JOHN JAMES (1785-1851). An American illustrator and naturalist who settled in Louisiana and explored the hinterlands of the Mississippi and Missouri rivers, pursuing the study of wildlife. In 1820 Audubon decided to concentrate on the work of illustrating all known North American birds. His pictures are classic examples of their kind, distinguished by fine draftsmanship and decorative sense and by the quality of the engravings, done by the English firm of Robert Havell, Jr.
☐ ALSO SEE 142-44, 251

AURICULAR STYLE. A 17th-century Netherlandish decorative style originated by silversmiths and applied to the carving of furniture ornament. The motifs include fish forms, bones, and earlobes.
☐ ALSO SEE 1655, *1936*, 1939, 1951

AUSTIN, JESSE. A 19th-century English engraver who used the technique of transfer printing to decorate ceramics.
☐ ALSO SEE 902, *903*, 1021, 1072-73, 1913

AVANTURINE LACQUER. A lacquer finish which imitates the color and sparkling quality of the mineral avanturine. It was used during the 18th century in France, sometimes for lining drawers in small chests or cabinets.

AXMINSTER. A type of carpet. Originally the term referred to rugs woven at Axminster in England in the mid-18th century where Turkish carpets were imitated on special looms. The loom made possible an unlimited number of colors, designs, and patterns. The Axminster carpet is tightly woven and the pile is usually cut. The back of the weave is heavily ribbed.
☐ ALSO SEE 608-11

JOHN JAMES AUDUBON

AZULEJOS. Spanish or Portuguese wall tiles decorated with sports or bullfight scenes. They were usually done in blue on white, and these tiles were used in the late Gothic period to cover the walls in place of tapestries.

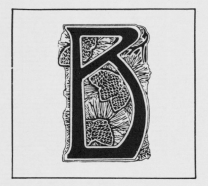

BACCARAT. Originally a French card game. The name of a fine crystal made in France and used to decorate chandeliers and sconces, and for table service.
☐ ALSO SEE 1545-49, *1578-79*, 1615

BACK POST. The two rear uprights of a chair which are continuations of the rear legs. These two elements are usually connected by a top rail and may have a split between them.

BACK STOOL. An upholstered chair without arms, or literally a stool with a back. This term was used to describe the simple seats of the 15th and 16th centuries.

BACON CUPBOARD. A late-17th-century English cupboard for holding bacon. The cupboard was usually the back of a settle which had an ornamented drawer under the seat.

BAG TABLE. A small 18th- and early-19th-century worktable which is usually distinguished by the cloth bag or pouch under the one or two drawers of the table. This design was popular in England and America. See *Pouch Table*.

BAGNELL. An early-18th-century Boston manufacturer of tall case clocks in the Queen Anne style. The works were of brass or wood and the cases of mahogany or maple.

BAGUETTE. A very small, convex bead molding. See *Barquette Molding*.

BAHUT. A large-footed chest, of the Middle Ages, which was used to hold tapestries, cushions, etc. It eventually evolved into a high cabinet. A 16th-century Italian Renaissance design is illustrated. See *Cassone*.

BAIGNEUSE. An upholstered daybed which was introduced during the French Empire period. The back piece sloped down, and it turned to form the sides; thus the arms or sides of this tublike unit angled from the back down to the front of the seat. It is similar to a *Méridienne*. See also *Grecian Sofa* and *Récamier*.

BAIL HANDLE. A handle or drawer pull which hangs downward in a reversed arch or half moon. The term usually refers to the brass drop handles introduced in the William and Mary period in England. Illustrated is a bail handle from a walnut side table of the period (late 17th century).

BACK POST

BACK STOOL

BAGUETTE

BAGUETTE

BAG TABLE

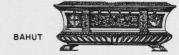

BAHUT

BAIL HANDLE

BALDACHINO

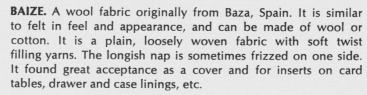

BAIZE. A wool fabric originally from Baza, Spain. It is similar to felt in feel and appearance, and can be made of wool or cotton. It is a plain, loosely woven fabric with soft twist filling yarns. The longish nap is sometimes frizzed on one side. It found great acceptance as a cover and for inserts on card tables, drawer and case linings, etc.

BALDACHINO. A canopy resting on columns, and usually used over altars or thrones in Italian Renaissance churches. The term was originally used to describe a fine, embroidered cloth of gold and silk which was used as a portable canopy over shrines, statues, etc., in processions. See *Canopy*.

BALDAQUIN BED

BALDAQUIN BED. The French term for a canopy or tester bed. A late-18th-century French or English canopy or "crown" bed. The fabric canopy extended over the bed but was attached to the wall rather than supported by pillars or bedposts extending up from the four corners of the bed frame. A Sheraton design is shown.

BALL-AND-CLAW FOOT

BALL-AND-CLAW FOOT. A bird's or dragon's claw grasping a ball or jewel. This is believed to be an old Chinese motif symbolizing world power. It appeared in Europe in Romanesque furniture and in the Dutch designs of the 17th and 18th centuries, and was popular in Georgian England in the first half of the 18th century. A carved Queen Anne chair of the early 18th century is illustrated.

BALL AND RING. A 17th-century turning used for furniture legs, decorations, etc. The turning consists of a series of ball-like turnings separated by flattened discs or rings.

BALL-AND-STEEPLE FINIAL. A wood turning popular in 18th-century American furniture. The lowest element of the finial was a sphere surmounted by a series of rings of graduated sizes which created a tapered, steeple-like element.

BALL FLOWER. A carved Gothic ornament, circular in shape, with a three-lobed or petal effect carved in the center. The ball flower was often a carved enrichment in the hollow or convex part of a molding. It was popular during the latter part of the 13th and most of the 14th century.

BALL FLOWER

BALL FOOT

BALL FOOT. A turned furniture foot of a spherical or nearly spherical shape with a narrow disc-like pad at its base. It was used extensively in 17th-century Flemish and English furniture, and is similar to a *Bun Foot*.

BALL LEG TIP

BALL LEG TIP. A small, ball-shaped foot with a cup or ferrule, usually made of brass. It fits over the end of a chair or table leg. A French directoire chair of the early 19th century, from Malmaison, is illustrated.

BALL TURNING. See *Knob Turning*.

BALLIN, CLAUDE (1614–1678). A celebrated French metal worker of the Louis XIII and Louis XIV periods. He created many vases and urns of great beauty, including this bronze vase from the park at Versailles.

BALLIN

BALLOON BACK

BALLOON BACK. The arced, or hoop-shaped chair back of the Hepplewhite period. The curved line starts in a concave form at the seat rail, then sweeps up in a bold convex arc creating a smooth loop. It is similar to the Montgolfier chair of the late 18th century in France, and was subsequently popularized during the Victorian era. See *Montgolfier Chair.*

BALUSTER

BALUSTER. A turned spindle column that supports a railing, functions as part of a balustrade, is used as a stretcher between chair legs, or is part of a chair back. It is commonly an elongated urn or vase shape. Split or half balusters were a favorite applied ornament in the English Restoration period of furniture. A baluster is also called a banister.

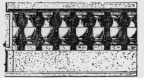

BALUSTRADE

BALUSTRADE. A continuous ornamental railing of stone, wood, or metal. It is a series of balusters topped with a rail, and serves as a decorative enclosure for balconies, terraces, stairways, etc. The balustrade was also used as a decorative motif on 18th-century English architect-designed furniture.

BAMBOO. A woody tropical plant used for furniture and ornament. Its distinctive nodular look became very popular in Europe in the 17th and 18th centuries because of the Chinese influence and the oriental or exotic quality of bamboo. Bamboo was also artificially reproduced as a wood turning in Europe and America. See *Bamboo-turned Chair.*

BAMBOO-TURNED

BAMBOO-TURNED. Wood turnings that simulate the nodular or jointed look of natural bamboo. It was favored in the late 18th and early 19th centuries for furniture.

BAMBOO-TURNED CHAIR. A refinement and development from the spool furniture of the mid-19th century in America. It was usually made of maple or other light hardwoods, and was often gilded or painted a light, fanciful color. The turnings resemble a stylized bamboo.

BANCONE. A 15th- or 16th-century Italian writing table which consisted of a flat writing surface over two paneled drawers. A recessed section, with drawers in its end, supported the two drawers. The entire piece rested on stretcher-connected pairs of legs called "running feet." See *Runner Foot.*

BANDEROLE

BANDEROLE. A ribbon-like motif, carved or painted; often the flat part of the ribbon was filled with an inscription. A Renaissance decoration. See *Ribbon Back.*

BANDING

BANDING. A narrow strip of veneer used as a border or edging on tabletops, drawer fronts, etc. It was usually made of a contrasting inlay, and was popular in 18th-century furniture.

BANDY-LEGGED. A colonial American term for bowlegged or cabriole-legged furniture of England and America in the early 18th century. Illustrated is a Queen Anne marquetry settee with bandy legs and ball-and-claw feet. Note the shell carving on the knees of the cabriole legs. See *Cabriole Chair* and *Cabriole Leg.*

BANDY-LEGGED

DISCOVERING ANTIQUES VOLUME / PAGE GUIDE	vol. contains pages	vol. contains pages	vol. contains pages	vol. contains pages
	3 • 253 to 376	7 • 749 to 872	11 • 1245 to 1368	15 • 1741 to 1864
vol. contains pages	4 • 377 to 500	8 • 873 to 996	12 • 1369 to 1492	16 • 1865 to 1988
	5 • 501 to 624	9 • 997 to 1120	13 • 1493 to 1616	17 • 1989 to 2112
1 • 1 to 128	6 • 625 to 748	10 • 1121 to 1244	14 • 1617 to 1740	18 • 2113 to 2236
2 • 129 to 252				

BANISTER BACK CHAIR

BANK

BANQUETTE

BAR TRACERY

BANJO CLOCK

BANNER SCREEN

BAR BACK

BARBER'S CHAIR

BANISTER. See *Baluster*. The term usually describes the split turned splats that make up a banister back chair of the late 17th century.

BANISTER BACK CHAIR. A late 17th-century English or American chair with split turned spindles or flat bars for the uprights of the chair back. A more elegant and polished variation on this type of chair back was popular in the Hepplewhite period (later 18th century). See *Bar Back*.

BANJO CLOCK. A 19th-century wall clock which resembles, in contour, an inverted banjo. See *Barometer Cases*.
□ ALSO SEE *109*, 111, 161

BANK. A long Gothic bench. See *Banquette*.

BANK OF ENGLAND CHAIR. A 19th-century English Regency chair. It is similar to a "tub chair" in that the arms start at the front post and sweep around the back in a continuous rising curve. The legs are usually cabriole, and the front edge of the seat is serpentine in form.

BANNER SCREEN. A fire screen. In the mid-18th century, the banner screen became a popular accessory, and the banner or shield was often made of tapestry or needlework. It was called, also, a "pole screen," since the screen moved up and down the pole. Some fire screens were made of carved mahogany in cheval form, with glass or silk screens.

BANQUETTE. The French term for an upholstered bench. Illustrated is an early-18th-century English example.

BANTAM WORK. A Dutch and English lacquering technique of the late 17th century. The design was usually etched into a black ground. This technique originated in Bantam in Dutch Java.

BAR BACK. Hepplewhite's term to describe the carved and shaped upright bars that are curved to fit the shield of an open shield back chair or sofa. A bar-backed sofa would be a three- or four-chair-back sofa.

BAR FOOT. See *Runner Foot*.

BAR TRACERY. Late Gothic tracery in which the stone was cut into bars and arranged in a variety of geometric patterns. It was a refinement from "plate tracery." See *Plate Tracery* and *Tracery*.

BARBER'S CHAIR. An 18th-century English corner or writing chair. A headrest was sometimes perched over the semicircular top rail. Sometimes the headrest was a continuous broad splat which extended up from the seat frame and was supported by the arms on either side. See *Triangle Seat*.

BARBET, T. A 17th-century late French Renaissance designer of elegant fireplaces and mantels.

BARBIZON SCHOOL. A mid-19th-century group of landscape painters who portrayed romanticized scenes of peasant life and the countryside. Included in this school of artists were Jean-François Millet, Théodore Rousseau, and Narcisse Diaz de la Peña.

BARCELONA CHAIR

BARGUEÑO

BARLEY SUGAR TURNING

BARGEBOARD

BARJIER

BARCELONA CHAIR. A late-17th-century and early-18th-century ladder-back type of chair of Spain. The top cross-slat was usually greatly enlarged and elaborately carved. The stretchers were ornamented with carved rosettes and chiseled grooves.

BARGEBOARD. The decorative woodwork that covers the joint between a gable end and the roof material of a pitched roof. The bargeboard appears under an overhanging gable. It was highly ornamented with jigsaw and cutout wood lacework at the end of the 19th and early 20th centuries.

BARGUEÑO. A Spanish cabinet and desk with a drop lid. It was introduced during the Plateresco period (16th and 17th centuries). The unit was a movable piece with the interior subdivided into many drawers and compartments. Bargueños were originally made of walnut, and later they were made in mahogany. The drop-lid front was either elaborately carved or inlaid with lacy pierced metal mounts, velvet panels, nacre, etc. The hardware was often very large, elaborate, and gilded.
☐ ALSO SEE 2135-36

BARJIER or BARJEER. Hepplewhite's term for an armchair or bergère. See *Bergère*.

BARLEY SUGAR TURNING. A spiral turning that resembles a twisted rope. It was much used in the mid- and late-17th century for furniture legs and stretchers. Illustrated is an upholstered chair of the Cromwellian period (mid-17th century in England).

BAROMETER CASES. In the 18th century, these were usually elegant mahogany cases banded with satinwood or boxwood and topped with a broken or swan's neck pediment. The dial was often surmounted by a circular mirror in a reeded frame. The "banjo" type was formed by a wide circular dial topped by a bulbous upper part. Adam and Chippendale designed many beautiful cases for this popular household accessory.

BAROQUE. French for "bizarre," "ugly," or "fantastic"; or from the Portuguese "barroco," which means a large irregular pearl. The Baroque period was a union of architecture, painting, and sculpture in the 17th and 18th centuries, to create an overwhelming and direct appeal to the senses of the beholder. It was a blend of illusionism, light and color, and movement with a new approach to classic art. The period is characterized by large-scale, bold details, sweeping curves, and a wealth of ornament. It was a period of religious emotionalism, and Bernini was one of the great architects of the period. The furniture and decoration of the Louis XIV period is also termed "baroque." Illustrated is the façade of the Church of SS. Vincent and Anastasia in Rome designed by Martino Longhi, another great designer in the baroque style. See *Bernini, Gian Lorenzo;* and *Borromini, Francesco.*
☐ ALSO SEE Austrian 253-78, 1652
   English 438, 446-55, 462-92, 501-05, 508-36, 544-52, 572-75
   French 1203-58, 1259-84, 1334, 1361, 1412, 1414
   German 264-71, 1641-66, 1686-87
   Italian 1821-46, 1852-53, 1857, 1860, 1864, 1879-1904
   Netherlandish 451-55, 1952, 1957-85

BAROQUE

BARQUETTE MOLDING

BARREL CHAIR

BAS-RELIEF

BARQUETTE MOLDING. A small semi-circular molding ornamented with beads or olive berries. See *Astragal*.

BARRED DOOR. Glass cabinet, secretary, and bookcase doors with wood fretwork. Because of the high cost of glass, the small precious pieces were set into the intricate, cutout, lacy wood framework. Illustrated is a Chippendale mahogany bookcase of about 1760. See *Fretwork*.

BARREL CHAIR. A semicircular chair, which is usually upholstered. It resembles a cylinder which has been cut in half vertically. An early-19th-century English Regency chair is illustrated.

BARRY, SIR CHARLES (1795–1860). An architect of the Classic Revival school in England in the early 19th century. He traveled in Egypt, Greece, and Italy, and introduced into England the fashion of "astylar" façades. By omitting the columns, pilasters, and porticoes from the fronts of his buildings, Barry more truly emulated the Renaissance look. Among his noted works are: the Reform Club in London based on the Farnese Palace, the Travellers' Club in London inspired by the Pandolfini Palace in Florence, Bridgewater House in London, and the Houses of Parliament in London in conjunction with *Augustus Welby Pugin*.

☐ ALSO SEE 943, 969, 990, *999*, 1000, 1907

BARTÉLEMY, JEAN SIMON. An 18th-century French painter and decorator of the Louis XVI period. He created a famous series of panels for Marie Antoinette's boudoir entitled "Love Assisting at the Toilet of Grace."

BARUM WARE. The English art pottery produced by C. H. Brannam, of particularly high quality during the period from 1879 to 1890.

☐ ALSO SEE *1092*, 1093

BAS-RELIEF. French for "low relief." A form of sculpture in which the design is only slightly raised up from the background. It is also known as "basso relievoo" in Italian. Illustrated are bas-relief panels by Jean Goujon for the Fountain of Innocents, 1549.

BASALT. A dark green or brown stone with columnar strata which was used in Egyptian statues, like the statue of a lion carved in green basalt, here illustrated. It became a favored material in the Empire period because of the "Egyptian" quality and its rich, strong coloring.

BASALT

BASALT WARE. A black porcelain pottery invented by Josiah Wedgwood in 18th-century England.

☐ ALSO SEE *782-83*, 785, 825

BASEBOARD. The horizontal board placed at the bottom of the wall and resting directly on the floor. It is usually trimmed with moldings. Illustrated is a wall area designed by Gilles Marie Oppenords, who introduced the Rococo style in France in the latter first half of the 18th century.

BARRED DOOR

SIR CHARLES BARRY

BASEBOARD

BASIN STANDS

BASKETWEAVE

BASSES

BASIN STANDS. Small Chippendale and Hepplewhite 18th-century washstands which were designed to hold minute handbasins.

BASKET STAND. A late-18th-century two-tiered worktable. The tiers were surrounded by galleries composed of small turnings or spindles, and the entire unit rested on a tripod base. It was similar to a Canterbury and a dumbwaiter. Sheraton designed many such tables.

BASKETWEAVE. A textile which is woven with large similar-sized warps and wefts. The weft crosses over alternate warp threads, creating an effect like that of a woven reed basket. This type of weave is used to make homespun and monk's cloth. An inlay technique that simulates the woven quality of a basket.

BASSES. The lower part of 17th-century English and French beds. The word is also used to describe the elaborate fabric treatments used to cover the basses. The fabric treatment was similar to what is today called the "dust ruffle." Illustrated is a state bed from Hampton Court Palace (late-17th-century England).

BASSET TABLE. A Queen Anne-style gaming table for the playing of five-handed basset, a popular 18th-century card game.

BASSO RELIEVO. Low-relief carving. See *Bas-Relief*.

BATAVIAN WARE. A type of 18th-century Leeds pottery. The surface was covered with brown slip, except for panels onto which painted designs were added.
☐ ALSO SEE 760

BAT'S WING BRASSES. An early American hardware design which resembles a conventionalized silhouette of a bat's wing outstretched. The design was used on handle plates and escutcheons.

BATTERSEA ENAMEL. The enameled copper articles made at York House in the Battersea district of London. The Battersea enamel firm produced small personal articles such as snuffboxes, patch boxes, and watch cases.
☐ ALSO SEE 592, *651-55*

BAXTER, THOMAS (1782-1821). One of the outstanding English porcelain decorators of his period. His decorations, which include figures, flowers, and landscapes, generally reflect the prevailing neoclassical trend and are highly detailed and carefully finished. Part of his reputation rests on his successful handling of feathers and shells, which were popular motifs of the period.
☐ ALSO SEE 948, *967*

BAXTER PRINTS. The prints produced by George Baxter (1804-1867), who revived the art of color printing with a new process making use of oil inks. This method made it possible to obtain unprecedentedly brilliant colors and elaborate detail. Baxter's works are mainly small portraits and biblical and historical scenes.
☐ ALSO SEE 999, 1072-73, 1142, 1145, 1844, *1845*, 1913

BAYEUX TAPESTRY

BEAD

AUBREY BEARDSLEY

BEAU BRUMMEL

BEAUFAIT

BAYEUX TAPESTRY. A French Romanesque embroidered tapestry commemorating the victory of the Normans in England.

BEAD. A small cylindrical molding that may be carved to resemble a continuous string of pearls or beads. An *Astragal*.

BEAD AND REEL. A decorative, half-round or bead molding with alternating circular and elongated oval shapes enriching the surface of the molding.

BEAD FLUSH. A small, almost circular applied molding that runs completely around a panel.

BEARDSLEY, AUBREY. An English illustrator and "high priest" of the "Art Nouveau" period of decoration in the 1890's. He is principally known for his work in the *Yellow Book,* 1894, and his illustrations for Oscar Wilde's *Salome.* Beardsley's designs influenced the interior and furniture designs of the time. See *Art Nouveau.*
☐ ALSO SEE 213-14, 239, *1160,* 1161

BEAR'S-PAW FOOT. A decorative furniture foot used by the French and English designers in the late 17th and early 18th centuries. It is a carved representation of a furry paw, sometimes combined with a ball. This furniture foot was occasionally used on Chippendale-type designs.

BEAU BRUMMEL. An early-19th-century Englishman's dressing table with adjustable mirrors, drawers, shelves, candlestands, etc. It was named after the famous dandy of the time of George IV. Sheraton designed several units of this type.

BEAUFAIT. The original spelling of "buffet." Illustrated is a 16th-century French buffet or cupboard. See *Buffet.*

BEAUVAIS. An art factory that specialized in textiles and tapestries, and was begun in France during the reign of Louis XIV. Boucher, during the period of Louis XV, designed many tapestries for the Beauvais looms, including the "Story of Psyche." Toward the end of the 18th century, Beauvais started to produce pile rugs. The most popular motifs used at Beauvais were love scenes and pastorals done in soft pastel colors. A Louis XV fauteuil covered in a Beauvais fabric is illustrated. See *Canapé* and *Causeuse* for other examples.
☐ ALSO SEE Tapestries 1306-10, 1552
  Carpets 1351

BED CHAIR. An early-18th-century Dutch innovation. It was an armed chair with a back that let down and a hidden leg that unfolded to support the lowered back. The legs and the lowered arms came together to make the center firm. The front rail was hinged so that the entire seat and back unit could come over and down. Often these "chairs" were made of nut wood or maple inlaid with tulipwood and styled with bandy (cabriole) legs and Dutch feet.

BED MOLDING. A small molding, or series of moldings, placed under a projection, as under the corona of a cornice. Illustrated is a late-17th-century cornice molding designed by William Penn.

BEAD AND REEL

BEAD FLUSH

BEAR'S-PAW FOOT

BEAUVAIS

BED MOLDING

BED STEPS

BEDROOM CHAIR

BED STEPS. An 18th-century English and American device used for getting in and out of high beds. The steps were often incorporated into other pieces of bedroom furniture, sometimes with a chamber pot container. Illustrated is a Sheraton bed step unit which converts into a stool with an upholstered top when not in use.

BED STOCK. The actual supporting framework of certain 16th-century beds in England and on the Continent. The front posts or pillars that supported the wood tester or canopy stood free of the bed proper, and the bedstock supported the bedding. Similar to the current "bed frame."

BEDROOM CHAIR. A light frame side chair, intended for use in a bedroom. Sheraton designed this type of chair at the end of the 18th and start of the 19th centuries. Often the chair frame was made of beech, stained or japanned, and equipped with a rush seat.

BEDSIDE CUPBOARD. A small bedside unit, which usually contained a chamber pot. It was also called a "pot cupboard." An 18th-century design.

BEDSTEAD. The supporting framework of a bed. Illustrated is an early-17th-century Jacobean oak bedstead with an arcaded head panel.

BEDSTEAD

BELL AND TRUMPET. See *Bell Turning.*

BELL SEAT. A Queen Anne chair seat with a rounded front (early-18th-century England).

BELL TURNING. A conventionalized bell-shaped turning that was popular during the William and Mary period. The turnings were used for furniture legs and pedestal supports (late 17th century).

BELL SEAT

BELLARMINES. Also called Greybeards, the 16th-century stoneware pieces from Cologne, made with bearded masks that were likened to the face of the Italian Cardinal Robert Bellarmine.
□ ALSO SEE 1628

BELLEEK. The porcelain ware from Belleek, Ireland, similar in appearance to Parian marble. Belleek made its appearance in the mid-19th century. It has a natural ivory-colored body that was often covered with a delicately tinted luster glaze.

BELLFLOWER ORNAMENT. A popular 18th-century carved motif used as a furniture and interiors enrichment. The decoration is based on conventionalized bell-shaped flowers or catkins, used in a continuous chain or swag or in graduated sizes as a pendant. It is similar to the "husk" design. See *Husk Ornament.*

BELLFLOWER ORNAMENT

BELLOWS. A blowing device used to create a blast of air when it is contracted, or its area is collapsed. It is often highly decorated, carved, or embellished and used as a fireplace accessory. Illustrated is a 16th-century Venetian bellows.

BELLOWS

BENCH

BELTER, JOHN HENRY (? -1865). A popular New York cabinet and furniture maker of the mid-19th century. He originated and worked with laminated plywood over 100 years ago. Belter's Victorian rococo designs were constructed mainly in rosewood, oak, and walnut. His furniture usually had heavily carved and curved frames, roll moldings, and naturalistic flower details.
☐ ALSO SEE *154*, 156-57

BENCH. A long stool or rectangular seating device. It is often backless or with a low back. See *Carreau* illustration.

BENCH TABLE. See *Settles*.

BENDED BACK CHAIR. See *Fiddleback Chair* and *Spoon Back*. This name is sometimes mistakenly given to a Hogarth chair because of its vase-shaped splat.
☐ ALSO SEE 482, 535

BENEMAN, GUILLAUME. An 18th- and early-19th-century French master ébéniste (cabinetmaker) for Louis XVI. He worked for Marie Antoinette at St. Cloud and later executed Percier's designs in the Empire style. Beneman's style was severely classic, and more in keeping with the Empire look. He used mahogany and elaborate gilt bronze mountings to enrich his designs.
☐ ALSO SEE 1459-60, 1505, 1520, 1529

GUILLAUME BENEMAN

BENJAMIN, ASHER (1773–1845). American publisher of handbooks for the guidance of carpenters and builders. He was greatly responsible for the generally high level of architecture and building during the Federal period.

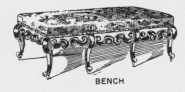
BENTWOOD FURNITURE

BENTWOOD FURNITURE. Furniture which has been made of wood that has been softened by steaming and then molded into curving forms. The term is particularly used to describe the furniture made in this manner by the Austrian, Michael Thonet, beginning in 1857. Modern contour furniture such as that created by Eames and Aalto is made in a similar fashion.
☐ ALSO SEE 187, 1721-25

BENTWOOD ROCKER. A typical rocking chair made by Thonet (at the end of the 19th century). It has swirling bentwood arms, back, and supports. A scrolly C- and S-shape decorated unit.

BERAIN, JEAN (1636–1711). A great French designer and decorator of the Louis XIV period. He designed furniture, tapestries, wood and metal accessories, and wall panels. Berain's style ranged from the Louis XIII tradition, through the chinoiserie, up to the elegance of the Régence. He is especially noted for his arabesque forms and the designs he created for Boulle's inlay technique. See *Boulle Work* and *Maître-Ébéniste*.
☐ ALSO SEE 480, 487-88, 536, 1193, *1216*, 1217, 1225, 1254, *1256-57* 1277, 1284, 1308, *1309*, 1339, 1401, 1652, 1830

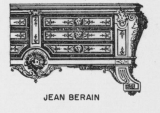
JEAN BERAIN

BERGAMA RUGS. The hand-knotted wool rugs from the Turkish town of Bergama (ancient Pergamum). Also known as Bergamo, Bergamot, or Bergamee rugs, they are made with the Ghiordes knot that distinguishes Turkish from Persian rugs. Bergamas are characterized by rich red tones, a long pile, and intricate geometric, floral, or arabesque designs. They are usually small, often of prayer-rug size.

BERGÈRE

BERGÈRE. An all-upholstered low armchair that usually has an exposed wood frame and enclosed sides. The upholstered arms are shorter than the length of the seat, and a soft loose pillow rests on a fabric-covered seat platform. It was introduced in the Louis XV period and was also popular in the Louis XVI period. Variations of the bergère are still produced today.
☐ ALSO SEE 1317, 1319, 1320, 1875

BERGERIES. A popular 18th-century rural scenic design in France and England. Pastoral landscapes were peopled with rustics or elegant gentlepeople dressed as farmers and shepherdesses. Paintings were made in this style, and the popular toile de Jouy prints featured bergerie designs. See *Toile de Jouy*.

BERLIN PORCELAIN. The hard-paste porcelain manufactured in Berlin, Germany. The early tableware of Berlin was decorated with relief and trellis work; by the last quarter of the 18th century neoclassical fashions prevailed.

BERLIN WORK. A form of embroidery popular in 19th-century England. Heavy worsted wool in brilliant colors was used in coverings for cushions, stools, screens, and chairs.
☐ ALSO SEE 54, *55*

BERNINI, GIAN (GIOVANNI) LORENZO (1598–1680). A great Italian architect and sculptor. The roots of his style were in Michelangelo, Caravaggio, and the classic forms. He used many materials together to achieve an exciting and emotional response from the viewer. Bernini did much work in and around St. Peter's and the Vatican in Rome, as well as suggested, but unused, plans for the east colonnade of the Louvre for Louis XIV. See *Baroque*.
☐ ALSO SEE 414, 442, 1412, 1823-24, 1826-27, *1846, 1852,*
   1853, 1854, 1860

BEWICK, THOMAS (1753–1828). An Englishman, considered to be the "Father of Modern Wood Engravings," who introduced white line engraving. See *Engraving*.
☐ ALSO SEE 710

BIBELOTS. The French term for "trinkets" or "knickknacks"; small art objects such as paintings, sculptures, snuffboxes, etc., created for personal use or as decorations. Illustrated is a gold box presented by the Empress Maria Theresa to Duke Charles of Lorraine in the latter part of the 18th century. The gold work was done by the jeweler, Franz Mach; the miniatures were painted by Antonio Bencini. See *Objet d'Art*.

BIBELOT

BIBERON. A Spanish ceramic drinking vessel with multiple spouts.
☐ ALSO SEE 2126, *2127*

BIBLE BOX

BIBLE BOX. A 17th-century carved box which contained the family Bible. The box was later made with a hinged sloping lid, which when closed served as a reading stand. The interior was sometimes fitted with compartments and small shelves. The desk was evolved from this piece of furniture. An oak piece of the early 17th century (Jacobean period) is illustrated.
☐ ALSO SEE 22, 420

BIBLIOTHÈQUE

BIBLIOTHÈQUE. A French term for a large bookcase or book press. Illustrated is a 19th-century bookcase by Wright and Mansfield made of juniper wood, and decorated with columns and moldings of ebony. Wedgwood plaques are set into the wood panels.

BIEDERMEIER. A German furniture and decoration style (1815–1848). An unaristocratic, clear and simple style, mainly Empire and classic in line but rendered "homey" and "bourgeois" with painted details in black and gold made to simulate carving. The furniture was made largely of fruitwoods and mahogany, and was characterized by arches, pediments, columns, simple escutcheons, burl woods, lyres, plumes, wreathes and rounded-back chairs. The name was derived from "Papa Biedermeier," a comic symbol of homey comfort, well-being, and middle-class contentment. Biedermeier furniture was also made in Austria and Northern Italy.

☐ ALSO SEE 156, 261, 959, 1579, 1691-95, 1708-16

BIEDERMEIER

BIENNAIS, MARTIN GUILLAUME. A noted 19th-century French Empire metalworker.

☐ ALSO SEE 1501, 1615

BILBAO MIRROR. A late-18th-century mirror, often with a marble or marble and wood frame. A pair of slender columns usually appears on the vertical ends of the frame. The name was derived from Bilbao or Bilboa, where it originated.

BILLET. A type of ornament which was peculiarly Norman and consisted of short cylinders and blocks. In 18th-century furniture, inlaid billet banding was used for decoration around cabinet drawers and doors.

BILLET

BIRDCAGE CLOCK. A late-17th-century English clock made of brass with exposed pendulum and weights. An openwork clock.

BIRDCAGE SUPPORT. In early American furniture, term for the double block construction which makes it possible for a tilt-top table to rotate and tilt. It resembles the outline of a cage. In other styles (e.g. 18th-century English) the birdcage was made of turned colonnettes.

BISCUIT. See *Bisque.*

BISCUIT TUFTING. A method of tying back upholstery and padding to create plump, square tufts on chair backs and seats. Buttons are usually sewn back taut in a regular square or diamond pattern. The excess padding is forced into the center of each square or diamond making a small "pillow." A late-19th-century German Victorian sofa is illustrated.

BISCUIT TUFTING

BISQUE. Pottery that has been fired once and has no glaze or a very thin one. At this point it is dull in color and is tan or red terra-cotta, depending upon the clay used. Bisque also refers to white, unglazed porcelain figurines and groups, made at Sèvres in France during the latter part of the 18th century.

☐ ALSO SEE Chinese 351
English 649, 848, *849, 850,* 947, 974
French *1290,* 1293, 1382-83, 1411-15, *1472,* 1473-74, 1543-44
German 1706
Russian 2059
Spanish 2156

BLACKWORK

BLACKWORK. A particular technique of embroidery of the English Tudor period (16th century). Patterns were picked out in black and silver thread, and these designs inspired many printed lining and wallpapers of the period. Blackwork embroidery became popular again at the end of the Elizabethan reign (after 1603).

BLACKAMOOR. A decorative statue of a Negro, usually in gaudy oriental-type costume. This was a popular motif during the Italian Renaissance and was revived in the Victorian period. The blackamoor was used as a pedestal for tables and torch holders.

BLANC DE CHINE. A white porcelain made in China, notably in Tê-hua in Fukien Province, southern China, and usually referred to by its French name. The colors in *blanc de chine* vary from creamy white to bluish white, and the pieces have a thick and lustrous glaze. The finest examples of *blanc de chine* are those pieces created in the 17th and 18th centuries, during the Ming Dynasty.
☐ ALSO SEE *286,* 288, 314, 563, 631, 1249, 1267, 1649

BLANC DE PLOMB. French for "lead white." Some Louis XV furniture which was ordered for the Petit Trianon was originally painted white, but dust and time grayed the furniture down to "gris Trianon," a soft gray color.

BLANKET CHESTS. 17th- and 18th-century American chests which had a lidded section on top, and sometimes one or two drawers below. These units were eventually replaced by the lowboy, the highboy, and the chest of drawers. See *Connecticut Chest* and *Hadley Chest.*

BLANKET CHEST

BLOCK FOOT. A cube-shaped foot usually used with a square, untapered leg. When the foot is tapered it is called a spade, taper, or therm foot. The block foot is also known as the "Marlborough foot," and was used by Chippendale in mid-18th-century England.

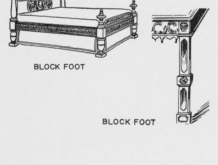

BLOCK FOOT

BLOCK FOOT

BLOCK PRINT. Fabric printed by hand, using carved wooden blocks or plates. The dye is rolled over the raised pattern on the block which is then pressed down, usually under pressure, on the fabric. If a two-color design is desired, two separate blocks are used. This technique was also used on early wallpapers and gilded leather tapestries.

BLOCKFRONT. A furniture front which is divided vertically into alternating convex and concave panels. The center panel is recessed between the two advancing side panels. This design is especially associated with John Goddard and the Newport School of 18th-century American furniture for chests, secretaries, highboys, etc. It is also called a "tub front."
☐ ALSO SEE 88, *90*

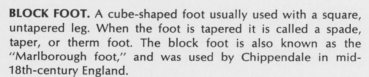

BLOCKFRONT

BLONDEL, JACQUES FRANÇOIS (1705–1774). A French architect of the period of Louis XV. He designed in a refined Rococo manner, and his interior "boiserie" is recognized by its straight, elegant, lined panels with Rococo corners and cornices.

JACQUES FRANÇOIS BLONDEL

BLUE-AND-WHITE CHINESE PORCELAIN. Porcelain decorated with designs in cobalt under a single glaze. According to recorded evidence, blue-and-white porcelain was first produced during the Sung Dynasty (920-1279), but did not become popular until the rule of the Ming (1368-1644). During the K'ang Hsi period (1662-1722) of the Ch'ing Dynasty, excellent blue-and-white ware was produced.

☐ ALSO SEE 76, 79, 285, *286, 311, 313,* 332-34, 350, 719, 1246

BLUNDERBUSS. A short musket with a widening barrel of brass or steel, widely used in Colonial America.

☐ ALSO SEE *30,* 31, *690, 1044,* 1046, 2151, *2152*

BLUNT ARROW LEG. The leg of an 18th-century American Windsor chair which ends in a ball-like tip. It resembles a spent practice arrow.

BOAT BED. A bed placed in an alcove with only one long side showing. A low, massive piece popular in the French Empire and Restoration periods, and in American furniture contemporary with these periods. It is similar to the gondola or sleigh bed. The boat bed was boat-shaped and often made in light-colored woods with contrasting wood marquetry. It was often raised up on a massive, steplike base.

BOBBIN TURNING. Turned legs and stretchers with bobbin-like swellings that were popular in the early 17th century. In the late-18th-century Windsor chair, this type of turning was sometimes used for stretchers. A Jacobean child's chair with bobbin-turned legs is shown.

BOBBIN TURNING

BOBÈCHE

BOBÈCHE. A socket with a wide rim for a candle or an electric bulb. The bobèche was originally used to catch the wax drippings, but today it is used as a decorative top to a candlestick, or as a device to hook prisms and crystals onto.

BOFET

BOFET. An early form of "buffet" from the original "beaufait." A 15th-century French buffet is illustrated. See *Crédence.*

BOFFET or BOFFET CHAIR. A three-legged, triangular, Scandinavian chair which was produced till the end of the 16th century. They were usually made of turnings and had carved ornaments.

BOFFRAND, GERMAIN. An 18th-century French decorator of the Louis XV style. He decorated the Palais Soubise for the Prince de Soubise.

BOIS DE FIL. See *Fil de Bois.*

BOISERIE. The carved woodwork and paneling of 17th- and 18th-century French interiors. The woodwork was often picked out in gilt, and could become quite elaborate as shown in this Louis XV salon. A gilt console table and mirror are to the left of the door. Note the trumeau (overdoor paneling with painting).

BOISERIE

BOLECTION MOLDINGS. A series of rounded moldings which project far beyond the panel or wall to which they are applied. A bolection panel (illustrated) projects from the wall surface, as opposed to a "sunk" panel.

BOLECTION PANEL

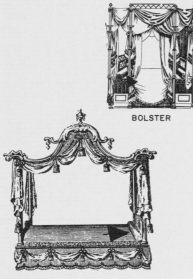

BOLSTER

BOLSTER

BOLSTER. A long, usually cylindrical, stuffed pillow or cushion that was popular in the late 18th century and early 19th century. A bolster is also an oversized pillow or back rest and may be wedge-shaped or rectangular.

BOLSTER ARM. A fat, rounded or cylindrical upholstered arm on a chair or couch which resembles a bolster. A 19th-century term

BOMBAY FURNITURE. Furniture manufactured in India after 1740 (the breakdown of the Mogul Empire). The furniture is a conglomeration of French and Portuguese styles and forms which are overlaid with typically elaborate and minute Indian carving. All this was brought about by the influence of France, England, and Holland on India at this time.
☐ ALSO SEE *1747*, 1748

BOMBÉ. French for "convex," "arched," or "humpbacked." A swelling or flowing curve, a surface which swells outward and then recedes. This line appears in commodes and chests at the end of the Louis XIV and the Régence periods in France, and reaches its height during the Louis XV or Rococo period. The term bombé often is given to the swollen, overblown commodes of this period. The bombé type of cabinet or drawer furniture also appears in the Venetian Rococo and Chippendale's French style. It is typical of a French base.
☐ ALSO SEE 663, 1271, 1278, 1858

BONADER. Wall hangings, painted on paper or canvas, of peasant subjects. These designs were created by Swedes and Swedish Americans in the 18th century.

BONE CHINA. An English porcelain that contains calcined bone ash mixed into the clay body. Invented at Bow, England, in the mid-18th century, bone china is softer than true porcelain but is easier to make; it is considerably more durable than soft-paste porcelain.

BONHEUR DU JOUR. A small upright lady's desk with a cabinet top and drawers. The desk area was usually covered with a let-down front. A small cupboard or bookshelf was often at the rear. A popular design of the Louis XVI period. Illustrated is a design by Reisener (late-18th-century France), which has been enriched with Sèvres plaques.
☐ ALSO SEE *1531*

BONNET TOP. A rounded, bonnet-shaped top portion of a highboy, secretary, etc. The bonnet top was prevalent in 17th-century and early-18th-century English and American furniture. Also called a "hooded top."
☐ ALSO SEE 57, 59, 60, 86, 88, 89

BONNETIÈRE. An 18th-century French cabinet, usually designed tall, narrow, and deep enough to hold hats and bonnets.

BOOK BOX. See *Bible Box*.

BOOK TABLE. A rectangular, circular, or hexagonal pedestal with either exposed shelves on all sides, or doors to cover the bookshelves. An 18th-century innovation similar to the pote or pole table.

BOMBÉ

BOMBÉ

BONHEUR DU JOUR

BONNET TOP

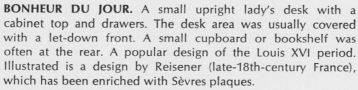

BOOKCASE. In the late 17th and early 18th centuries, the book-case resembled the china cabinet of the times. In the mid- and late 18th century, the bookcase took on a new importance, and usually was made in two parts: a glazed door section on top of a closed cupboard. The area below had either additional shelves or drawers. The bookcase top was sometimes used with a writing desk below. Illustrated is a Sheraton-type design.

BOOKCASE

☐ ALSO SEE American (19th century) *217*
Austrian (19th century) 1919
English (17th century) *448,* 450
(18th century) 574-75, *672, 788, 857,* 873-77
(19th century) 960
French (18th century) 1226/ (19th century) 1532

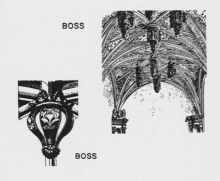

BORNE

BORNE. A round or oval type of French sofa with a separating pillar or rail in the center which serves as a back. This seating device was popular in public areas during the Victorian period. These upholstered poufs were usually located in the center of a room, and people sat all around on the circular seat.

BORROMINI, FRANCESCO (1599–1667). An Italian Baroque architect who introduced the undulating façade in the San Carlo alle Quattro Fontane, in Rome. It was the prototype for late-18th-century English "crescents," and appears in altered forms in contemporary architecture. The curved façade presents a picture of animation, movement, and organic growth. These same properties are seen in his St. Ivo's in Rome. It is an interpretation of inner and outer space. Illustrated is the front façade of his Church of the Four Fountains in Rome (1667).

FRANCESCO BORROMINI

☐ ALSO SEE 1823-24, *1825,* 1826, 1854, 1860

BOSS. The projecting ornament which is placed at the inter-sections of moldings or beams. Angel heads, flowers, or foliage and animal heads are common motifs. In Gothic architecture it is often a hanging, ornamental pendant at the meeting of ribs in vaults. See *Cul-de-Lampe.* On furniture, the boss is a small oval or semicircular applied ornament found in 17th- and 18th-century English and American designs.

BOSS

BOSS

BOSSE, ABRAHAM (1611–1678). A French designer, painter, and architect under Louis XIII and Louis XIV.
☐ ALSO SEE *1256,* 1654

BOSTON ROCKER. A rocking chair, or a chair on curved sup-ports. The wooden seat usually curves upward in the rear and dips down in front. The chair is often spindle-backed and ornamented with a painted design on the wide top rail. An early-19th-century American design.

BÖTTGER, JOHANN FRIEDRICH (1682-1719). A German al-chemist who was instrumental in developing the first true Euro-pean porcelain. In 1708 Bottger succeeded in producing white unglazed ware, and the next year he developed a satisfactory glaze. The Meissen factory was established in 1710 to manu-facture the porcelain.
☐ ALSO SEE 261, 275, 1646-50, 1962, 2056

BOSTON ROCKER

BOTTLE END GLAZING. Glazing of cabinet doors in the 18th century that resembled bottle bottoms leaded together. A bull's-eye effect in a circular glass disk. See *Crown Glass.*

FRANÇOIS BOUCHER

BOTTLE TURNING. A Dutch wood turning which resembles a bottle and appears in William and Mary furniture in late-17th-century England.

BOUCHER, FRANÇOIS (1703–1770). The French boudoir artist and decorator of the 18th century. Boucher specialized in voluptuous and sensuous art, and he was a favorite designer of Mme de Pompadour. In 1765, he was made Court Painter to Louis XV. Among his assignments was that of inspector at the Gobelins Factory, where his style influenced the products, including the use of an oval medallion or frame which appears on tapestries and on Sèvres china.

☐ ALSO SEE 736, 1299, *1300, 1306,* 1307-08, *1311, 1318, 1335,* 1350, *1374-76, 1375,* 1377, 1413, 1469, *1470*

BOUCHER, JULES FRANÇOIS (1736–1781). The son of François Boucher, the famous painter of the Louis XV period. He painted and designed panels and interiors in keeping with the Louis XVI style. One of his chair designs is illustrated here.

BOUCHON. A cork pad covered with baize on one side and leather on the other. It was used, in the 18th century, as a removable cover over the marble top of a bouillotte table. The bouchon filled the space between the actual tabletop and the surrounding brass gallery, thus creating a level surface.

JULES FRANÇOIS BOUCHER

BOUILLOTTE LAMP. A late-18th-century candlestick-like lamp. It often was a three- or four-armed candlestick set into a brass galleried base, and a shallow shade, usually metal, covered and protected the flames of the candles. A decorative brass handle finial above the shade made the lamp portable. The bouillotte lamp was originally associated with the small galleried tables they were set upon. See *Bouillotte Table.*

BOUILLOTTE TABLE. An 18th-century French small circular gaming table, with a brass or bronze gallery edge. The table usually had two small drawers as well as a pair of candle slides set into the apron, below the marble top. Originally used for playing bouillotte, a card game. See *Bouchon.*

BOUILLOTE TABLE

BOULARD, JEAN-BAPTISTE (1725-1789). A cabinetmaker (ébéniste) and sculptor of the Louis XVI period, noted for the magnificent bed he created for Fontainebleau.

JEAN-BAPTISTE BOULARD

BOULLE, ANDRÉ CHARLES (1642–1732). Boulle and his four sons were French master cabinetmakers. Boulle designed rich, ornate, massive pieces often in his own particular veneer technique of tortoiseshell and brass inlay. In 1672, Boulle was appointed head cabinetmaker to Louis XIV. Besides his noted "Boulle-work" technique, he also designed the parquet floors, mirrored walls, and inlaid panels in the Versailles Palace. His designs were opulent and full of scrolls, flowers, and arabesques. See *Boulle Work.* An armoire of Boulle work is used to illustrate *Le Brun, Charles* and *Le Roi Soleil.* Here, illustrated, is a Boulle commode in the Régence style.

☐ ALSO SEE 481, 1205, 1224-28, *1259,* 1261, *1262,* 1276-78, 1284, 1330-31, 1354, 1361

ANDRÉ CHARLES BOULLE

BOULLE, P. Born in France in 1619. The "head cabinetmaker" to Louis XIII. See *Ébéniste.*

DISCOVERING ANTIQUES VOLUME / PAGE GUIDE	vol.	contains pages	vol.	contains pages	vol.	contains pages	vol.	contains pages
	3 •	253 *to* 376	*7* •	749 *to* 872	*11* •	1245 *to* 1368	*15* •	1741 *to* 1864
vol. contains pages	*4* •	377 *to* 500	*8* •	873 *to* 996	*12* •	1369 *to* 1492	*16* •	1865 *to* 1988
1 • 1 *to* 128	*5* •	501 *to* 624	*9* •	997 *to* 1120	*13* •	1493 *to* 1616	*17* •	1989 *to* 2112
2 • 129 *to* 252	*6* •	625 *to* 748	*10* •	1121 *to* 1244	*14* •	1617 *to* 1740	*18* •	2113 *to* 2236

BOULLE WORK

BOULLE WORK. The special inlay technique of Charles André Boulle, using tortoiseshell and German silver, brass, or pewter. A sheet of metal (usually brass) and a sheet of tortoiseshell were glued together, and the design was cut out of both pieces at the same time. The piece of brass which dropped out during the cutting could then be set into the tortoiseshell, making a decorative inlay (première partie); or the tortoiseshell could be used to fill in the brass sheet (contrepartie). Boulle work is most often associated with the Louis XIV and Régence periods. See *Première Partie, Contrepartie,* and *Marquetry.*

BOULTON, MATTHEW (1728-1809). An English manufacturer, artist, engineer, and industrial leader. He helped develop James Watt's steam engine.
☐ ALSO SEE *696,* 699, *853,* 854, 860-64, 872, 982, 2067

BOURBON PERIOD. The classic part of the French Renaissance period, dating from about 1589 to 1730. It encompasses the reigns of Henry IV, Louis XIII, and Louis XIV, and the Régence. Illustrated is a chair of the Louis XIII period done in the Italian style.

BOURBON PERIOD

BOURBON STYLE. See *Charles X Period.*

BOUTET, NICHOLAS-NOEL (1761-1833). A French gunsmith, maker of official presentation weapons under the First Empire. These *armes de luxe* are considered among the finest examples of European firearms craftsmanship.
☐ ALSO SEE 1441, 1523-27, 1616

BOW BACK

BOW BACK. An 18th-century Windsor-type chair with the hooped or curved back continuing in its sweep down to the arms or chair seat.

BOW FRONT. A convex or "swell front" shape, typical of mid- and late-18th-century chests, commodes, sideboards, etc. This curved line was especially popular in England with Adam (illustrated) and Hepplewhite.

BOW FRONT

BOW PORCELAIN. The soft-paste porcelain manufactured in London around the middle of the 18th century. The Bow factory was probably the largest center of porcelain production in England during this period. It was chiefly known for tableware in white, imitating Chinese models and decorated with Oriental designs in underglaze blue.
☐ ALSO SEE 588-92, 739-40, *741,* 1575

BOW TOP

BOW TOP. The top rail of a chair with an unbroken curve between the uprights.

BOX BED. A bed enclosed on three sides, or sometimes a bed that folds up against the wall. In the French Gothic period, the open side was usually draped or shuttered to provide privacy and keep out the drafts. Illustrated is a 10th-century Anglo-Saxon box bed showing drapery used as a screen. See *Lit Clos.*

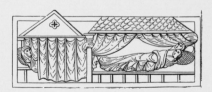

BOX BED

BOX SETTLE. A chest or box that functions as a seat and has a hinged lid that serves as the cover to the chest-seat. This piece was popular in the early English Renaissance (Tudor and Elizabethan), and also in 17th- and 18th-century Provincial American furniture.

BOX SETTLE

BOX SETTLE

BOX STRETCHER

BRACED BACK

BOXWOOD

BOX STOOL. A Renaissance simple seating unit which consisted of a box with a flat hinged top that functioned as a seat.

BOX STRETCHER. A square or rectangular reinforcement at the furniture base, created by the turned or squared stretchers which are found between the legs of a table, chair, or cabinet.

BOXWOOD. A very dense, light-colored, and grained West Indian wood which is used almost entirely for inlays and small decorative articles. During the 16th century it was used as an inlay wood on walnut and oak, and in the late 18th century it was used for border edge work on satinwood pieces.

BRACED BACK. A term applied to a Windsor-type chair whose back is reinforced by two spindles projecting up from an extension behind the seat up to the chair rail. It is also called a "fiddle-braced back."

BRACKET

BRACKET. In furniture, a shaped support between the leg and the seat of a chair, or the leg and the top of a table. A bracket is also a decorative wall-hung shelf and a sconce or wall fixture. In architecture, a supporting element which projects from a wall or pier at a right angle, and helps to carry the weight of a beam or architectural member, like a cornice, etc.

BRACKET CANDLESTICK. A sconce or applique. A decorative wall-hung unit with a candlestick projecting forward. Illustrated is a late French Renaissance design from the Versailles Palace. See *Bronze-Doré* illustration.

BRACKET CANDLESTICK

BRACKET CLOCK. A small clock designed to be set on a projecting wall-hung bracket. It is a shelf clock rather than a wall-hung clock.

BRACKET CORNICE. An ornamental cornice supported by a series of brackets. An interior wooden version of a corbel table. See *Corbel Table*.

BRACKET CLOCK

BRACKET CORNICE

BRACKET FOOT. In cabinetry, a popular furniture leg in 18th-century English and American designs. The foot has a straight corner edge and a curved inner edge. In English furniture the leg is usually longer than it is high. It is also called a "console leg."

BRADLEY, WILL (1868-1962). An American graphics designer and typographer whose posters are among the best American examples of the Art Nouveau style.
☐ ALSO SEE *212*, 213-14

BRADSHAW, GEORGE AND WILLIAM. Cabinetmakers and upholsterers of the mid-Georgian period in England.

BRADY, MATTHEW (1823-1896). An American pioneer photographer. Authorized to accompany Union armies during the Civil War, he compiled an extensive photographic record of the war, including pictures taken on the battlefield.
☐ ALSO SEE *147*, 148, 175

BRACKET FOOT

BRAGANZA TOE. See *Spanish Scroll Foot*.

BRAGANZA TOE

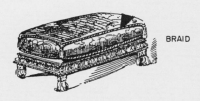

BRAID

BREAKFAST TABLE

BRIDAL CHEST

BRATTISHING

BREAKFRONT

BREWSTER CHAIR

BRAID. A narrow strip made by intertwining several strands of silk, cotton, or other fabric. It is used as a trimming, a binding, or a finishing edge. A late-17th-century footstool is illustrated. The pillow is edged with braid.

BRASSES. Hardware or decorative handles, escutcheons, hinges, etc., made of brass.

BRATTISHING. A cresting like an ornamented or pierced parapet. A decorative leaf design used as a cresting device on the top of English Tudor screens or paneling. The motif is also called "Tudor Flower."

BREAKFAST TABLE. Chippendale's name for an elegant, small, four-legged table, often with a pierced gallery and fretwork trim. The table sometimes had a long narrow drawer.

BREAKFRONT. A case piece of furniture whose front is formed on two or more planes; the central portion is either advanced or recessed from the two ends. It is particularly descriptive of bookcases, cabinets, and secretaries of the 18th century in England and America.

BREGUET, ABRAHAM LOUIS (1747-1823). A French clock- and watchmaker under Louis XVI, designer of a mechanism for winding and synchronizing watches. His designs embodied a remarkable combination of elegance and scientific utility.
☐ ALSO SEE 1419-22, 1492

BREWSTER CHAIR. An early New England chair with turned spindles and a rush seat. Named after Elder Brewster. The chair usually has a double row of spindles on the back. The Brewster chair resembles Provincial Jacobean furniture and is similar to the *Carver Chair,* which, however, has horizontal rails on the back.
☐ ALSO SEE 20-21

BRIDAL CHEST. A "hope chest." A chest to hold linens, dower, etc. See *Cassone, Connecticut Chest.* A 17th-century Flemish Renaissance bridal chest is illustrated.

BRIGGLE, ARTUS VAN (d. 1904). An American Art Nouveau potter known for his use of matte glaze and his practice of deriving decorative elements from basic form.
☐ ALSO SEE 193-94, 207

BRISÉ FAN. An ivory fan, popular in 18th-century England, composed entirely of sticks and guards, with up to thirty pierced or painted blades linked around the perimeter with ribbons.
☐ ALSO SEE 567-69, 1333

BRISEAUX, CHARLES ÉTIENNE (1680–1754). A French rococo architect and interior designer. In his boiserie panels he preferred straight sides with a moderate amount of curvature on top.

BRISTOL CERAMICS. The pottery and porcelain made in Bristol, England. A pottery center from the Middle Ages, Bristol produced much notable ceramic ware in the 18th century, including tin-glazed earthenware, known as delftware, and both soft-paste and hard-paste porcelain. Some Bristol hard-paste ware is highly elaborate, decorated with flowers and foliage in leaf-green or deep red.
☐ ALSO SEE 678, 740, 742, 809, 846-50

BRISTOL GLASS. The decorated and colored glassware produced in Bristol in the 17th and 18th centuries. Deep blue, purple, and green glass were used, and such articles as snuffboxes, candlesticks, decanters, and finger bowls were produced. Opaque white glass (milk glass) was used in the manufacture of vases, beakers, jars, and similar articles, with enameled decoration, in imitation of porcelain.

☐ ALSO SEE 904

BRITISH COLONIAL. The Georgian-like furniture, interiors, and architecture of the 18th century which was developed by the English Colonials in the West Indies, India, and parts of Africa. Basically, it resembled the styles current and popular in England at that time, but it was interpreted by native craftsmen in native woods with native details.

BROCADE. From Low Latin for "to embroider" or "to stitch." Originally a fabric of silk, satin, or velvet, variegated with gold and silver or raised and enriched with flowers, foliage, and other ornaments. The fabric resembles embroidery and is woven on a jacquard loom. The threads do not appear on the surface, but are carried across the width of the fabric on the reverse side. Brocade is much favored for drapery and upholstery in period and traditional rooms.

BROCATELLE

BROCATELLE. Originally an imitation of Italian tooled leather. A heavy fabric which resembles damask, with a pattern which appears to be embossed. The pattern is usually a silk weave against a twill background. Also, a calcareous stone or marble having a yellow ground, flecked with white, gray, and red.

BROCATELLE VIOLETTE. The most French of all marbles. A stone or marble with a purplish undertone. It is usually richly grained and patterned.

BROCHÉ. A silk or satin ground fabric similar to brocade, with small raised floral designs made to resemble embroidery. Threads that are not used on the surface design are carried only across the width of the design on the reverse side, rather than across the entire reverse side as on brocade.

BROKEN ARCH

BROKEN ARCH. A curved or elliptical arch which is not completed or joined at its apex. The open center section is sometimes filled with a decorative device like an urn, finial, etc. Illustrated is a late-17th-century English china cabinet.

BROKEN ENTABLATURE

BROKEN ENTABLATURE. An entablature which does not make a straight even projection out from the building but projects farther over the individual pilasters and columns than it does in the spaces between the pilasters or columns. Illustrated is the Renaissance Church of St. Zachary (S. Zaccaria) in Venice.

BROKEN FRONT. Like a blockfront or breakfront. The front of the piece of furniture is made up of different planes. The center section may project beyond the side sections. Illustrated is an English bookcase of the first half of the 18th century, with a typical classical pediment on top. See *Blockfront* and *Breakfront*.

BROKEN FRONT

BROKEN PEDIMENT

BROKEN PEDIMENT. An architectural element frequently used on 18th-century English furniture on top cabinets, bookcases, curio cabinets, corner cabinets, highboys, etc. The triangular pediment is interrupted at its apex (crest), and the open central area is often filled with a decorative urn, finial, shell, etc.

BRONZE. A metal originally used for sculpture in ancient Greece and Rome as well as China and Africa. It is a compound made up mainly of copper and tin. As bronze ages and reacts with chemicals, it takes on a greenish tint and matte surface called a patina. A patina can be chemically induced. Bronze has been a popular material for cast sculpture since the 15th century. Illustrated is an ancient Pompeiian bronze figure.
□ ALSO SEE *146*, *338*, *339*, *1183*, 1226, *1421*, 1518-22, 1554-58, 1566-69, *1604-06*, *1610*, 1619, *1621*, 1630-33, 1651, 1816-18, 1846, 1861

BRONZE

BRONZE D'AMEUBLEMENT. Bronze furniture mounts: handles, escutcheons, drawer pulls, etc.

BRONZE-DORÉ. Gilded bronze. Illustrated is an 18th-century Italian bracket candlestick with a bronze-doré finish. See *Ormolu or Ormoulu.*

BRONZE-DORÉ

BRONZE FURNITURE. A type of metal furniture used by the ancient Greeks and Romans. The designs could be light and open since the material was so strong. In the late Renaissance and Empire period, bronze was again popular for tables, bases, etc., as well as for mounts, hardware, and trim. Illustrated is a Roman bronze lampstand found in Pompeii. See *Bronze-Doré* and *Ormolu or Ormoulu.*

BRONZE FURNITURE

BRUGES TAPESTRY. The Flemish tapestry hangings produced in the weaving center of Bruges from the beginning of the 16th century. A famous example is the *History of San Anatoile,* a set of fourteen pieces.
□ ALSO SEE 2119, 2122

BRUSSELS CARPET. The carpeting named for the city of Brussels, Belgium, where it was originated. Woven with a three- or four-ply worsted yarn, it has uncut loops drawn up to appear on the surface and form a pattern. The backing is usually of cotton. Because of its deep, uncut pile, Brussels carpet is noted for its long wear. This type of carpeting was introduced at the important English carpet-manufacturing town of Wilton in the mid-18th century.
□ ALSO SEE 609

BUCKET ARMCHAIR. A Regency-type armchair, similar to the spoon-back chair. The arms rise in a scroll from the middle of the side rails of the seat, then form a continuous curve to create the top rail of the chair. The rounded back is often filled in with caning.

BUCKET ARMCHAIR

BUCKLAND, WILLIAM. An indentured servant, who was brought to America from England in 1755 to serve as "architect" for Gunston Hall near Mount Vernon in Virginia. This was the home of George Mason, author of the Virginia Declaration of Rights. Buckland was responsible for the exterior and interior woodwork, which is considered some of the most beautiful of the period. He also designed the exquisite woodwork in Edward Lloyd's house in Annapolis, Maryland. The Hammond-Harwood House in Annapolis is considered to be his masterpiece.

BUEN RETIRO. See *Capo di Monte.*

BUFFET

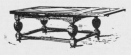

BULBOUS FORM

BULL'S-EYE MIRROR

BUREAU BOOKCASE

BUFFET. A cupboard or sideboard. A side table sometimes with cupboards or shelves. Early Renaissance buffets resembled medieval cupboards and were supported on bases. The entire piece was usually decorated with columns, medallions, and arabesques. Illustrated is a late-18th-century Sheraton-type buffet. See *Crédence, Desserte.*
☐ ALSO SEE 20, *1192*, 1194, 1446, 1916, 1948, *1952*

BUILT-IN FURNITURE. Elements of furnishing like cabinets, seats, beds, chests, etc., built into the room as an integral part of the interior architecture, a practice that dates from the earliest interiors.

BULBOUS FORM. A heavy, melon-like wood turning that was popular for furniture supports and bases during the early Renaissance in Holland, England, France, and Italy.

BULFINCH, CHARLES (1763-1844). The first professional American architect, from Boston. Based on the English Georgian style of architecture, Bulfinch's buildings are characterized by elegant proportions and the use of the classical orders. Among his important works are the Statehouse in Boston, the University Hall at Harvard University, and the Massachusetts General Hospital. Bulfinch was responsible for the completion of the Capitol building in Washington, D. C.
☐ ALSO SEE 68, 132, 779

BULL'S-EYE. A circular or oval window. A circular distortion in the center of a disk of crown glass. In French it is known as "oeil-de-boeuf." See *Crown Glass.*

BULL'S-EYE MIRROR. A round mirror, often with a convex or concave glass set in an ornamental frame. The period of decoration of the frame may vary. A *Girandole.*

BUN FOOT or Flemish Foot. A furniture support resembling a slightly flattened ball. A device used on Flemish, late French Renaissance, and English late-17th-century furniture.

BUREAU. Originally the fabric used to cover a table which was to be used as a writing surface. A desk. A writing table with "pigeonhole" compartments. According to Sheraton, in late-18th-century England, "a common desk with drawers." In the 19th and 20th centuries in America, a chest of drawers used in a bedroom, or part of a bedroom suite.
☐ ALSO SEE *90, 537*, 1194, 1238, 1389, 1607, *1608-09, 1858*

BUREAU À CYLINDRE. French for a rolltop desk. Illustrated is the famous "bureau du roi" (king's desk) begun by Oeben and completed by Riesener. It was created for Louis XV. The rolltop desk is also called a bureau à rideau.

BUREAU À PENTE. French for a folding, slant-lid desk.

BUREAU À RIDEAU. French for a rolltop desk. See *Bureau A Cylindre.*

BUREAU BOOKCASE. A desk with a cabinet over the writing surface, according to Chippendale in 18th-century England.

BUREAU COMMODE. A Louis XIV large writing table with drawers.

BUILT-IN FURNITURE

BULL'S-EYE

BUN FOOT

BUREAU À CYLINDRE

BUREAU

BUREAU EN DOS D'ÂNE. A Louis XV drop leaf desk which took its name from its contour. The top of the desk resembled "the back of an ass." The desk stood on tall cabriole legs with a slant-fronted unit on top. The slanted front dropped down to become a flat horizontal writing surface.

BUREAU MAZARIN. A French writing table which became popular during the 17th century. There were drawers on each side of a central kneehole, and the entire table was supported on two sets of four legs.
☐ ALSO SEE 1226, *1237*, 1238

BUREAU PLAT

BUREAU PLAT. A flat writing table or desk. Illustrated is a Louis XVI design by Riesener with decorative hardware and mounts by Gouthière.
☐ ALSO SEE 1226, 1238, *1276*, 1278-79, 1389, 1531

BUREAU TABLE. A kneehole table designed by Goddard of Newport, Rhode Island, in the late 18th century.

BURGOMASTER CHAIR. See *Roundabout Chair.*

BURGUNDIAN STYLE. A provincial French Renaissance furniture style of the Rhone Valley area. It was typically Renaissance in its use of architectural elements, and it was noteworthy for its massive construction and high-relief carved decoration. The two-tiered cupboard (cabinet à deux corps) with carved human or allegorical figures is typical of the Burgundian style. Hughes Sambin of Dijon, the architect, is believed to be largely responsible for the Burgundian style. In 1570 he published a book of engraved ornaments, architectural details, etc. See *Cabinet à Deux Corps* and *Sambin, Hughes.*

BURGUNDIAN STYLE

BURMANTOFTS FAIENCE. A very durable, decorative earthenware produced in England by Messrs. Wilson & Company after 1880. It was a popular decorative material for the interiors and exteriors of houses and for art pottery. The shapes of Burmantofts faience are derived from Oriental or Persian models.
☐ ALSO SEE *1168-69*, *1171*, 1172

BURMESE GLASS. An American art glass patented in 1885 by the Mount Washington Glass Company. This opaque glass contained gold and uranium oxides which produced a color gradually shading from delicate pale yellow to rich pink.
☐ ALSO SEE *180*, 181, *182*

BURNE-JONES, SIR EDWARD COLEY (1833-1898). An English painter and decorative artist. His most important decorative works are stained-glass designs, characterized by the use of mannered figures against leafy backgrounds. An outstanding example of his work in this field is the St. Frideswide window (1859) in Christ Church Cathedral, Oxford.
☐ ALSO SEE 210, 214, 1058, 1078, *1079*, 1080, 1082-84, *1085*, *1158*, 1159, 1608, 1917, 1919

BURO TABLE. An early American (early-18th-century) term for a bureau on legs, and usually with drawers.

BURR. A veneer made from transverse slices of the gnarled roots of the walnut tree. It was popular in England from the mid-17th century up to the beginning of the 18th century.

BUST

BURSLEM, STAFFORDSHIRE. The first North Staffordshire town to become an important center of pottery manufacture and trade. Manufacturers included Josiah Wedgwood and the Malkin, Lockett and Warburton families.
☐ ALSO SEE 923-27

BUST. A painting or sculpture of a human head and shoulders, sometimes including the chest or breast. It may be used as a freestanding piece of art, or incorporated into an architectural niche, set on a pedestal, or used as a finial in a broken pediment. Illustrated is a section of a room designed by James Paine in the mid-18th century.
☐ ALSO SEE 825, 926, *927*, 1064, 1383, 1485-86, *1606, 1674*

BUTCHER FURNITURE. The heavy, architectural furniture produced by Duncan Phyfe after 1825. The massive scrolled quality that was characteristic of the Second or Late Empire in France. See *Second Empire or Late Empire*.

BUTTERFLY TABLE. A Colonial American drop-leaf table with a broad butterfly winglike bracket to support the raised leaf.
☐ ALSO SEE 22

BYZANTINE

BYZANTINE. Of the Byzantine Empire. Constantinople became the seat of the Roman Empire A.D. 330, and after the fall of Rome in 476, it became the seat of the Byzantine Empire until 1453. The name "Byzantine" is derived from the original town of Byzantium, which was renamed Constantinople by the Emperor Constantine. The Byzantine designs that flourished here were composed of Roman forms overlaid with Near Eastern motifs. The dome on pendentives, the rounded arch, and mosaics play an important part in Byzantine architecture. Some of the Byzantine motifs still appear in Russian and south European decoration.
☐ ALSO SEE 1796

BUTTERFLY TABLE

CABBAGE ROSE. A flamboyant, overblown rose which was extremely popular in the Victorian era. It appeared on carpets, wallpapers, silks, and chintzes and was often combined with lovers' bowknots, doves, and cherubs.

CABINET. A general term from the French for "closet" or "receptacle." In current usage it refers to case furniture with shelves and/or cabinets, or a wooden or metal housing to contain an object (i.e., television set, radio, etc.). Illustrated is a 16th-century French Renaissance cabinet with carved door panels and architectural motifs.
☐ ALSO SEE American *20*, 106, *107*, 216, *217*
   Austrian *1729*
   Chinese *292*
   English 421, 448, *480*, 483, *732, 856, 990*, 1009, 1088-89, *1129-30*, 1917-18
   French *1192*, 1194, *1203, 1204, 1225*, 1226, *1410, 1444, 1610*
   German 1622, 1624, *1653, 1655, 1711*
   Indian *1745*
   Irish *1776*
   Italian 1798, 1829, *1831*, 1854

CABINET

Japanese *291, 292,* 293
Netherlandish 2134, 1948, 1950, *1951*
Scottish *2100,* 2102
Spanish 2135-36

CABINET À DEUX CORPS. A late-16th-century Renaissance case piece consisting of one cupboard or cabinet set upon a second and usually larger one. These pieces were often carved and ornamented with classic motifs, and had caryatid supports at the corners of the lower unit.

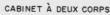

CABINET À DEUX CORPS

CABINET SECRÉTAIRE. A desk with a cabinet set above the writing surface. The cabinet may have glass, metal, grill, or wood-paneled doors. It was a popular innovation of the 18th century in France and England. A late-18th-century Sheraton design is illustrated.

CABINET SECRÉTAIRE

CABINET VITRINE. A cabinet with glass doors. It is essentially a display case, and was first popularized in the late 17th and early 18th centuries when porcelain from China was rare and precious, and collections of "China" articles were worthy of display. Illustrated is an 18th-century Hepplewhite design which served as a bookcase.

CABINET VITRINE

CABOCHON. From the French "caboche," a hobnail. A round or oval convex polished stone. A concave or convex shape used as a carved enrichment on furniture, sometimes surrounded by ornamental leaf carvings. It is found in Rococo furniture and decoration.
☐ ALSO SEE *1013*, 1752, 1936

CABOCHON

CABRIOLE CHAIR. A small chair with a stuffed back made in the mid-18th century in England during Chippendale's French period. The term is an anglicized version of "cabriolet." It does not refer to the cabriole leg. See *Cabriolet* and *French Chair.*

CABRIOLE CHAIR

CABRIOLE LEG. From the French "cabrioler," to leap or caper. A conventionalized animal's leg with knee, ankle, and foot adapted in wood as a furniture leg or support. It was greatly favored by designers in the late 17th and 18th centuries for French, English, Flemish, and Italian furniture. The leg curves outward toward the knee and then in and downward to the ankle, making an S shape. In the Queen Anne period the knee was often adorned with a shell. In early Georgian furniture the leg was often embellished with lion masks, satyr masks, or cabochon and leaf ornaments. The cabriole leg reached the height of refinement and ornateness during the Louis XV Rococo period, and is considered a typical Rococo feature. An 18th-century Chippendale secretary is illustrated.

CABRIOLE LEG

CABRIOLET. A small Louis XV chair with a concave back and cabriole legs. In the Louis XVI period the name was applied to a chair with an oval, hollowed-out back. The top of the frame was often decorated with a ribbon and bow as though the chair back were a frame ready to be hung. Illustrated is a Hepplewhite adaptation. A cabriolet is also a two-wheeled, one-horse carriage. See *Cabriole Chair.*
☐ ALSO SEE *1316*, 1319, 1340

CACHE-POT. A pot made of china, wood, or porcelain, and used as a container or flowerpot holder.
☐ ALSO SEE 466, 1575

CABRIOLET

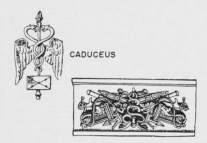

CADUCEUS

CACQUETEUSE

CACQUETEUSE (chaise de femme). An early French Renaissance conversational chair with a high, narrow back and curved arms. A prototype for the smaller scaled "fauteuils" of the 18th century. A 16th-century French Renaissance chair is shown. See *Caqueteuse* and *Caquetoire*.

CADUCEUS. A wand or staff, entwined by two serpents, and surmounted by a pair of wings. In classic times it was the symbol for Mercury's rod. The motif appears in carved and painted form in the Louis XVI period. The caduceus is currently the symbol of the medical profession.

CAFFIERI, JACQUES (1678-1755). A French cabinetmaker and sculptor in bronze, who worked for Louis XV in the Rococo style.
☐ ALSO SEE 1361, 1362, *1388*, 1411

JACQUES CAFFIERI

CAFFIERI, JEAN-JACQUES (1725-1792). A great French artisan of ormolu metal mounts for Rococo furniture. He worked under Jean-François Oeben, the "king's cabinetmaker" to Louis XV.
☐ ALSO SEE 92

PHILIPPE CAFFIERI

CAFFIERI, PHILIPPE (c. 1634–1716). A French sculptor in metal, wood, and marble. He was considered the greatest metal carver of his time, and he specialized in decorative furniture mounts. Caffieri worked under Le Brun at the Gobelins Factory during the reign of Louis XIV. The illustrated pedestal was designed by Boulle, the metalwork was executed by Caffieri.
☐ ALSO SEE 1361, 1362, *1388*, 1411

CAFFOY. A rich 18th-century fabric used for hangings and draperies in state rooms.

CAGEWORK. A pierced and chased sleeve of silver overlaying a plain, usually gilt, base.
☐ ALSO SEE *437*, 438

CAISSONS. Sunken panels in a ceiling or dome. They are also called "coffers" or "lacunaria." They are found in classic Greek and Roman architecture. This same motif was simulated in wood in English Renaissance interiors, and interpreted in plaster composition or gesso in Adam brothers interiors in mid-18th-century England. This ceiling, arch, or dome enrichment is also found in French and Italian Renaissance structures, especially in domed buildings.

CAISSONS

CALCUTTA PAINTING. A type of British East India Company painting that evolved in Calcutta in the early years of the 19th century. In Calcutta paintings, the artist would portray the house and family of a particular Englishman, his staff of servants, his carriages, horses, and pets. See *Company Painting*.
☐ ALSO SEE *1754*, 1756, *1757*

CALLIGRAPHY

CALLIGRAPHY. The art of free rhythmic handwriting. The brushstrokes used by the Chinese in producing their written characters. In painting, it refers to free and loose brushwork.
☐ ALSO SEE American 175, *177*
    Chinese 308

CALLOT FIGURES. The porcelain figures modeled after the engravings of grotesques by Jacques Callot (1592-1635). The famous dwarf subjects of his engravings were reproduced in porcelain factories in Meissen, Vienna, and Chelsea.

CAMAÏEU. French for "monochromatic." Shades and tints of a single color.
☐ ALSO SEE 277, 1267, 1273, *1292*, 1336, 1593

CAMBRIC. A soft, white, loosely woven cotton or linen fabric originally from Cambrai, France. True linen cambric is very sheer; coarser versions are used for linings.

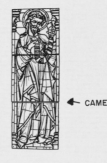

← CAME

CAME. The soft metal strip used as the divider between adjacent pieces of glass in a stained or leaded glass window.

CAMELBACK

CAMELBACK. A chair back with a serpentine curved top rail. A late Chippendale- (illustrated) or Hepplewhite-type chair. The term may originally have been applied to the 18th-century shield-back chair.

CAMELBACK SOFA. An upholstered couch in the mid-18th-century Chippendale tradition. The sofa back has a serpentine line which rises from the roll-over arms to a high point in the middle of the couch back.

CAMELBACK SOFA

CAMEOS

CAMEO. A low-relief carving. A striated stone or shell which is carved in relief. Cameos were used for decoration on English furniture of the late 18th century. Illustrated is a pair of ancient Roman cameos.
☐ ALSO SEE English 368, 802
French *1312*
German 1701
Italian 1820
Scottish *2086*, 2087, *2088-89*
Sulphide 1547, 1579, 1715

CAMEO BACK. An oval-framed chair back with an upholstered oval insert. It was popular in the Louis XVI, Adam, and Sheraton styles. The cameo-back chair is similar to the Louis XV "cabriolet," and Heppelwhite's "oval-back chair." See *Le Medaillon* and *Oval Back*.

CAMEO BACK

CAMEO GLASS. An ornamental glass in which layers of two different colors are fused and a relief is carved from the upper layer. It is used for jewelry and also for small decorative pieces such as vases.
☐ ALSO SEE *178*, 182, 1110-14, 1243, 1592-93

CAMLET. A rich fabric, made of camel's hair, which originated in the Orient. It was made in France in the 14th century from hair, wool, and silk, and it was used and manufactured in England in the 17th and 18th centuries.

CAMPAGNOLA. The Italian term for "provincial" furniture; furniture made in the outlying districts in a simple, unsophisticated manner.

CAMPAIGN CHEST. Originally a portable chest of drawers used by officers on their campaigns. The units were reinforced with metal edges and corners to withstand the rough traveling conditions. In current usage, somewhat like a "bachelor chest," often lacquered and embellished with metal corner strips, corner pieces, and pronounced hardware. It usually sits flush on the floor.

CANAPÉ

CANAPÉ

CANAPÉ. Originally, a 17th-century small, two-seater couch covered with a canopy. The canopy was later removed and the name applied to a small sofa. A Louis XVI canapé or sofa covered with Beauvais tapestry is here illustrated. The woodwork was carved and gilded. See *Tapet* for a 15th-century canapé.
☐ ALSO SEE *230, 1610*

CANAPÉ À CORBEILLE. A kidney-shaped sofa. The ends curve in so that the sofa takes on the appearance of a wide topped basket. Corbeille is the French word for a wide basket or breadbasket.

CANDELABRUM. A branched, highly ornamental candlestick, lampstand, or hanging lighting unit or chandelier. See *Chandelier*.
☐ ALSO SEE *403, 663, 852, 853, 961, 964*
French *1216,* 1304, *1305,* 1520,

CANDELABRUM

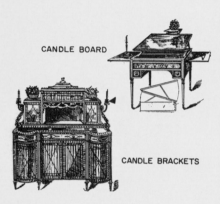

CANDLE BOARD

CANDLE BOARD. A small shelf, under the writing surface of a desk, which slides out and is used to hold a candlestick. An 18th-century English furniture device. Illustrated is a Sheraton drawing table.

CANDLE BRACKETS. Brackets set into the base of the upper part of a secretary and meant to be used as candlesticks. Illustrated is an early-19th-century Sheraton design.
☐ ALSO SEE *1827,* 1830

CANDLE BRACKETS

CANDLESTAND. A light table used for candles, vases, and other small ornaments. It is usually associated with tripod-type furniture. The candlestand was made in the early Georgian period, and continued in use up through the 18th century. A Chippendale design is illustrated.
☐ ALSO SEE *705, 718*

CANDLESTAND

CANDLESTICK. A socketed holder made of metal, wood, china, or pottery. It can be a simple tube with an opening at one end to receive the candle and a flattened base at the other to set securely on a flat surface, or it can be elaborately decorated.
☐ ALSO SEE American *34, 61, 70, 84, 120, 122, 180, 192*
Austrian *1735*
Dutch *1964*
English *549,* 552, *598, 653, 662, 663, 674, 742,* 760, 852, 853, *906,* 984, *1165, 1167*
French 1196, *1198,* 1200, *1300, 1358, 1381*
Italian 1830, *1902,* 1903-04
Scottish 2081
Spanish 2130

CANDLESTICK

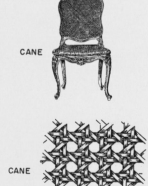

CANE

CANE

CANE. From the Latin for "reed." The stems of certain palms, grasses, or plants like bamboo and rattan. The reedlike material is plaited or woven into a mesh which is yielding, and therefore comfortable to sit on or lean back against. Cane was used as a decorative and elegant seating and chair-back material in the Louis XIV, XV, and XVI periods in France, and in the 17th- and 18-century designs in England and Holland.

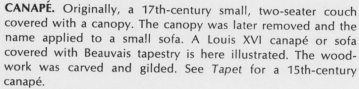

It is still a popular material, and is also currently used for decorative inserts in screens and case furniture.
□ ALSO SEE *154*, 155, *448*, 449, 481, *483*, *1086*, 1237, *1259*, *1550*, *1553*, 1721, 1747, *1855*, 1858, *1949*

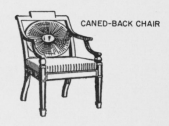
CANED-BACK CHAIR

CANED-BACK CHAIR. A popular chair back of the latter part of the 18th century. An intricately woven pattern of cane was set into a round or oval frame, which usually had an inlaid wood center. The cane appears to radiate out from the center medallion. A Sheraton design is illustrated.

CANEPHORA

CANEPHORA. A sculptured female figure with a basket on her head. Originally it was used as a classic structural decoration somewhat like a caryatid. (See *Caryatids* and *Atlantes*.) It was used as an ornamental support for furniture and shelves in the French and Italian Renaissance.

CANOPY. From the Greek for "a net to keep out gnats." A covering, usually of drapery, over a piece of furniture, like the Sheraton bed illustrated. See *Canapé* and *Tester*. In architecture, a shelf, hood, or roof projecting from a building. See *Baldachino*.

CANOPY BED

CANOPY BED. A bed with a fabric roof over it. The canopy is often supported by four posts, one at each corner of the bed, or suspended from above. An early-19th-century American version of a Sheraton design is illustrated. See *Angel Bed*, *Four-poster Bedstead* and *Tent Bed*.

CANOPY CHAIR. A late-15th-, early-16th-century stately chair with a broad back that angles upward over the seat to form a projecting canopy. The design was usually heavily enriched with carved ornament. It was the probable forerunner of the smaller, wider, and more intimate 17th-century *Canapé*. See *Chayers à Dorseret*.

CANTERBURY. An ornamental stand having compartments for papers, books, envelopes, etc. A sort of portable magazine rack of the 18th century. It was probably originally designed to carry trays, plates, cutlery, etc., and serve as an auxiliary piece for tea service or dining.
□ ALSO SEE *1009*

CANOPY CHAIR

CANTON CHINA. A traditional blue-and-white oriental china imported from China from the 17th century up to modern times.

CANTON CHINA

CANTONNIÈRE

CANTONNIÈRE. The French word for "valance." It especially refers to the elaborate valance arrangements used on French state beds in the 16th and 17th centuries. See *Lambrequin* and *Valance*.

CAPITAL. The head of a column or pillar. The capital is placed directly over the shaft and immediately under the entablature. Each of the classical architectural borders has its own particular capital. The column and capital have been used as decoration and for functional supports on Renaissance and Louis XVI furniture. See *Composite Order*, *Corinthian Order*, *Doric Order*, *Etruscan Order*, and *Ionic Order*.

CAPITAL

CAPO DI MONTE. A Spanish porcelain factory founded by King Charles III in 1743. In 1760, the plant was set up in Buen Retiro, and this type of porcelain is also known by that name. Figures and groupings of soft paste were made here, in typically Rococo patterns and vivid colors. Large plaques and wall brackets of Capo di Monte were used to decorate the palaces in Madrid and Aranjuez. Capo di Monte-type ware is still used today for ornamental lamps and vases.
☐ ALSO SEE 373, 1886-90, 2153, 2156

CAPRICCIO. Italian for "caprice." A fanciful landscape composition of the 18th century.

CAQUETEUSE. A "conversation chair" with a high wood back, and the seat sometimes arranged to turn on a pivot. It was an early French Renaissance design that was introduced into England in the 16th century. The front of the chair seat was usually wider than the back. Illustrated is a 16th-century French example. See *Cacqueteuse*.

CAQUETEUSE

CAQUETOIRE. A small, light, four-legged conversation chair of the mid French Renaissance. The back of the seat is narrower than the front, and the arms are curved inward from the front to the chair back. See *Cacqueteuse*.
☐ ALSO SEE 363, 364, 1193, 2133, *2134*

CAQUETOIRE

CARD CUT. A Chinese-style fretwork or latticework design. The pattern is carved in low relief rather than pierced or cut out. Chippendale used this type of decoration on some of his cabinets and secretaries.

CARD CUT

CARD TABLE. A small folding table used for gaming. This type of table originated in the 17th century and was especially popular in the William and Mary and Queen Anne periods. Early card tables had depressions at the four corners of the tabletop to hold candles, and often, four additional wells or "guinea holes" for holding the money in use during the gaming. The tabletops were often covered with green baize. The styles of card tables varied with the succeeding periods. Illustrated is a Queen Anne card table with cabriole legs with shell motif on the knee. See *Dished* and *Mechanical Card Table*.
☐ ALSO SEE 133, 450, *479*, 483, 535, *573*, *761*, 762-65

CARD TABLE

CARLIN, MARTIN. An 18th-century French master cabinet-maker to Louis XVI. He produced charming, delicate furniture in rosewood, with Sèvres porcelain inlays. Carlin was also a founder and chaser of metal furniture mounts, and one of the earliest exponents of the Classic Revival. He often used independent, or detached, balustrade columns to support the friezes of cabinets. These columns were made of wood, bronze gilt, or the two combined. Another decorative device frequently used by Carlin was the fringe of drapery pinched in with small tassels.
☐ ALSO SEE *1286*, *1289*, 1456-60, 1491-92

MARTIN CARLIN

CARLTON TABLE. A writing table on legs with a raised back and sides, and fitted with pigeonholes, small drawers, and fittings for pens and inkwells. The desk made its appearance at the end of the 18th century in England, and was usually made of of mahogany or satinwood with inlay trim. Sheraton referred to this as a "ladies' drawing and writing table."

CARLTON TABLE

CAROLEAN PERIOD

CAROLEAN PERIOD. The period in English furniture and interior design which spanned the years 1660–1688, also referred to as the Restoration, Late Stuart, or part of the Jacobean period. Illustrated is an oak chest of the period with geometric panels and lunette carving.

CAROLINGIAN. The period in architecture and art in western Europe from about the 7th to the 10th centuries. It was roughly the dynasties before, of, and after Charlemagne. See *West Work*.

CARPET. In the 16th and 17th centuries, the term referred to a woven table covering. In the late 17th century, it assumed the meaning we now give it: a floor covering. See *Tapet*. Illustrated is a carpet pattern of the early-16th-century German Renaissance.
☐ ALSO SEE English 415, 585, 607-11, 1084, *1085*, 1927, 1928-29
　　French 1347-51
　　Indian 1763, 1764, 1861
　　Persian 1998, *1999*, 2005-09
　　Turkish 2178-81

CARPET

CARQUEVILLE, WILL. An American Art Nouveau graphics designer of the late 19th and early 20th centuries. In Carqueville's work, objects and people are reduced to abstract areas of bright color, subtly balanced with background voids and with lettering.
☐ ALSO SEE *211*, 212

CARREAU

CARREAU. From the French for "square." A square tile or brick. A loose, stuffed cushion used on chairs and settles before upholstery, as known today, came into use. A squab cushion. Illustrated is a French 15th-century bench with movable backrest. See *Squab*.

CARTEL (Clock). A hanging wall clock. In the Louis XV and Louis XVI periods it was often highly ornate and fanciful in design, and made of ormolu. See *Régulateur* and *Regulator*.

CARTER, EDWARD. A 17th-century English designer-architect who, with John Webb, executed many of Inigo Jones's designs. His own work was much in the style and tradition of Inigo Jones, as illustrated.

EDWARD CARTER

CARTER, J. A late-18th-century English designer who worked mainly in the Adam brothers tradition. He designed classic-inspired ceilings, panels, chimneypieces, gates, grates, architectural pedestals, shop fronts, and doorways.

J. CARTER

CARTER'S GROVE. A typical Georgian house of the mid-18th century in America. It was built for Carter Burwell in James City, West Virginia, in 1751. The great central hall opened into four rooms, two of which were coupled with antechambers. The main part of the house was flanked by a kitchen and a service building (flankers). David Minitree was the builder of this brick structure done in Flemish bond.

CARTER'S GROVE

CARTON-PIERRE. A Robert Adam, mid-18th-century English technique of "carved ornament" using a gesso-like composition applied to the surface of wood, panels, and ceilings. See *Anaglypta*.

CARTONNIER

CARTOUCHE BACK

CARYATIDS

CARTOUCHE

CARVING

CARTONNIER. A decorative 18th-century pasteboard box used to hold papers. The box was usually ornamented and lavishly decorated.

☐ ALSO SEE *1343*, 1388

CARTOON. From the Italian "cartone," a big sheet of paper. A full-sized drawing for a painting, worked out in detail, and ready to be transferred to a wall, canvas, or panel. One of the steps in the preparation for a fresco or wall mural.

☐ ALSO SEE 416, 427-29, 1180, 1181, 1219, 1310, 1349, 1968-71, 2120-22, *2159*

CARTOUCHE. In architecture, usually a sculptured ornament in the form of a scroll unrolled, which often appears on cornices. The cartouche is frequently used as a field for inscriptions, and as an ornamental block in the cornices of house interiors. A conventionalized shield or oval. An ornate frame.

CARTOUCHE BACK. An upholstered chair back of a side chair or fauteuil which is scroll- or cartouche-shaped. Illustrated is a Louis XV fauteuil which is upholstered in Beauvais tapestry. The tapestry has a multicurved shield effect, and is, in turn, set into the cartouche frame of the chair.

CARVER CHAIR. An early American wood-turned chair with a rush seat. A straight, square-looking chair named after a chair of that design belonging to Governor John Carver of Plymouth. The rear legs continued up to form the uprights of the back. A single row of vertical and horizontal spindles was set between the uprights. Mushroom-shaped turnings usually acted as finials on the uprights. It is closely related to the Brewster chair. See *Banister Back Chair* and *Brewster Chair*.

☐ ALSO SEE 20-21, *22*

CARVING. A sculptured, incised, gouged, or appliquéd three-dimensional decoration or ornament. Illustrated is an early Georgian (early-18th-century) sideboard which is heavily carved and gilded.

CARYATIDS. In architecture, sculptured female figures used in place of columns or pilasters to support entablatures. The caryatid is a decorative figure used as a supporting member of a design. It appears in classic architecture and decoration, and again in the Renaissance and Empire periods. The male version of the caryatid is the Atlas. Illustrated is the Hall of the Marshal (no longer extant) in the Tuileries, Paris, as designed by Charles Percier and Pierre Fontaine in the early-19th-century Empire style. See *Canephora*. The famous "Porch of the Maidens" in the Erectheum consists of caryatid supports.

CASEMENT, WILLIAM. A late-18th-century English furniture designer, who contributed to the *Cabinet Makers' London Book* of prices for designs of cabinetwork.

CASHMERE WORK. Referring to Kashmir in India. A "mirror-mosaic" form of decoration in Indian furniture of the 18th and early 19th centuries. Small pieces of mirror were inlaid into the small, carved, geometric patterns of a panel or surface.

CASKET

CASKET. A box or miniature chest usually lavishly ornamented and made of wood, ivory, and precious metals. A container for trinkets, jewels, etc. A Byzantine ivory casket is illustrated.
☐ ALSO SEE 394, *438*, 651, *654*, 1106-07, *1108*, 1196, 1228, *1262*, *1812*, 1813, 1940, 2070, 2129

CASO-RILIEVO. An Italian word for a relief carving in which the highest parts of the sculpture are on a level with the surface that surrounds the relief. It is also called "intaglio rilievato."

CASSAPANCA. Derived from the Italian "cassone" (chest) and "banca" (bench). A mid-Renaissance Italian, long, wooden, hinged-top chest with wooden arms and a back. It functioned as a bench as well as a chest. A prototype of the box settle. See *Box Settle*.
☐ ALSO SEE 1802

CASSAPANCA

CASSAWS. A late-17th-century English wallpaper which resembles a silk damask.

CASSETTE

CASSETTE. The French word meaning "casket." It sometimes assumed monumental proportions. Illustrated is a 14th-century French wood cassette.

CASSOLET or CASSOLETTE. A small box, made in a variety of shapes, for holding or burning perfumes. The term also applies to a covered urn-shaped vase sometimes with a top that reverses to become a candle holder.
☐ ALSO SEE *1521*

CASSONE. An Italian decorated hinge-topped chest. It was usually used as a marriage chest which contained the bride's household linens. This 14th- to 16th-century chest was richly decorated and carved with gilt moldings, and often had painted front and back panels. The panels were from 4' to 6' long and about 18" in height. See *Cassapanca, Chest,* and *Marriage Chest*.
☐ ALSO SEE 1798, 1800-03, 1862-63

CASSONE

CASSOON

CASTLE DURANTE MAJOLICA. The majolica were produced at Castel Durante, Italy. The finest examples date from the beginning of the 16th century.
☐ ALSO SEE 1805, 1807, 1809, 1941, 1950

CASTERS

CASTERS or CASTORS. Small wheels on swivels which are applied to legs or bases of furniture to make it movable.
☐ ALSO SEE 865-66

CASTLEFORD POTTERY. The ware made at Castleford near Leeds, Yorkshire, England, by David Dunderdale between about 1790 and 1821. The most typical Castleford, produced about 1815, is cream-colored stoneware with blue outlines and relief patterns of figures or flowers. A fine white stoneware was also manufactured.
☐ ALSO SEE 644, *645*

CATENARY

CATENARY. Chainlike. A swag or festoon. See *Festoon* and *Swag*.

CATENARY ARCH. The arc or curve formed by a cord or chain of uniform density hanging freely between two points of suspension. The console with the catenary arch trim illustrated was designed by Charles Normand in the French Empire period.

CATENARY ARCH

CATKINS

CATHÉDRALE STYLE or FAUX GOTHIQUE. The Gothic revival style in France. In the first half of the 19th century, the Gothic style enjoyed a brief vogue in France. The *Cathédrale* style is fairly easily distinguishable by a certain shallowness of ornament and by the wood used, which was nearly always mahogany or maple.
☐ ALSO SEE 988, *1551*, 1552

CATKINS. A decorative 18th-century motif like the bellflower or husk ornament. It was usually used as a pendant, or as a chain of stylized and graduated bell-shaped flowers. A late-18th-century Hepplewhite girondole is illustrated. See *Bellflower Ornament* and *Husk Ornament*.

CAUDLE CUP. A two-handled cup, three to six inches in height, used for drinking hot spiced drinks.
☐ ALSO SEE *34, 35*, 437, 464, *466*, 550, 1382

CAUGHLEY PORCELAIN. An English soft-paste porcelain, made in Caughley, Shropshire, in the 18th and early 19th centuries. From 1776, the porcelain was decorated by means of transfer printing in an underglaze bluish color. The Caughley willow pattern was especially popular.
☐ ALSO SEE 740, 742, 872, 882-86, 1019

CAUSEUSE

CAUSEUSE. A wide armchair, or a small sofa with open sides. The back and seat were often covered with Beauvais tapestry in the 17th and 18th centuries. The causeuse is similar to a marquise, love seat, or settee. Illustrated is a typical Louis XVI design covered with a Beauvais tapestry.

CAUVET, GILLES-PAUL (1731–1788). A leading French designer of interiors, furniture, and metal ornament in the Louis XVI period. His work is reminiscent of the Louis XV style.

CAVETTO. A quarter-round, concave molding. In late-17th-century English furniture, the cavetto molding was often veneered crosswise. See *Cove*.

CAVETTO

CAVO-RELIEVO. Italian for "intaglio."

CEDAR CHEST. A long, low chest, either made completely of, or lined only with, cedarwood. The chest is used for the storage of linens, blankets, and woolens. It can be styled to suit any period and is also often referred to as a "hope chest." Illustrated is a 15th-century carved cedar chest. See *Cassone*.

CEDAR CHEST

CELADON. A light-grayish sea-green color. The word is also used to describe pottery or Chinese porcelain of this pastel, sea-green color.
☐ ALSO SEE 287, *310*, 314, 403, *1573*

CELATURE

CELATURE. A method of decorating metal surfaces by embossing or cutting into the metal.

CELLARETTE. A portable or movable cabinet or liquor chest with a place for bottles, glasses, etc. A Sheraton design is illustrated. Also, the drawer of a sideboard fitted with divisions to hold bottles, and often lined with lead. See *Sarcophagus*.

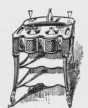

CELLARETTE

BENVENUTO CELLINI

CENTER OTTOMAN

CERAMIC

CHAIERE

CENTAUR

CENTER TABLE

CHAIR

CELLINI, BENVENUTO (1500–1571). An outstanding Italian Renaissance goldsmith, sculptor, and adventurer. A beaten silver goblet of his design is shown. See *Tazza* for another illustration of Cellini's work.

☐ ALSO SEE *1183*, 1199, 1200, 1202, 1242, 1799, 1819

CENTAUR. A decorative figure with the forepart of a human male, but the body and legs of a horse. It appeared in ancient Greek mythology, and reappeared in Renaissance and later designs.

CENTER OTTOMAN. See *Borne* and *Confidante*.

CENTER TABLE. A large table which stands in the center of a hallway or large room. It is similar in use to the rectangular library table. Illustrated is an Elizabethan room with a center table. See illustration of *Venetian Gilt*.

CERAMIC. A product of baked clay. It may be pottery, tile, earthenware, etc. A 17th-century English stoneware jug is illustrated.

CERCEAU, JACQUES DU. A 16th-century French architect and furniture designer under Henry IV. See *Du Cerceau, Jacques Androuet*.

CERTOSINA. An Italian term for an inlay of marble, ivory, or blond woods on a darker background. It has an oriental character since it is generally set into small geometric patterns. See *Intarsia or Tarsia and Intarsi*. The name was derived from the Carthusian monks who excelled in this type of inlay work.

CHAFFEUSE. A low, fireside chair. Originally the seat was so low that the knees of a seated person were higher than his lap. It was used by nursing mothers to cradle children between their knees and body. It is also spelled "chauffeuse."

CHAIERE or CHAIRE. A French Gothic term for a thronelike wood-carved chair. See *Chaire*. Illustrated is a 14th-century interior.

CHAIR. Derived from the Old French "chaiere." A seat with a back for one person. A chair usually has feet, legs, stretchers, brackets, apron, seat frame, rails, arms, splat, and top rail. Illustrated is an ancient Greek klismos.

☐ ALSO SEE American (17th century) 19-20, *21-22*
    (18th century) *58*, 59-60, *86*, 88, *89*, 90, *104*, 106, *183*, 184
    (18th-19th centuries) 134, *136-37*
    (19th century) 133-37, *154*, 155-56, 184-87, 216, *217*
  Austrian (19th-20th centuries) 1721-25
    (20th century) *1727*, 1728
  Belgian (19th-20th centuries) *230-33*
  Chinese (17th century) *290*
  English (16th century) 362-64, *365*, 367
    (16th-19th centuries) 496-98
    (17th century) 418-19, *421*, *447-48*, 449, 481-82
    (18th century) *532*, 535, 574-75, *606*, 703, 705, *786*, 790, *840*, *841*, *842*
    (18th-19th centuries) *932-33*, *956*, *958*
    (19th century) *986-89*, *1009*, *1082*, 1083, *1085*, *1086*, *1126*, 1916, *1918*
  French (16th century) *1191*, 1193
    (17th century) 1234-35, *1236-37*, *1238*

(18th century) *1259-60, 1308, 1310, 1317,* 1319, *1389,*
1390, *1447, 1503,* 1504, *1505-06*
(19th century) *1529,* 1530, 1532, 1550-53
German (18th century) *1652, 1654, 1655, 1687*
(19th century) *967*
Indian (18th century) *1745, 1746*
Irish (18th century) *1775*
Italian (16th century) 1802, *1803*
(17th century) *1828,* 1829, *1830, 1831*
(18th century) *1855,* 1858
Netherlandish (16th century) *2132,* 2133, 2134
(17th century) *1949,* 1950
Russian (18th-19th centuries) *2065, 2066,* 2067
Scottish (19th-20th centuries) *2099,* 2100, *2101*
Spanish (16th century) 2135-36

CHAIR RAIL

CHAIRE

CHAIR TABLE

CHAIRE À HAUT DOSSIER

CHAIR AND A HALF. An 18th-century English chair with overly generous proportions. The chair usually had wings or cheeks, and the seat was smaller than a two-seater love seat but larger than a regular upholstered chair. It is similar to the French "marquise" in proportions and was also called a *Drunkard's Chair.*

CHAIR BED. A chair or settee with a draw-out arrangement that converts into a bed. An 18th-century English innovation. See *Bed Chair.*

CHAIR RAIL. The top molding of a dado, also called a "dado cap." The chair rail is usually placed about 30″ off the ground, and the wall area below the molding is called the dado. The wood strip originally was used to protect the plaster wall from being damaged by the top rail of chairs. An 18th-century English room designed by Halfpenny is illustrated. See *Dado.*

CHAIR TABLE. A chair that converts into a table when the hinged back is dropped to a horizontal position. Illustrated is a 17th-century Stuart period chair. See *Table Chair.*
☐ ALSO SEE 419

CHAIRE. A French term for an early Renaissance choir stall. It resembles a chest (or boxlike seat) with a tall, heavily carved back. The arms were also carved. In the Gothic period it was also called a "chayère" and its thronelike proportions made it the special seat for the lord or head of a family.

CHAIRE À HAUT DOSSIER. A 16th-century French Renaissance high-back chair. It was usually ornately carved and covered in leather or tapestry.

CHAISE. French for "side chair."

CHAISE À ACCOUDOIR. See *Cockfight Chair* and *Fumeuse.*

CHAISE À BRAS. A Renaissance armchair. Illustrated is an English version from the 16th century.

CHAISE À CAPUCINE. A low slipper chair. The name is probably derived from the Capucin nuns who might have used this type of chair.

CHAISE À PORTEURS. A sedan chair. It originally was an enclosed covered chair which seated one person and was suspended between two poles. The two poles were carried

CHAISE À BRAS

CHAISE BRISÉE

CHALICE

SIR WILLIAM CHAMBERS

CHANDELIER

CHAISE LONGUE

CHAMBER HORSE

CHAMFER

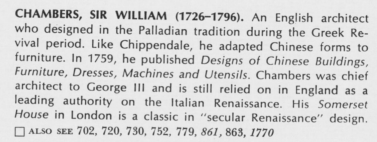

CHAMFER

by porters. Present-day variations are hooded and winged chairs that simulate the enlosed look of the chaise à porteurs. See *Sedan Chair*.

CHAISE BRISÉE. A *Chaise Longue* in two parts, one of which is the footrest. Also, a folding chair.

CHAISE LONGUE. A long chair for reclining or stretching out. A *Duchesse*. It is an upholstered chair with a very elongated seat supported by extra legs.
☐ ALSO SEE *1532*

CHALICE. A cup or goblet used in church ceremony, and often made of precious metals beautifully ornamented and jeweled.
☐ ALSO SEE 1811, 2130, *2131*

CHAMBER HORSE. An 18th-century English exercising mechanism designed by Sheraton. It was a bellows-like affair made up of several wooden boards separated by coils, and covered over with leather equipped with air vents. This "bellows" was set on a wood base with "arms," and a front step. The individual sat on the bellows-pillow, held onto the arms, and bounced up and down, much as one would today ride a vibrator.

CHAMBERS, SIR WILLIAM (1726–1796). An English architect who designed in the Palladian tradition during the Greek Revival period. Like Chippendale, he adapted Chinese forms to furniture. In 1759, he published *Designs of Chinese Buildings, Furniture, Dresses, Machines and Utensils*. Chambers was chief architect to George III and is still relied on in England as a leading authority on the Italian Renaissance. His *Somerset House* in London is a classic in "secular Renaissance" design.
☐ ALSO SEE 702, 720, 730, 752, 779, *861*, 863, *1770*

CHAMBLIN, M. DE. Early 18th-century French Régence designer and decorator.

CHAMFER. The edge of a corner that is beveled or angled off. A splayed effect. A Chippendale press or wardrobe with chamfered edges is illustrated. See *Bevel* and *Canted*.

CHAMPLEVÉ. A type of enamelware in which the pattern is grooved out in a metal base and the grooves are then filled with colored enamels. The thin raised lines that separate the enamel color are similar to the cloisons in *Cloisonné*.
☐ ALSO SEE *908*, 909-10, *1195*, 1196, 1197, *1751*, 1752, 1843, 2064, 2069, *2070*

CHANDELIER. A hanging lighting fixture. A pendant unit with branches to hold candles or lights. It is often decorated with prisms and crystals. Crystal chandeliers were introduced into England by the French émigrés of 1685.
☐ ALSO SEE 261, *1866*, 2054

CHANTILLY LACE. A bobbin lace with a delicate ground. The design is outlined by a cordonnet of thick silky threads. See *Valenciennes Lace*.

CHANTILLY PORCELAIN. The porcelain manufactured in Chantilly, France, from about 1725 until about 1800. The factory produced a fine soft-paste porcelain with enamel colors over an opaque white glaze containing tin ashes.
☐ ALSO SEE 1265-68, 1363, 1367, 1491, 1575

CHASING

CHÂTEAU DE CHAMBORD

CHAYERS À DORSERET

CHARLES X PERIOD. From 1824 to 1830, part of the Restoration period in France. A mixture of Louis XVI and late Empire styles and Rococo and Renaissance detail.

CHASING. A method of ornamenting on any metal surface. The pattern is produced by embossing or cutting away parts of the metal. A burin or graver is also used in this technique. Chasing with a burin is also done on marquetry, on metal mounts for furniture, or on Boulle-type metal inlays. Chasing, as a form of metal enrichment, reached its peak during the 18th century in France. See *Lalonde* and *Repoussé*.
☐ ALSO SEE 436-38, 1199-1202, *1938*, 1939, 2024

CHÂTEAU. A French country residence, usually the country home or suburban manor of a nobleman. Illustrated is the French Renaissance Château d'Écouen by Jean Bullant.
☐ ALSO SEE 1178-83, 1191-92, 1313-14, 1529-30, 1536-37

CHÂTEAU DE CHAMBORD. Built in 1526 in the Loire district of France by Pierre Nepveu. In plan this semifortress consists of a rectangle inside a rectangle. The famous double spiral staircase is another architectural feature. It is a stone cage topped with the lantern, here shown. The structure is a combination of Renaissance details and Gothic construction. The high-pitched roof, ornate dormers, and beautiful chimneys make this a typically French, Early Renaissance building.
☐ ALSO SEE *1178*, 1179, 1191

CHÂTEAU DE GAILLON. Built between 1497 and 1509 by Pierre Fain for Cardinal Georges d'Amboise. It is a classic of the early French Renaissance Rouen school. It has an irregular plan, moats, drawbridges, round corner towers, turrets, high roofs, and dormers. It is a curious yet delightful blend of Renaissance details and medieval charm.

CHAUFFEUSE. A small fireside chair with a low seat of the early French Renaissance. See *Chaffeuse*.
☐ ALSO SEE 1532

CHAYERS À DORSERET. Late-14th- and early-15th-century Gothic canopied chairs. They were usually carved of oak or chestnut, elaborately gilded, and highlighted with color. The chayer (or chaire) was massive and thronelike. The illustrated canopied chair is a 15th-century French example. The back of the chair was lined with tapestry. See *Canopy Chair*.

CHEEK PIECES. The "wings" or "fins" of the tall easy chairs designed in 18th-century England. These cheeks were designed to keep draughts from the head of the person seated in the chair. See *Draught Chair*, *Grandfather Chair*, and *Wing Chair*.

CHEESEBOX SEAT. A chair seat, made of rush, which is round or bell-shaped and has a thin rim of wood bent around the edge. Cheesebox seats were used in early 19th-century American furniture.

CHEF D'OEUVRE. French for "masterpiece."

CHELSEA PORCELAIN. A soft-paste porcelain manufactured in the Chelsea section of London from about 1745 to 1784. Chelsea porcelain is classified according to the four major changes in design and texture of paste that occurred during the fac-

CHÂTEAU

CHÂTEAU DE GAILLON

CHEEK PIECES

tory's existence, and it Is named according to the potter's mark used during each period.
☐ ALSO SEE *560*, 561-64, 623, 649, 739, *1573*, 1575

CHELSEA TILE. A type of American tile. In about 1880, Chelsea, Massachusetts, became a center for tile manufacture. The best-known tiles, produced by John G. Low, are notable for their decoration, which consists of paintings in relief by Arthur Osborne.
☐ ALSO SEE 190, 194

CHEQUER. One of the squares in a chequered or checkered pattern. An inlay design. Illustrated is chequered ashlar work from Austin Hall, Harvard University.

CHEQUER

CHERRYWOOD. A light to dark reddish grained wood resembling mahogany. It darkens with age. Cherrywood is used for small carved articles and French and American 18th-century Provincial furniture. It is also popular for inlays and marquetry. The figure varies from plain to a rich mottle. Black cherrywood is found in United States, in the Appalachians, mainly in Pennsylvania and West Virginia. French cherry is found in France and England. Wild cherry is found in England, Europe, and Asia Minor.
☐ ALSO SEE *86*, 87, *185*, 1446

CHERUB HEAD

CHERUB HEAD. A popular decorative motif which appears in Renaissance church or secular architecture. The motif was used either singly or in groups, in medallions, on corner blocks, in capitals, panels, and as furniture decoration. See *Têtes d'Anges*.

CHESS TABLE. A tabletop with a checkered pattern either painted or inlaid upon it. In medieval Europe, the tops of chests were sometimes decorated with checkerboards.
☐ ALSO SEE 1010, *1747*

CHESS TABLE

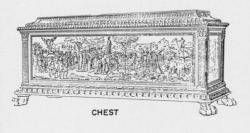
CHEST

CHEST. Originally, a container or box with a hinged lid. Drawers were added to the chest in the mid-17th century, and the chest of drawers evolved. Chests in the medieval period were architectural in concept and decoration. Illustrated is a 15th-century Italian chest or cassone.
☐ ALSO SEE American (17th century) *18*, 19-20
   English (16th century) 363-64
     (17th century) *418*, 420, 449
     (18th century) 535
   German (16th century) 1623, 1624
     (17th-18th centuries) *1654*, 1655
   Italian (16th century) 1798, 1800-03
   Netherlandish (16th century) *2132*, 2133-34
     (17th-18th centuries) 1655
   Spanish (16th century) 2135

CHEST OF DRAWERS. A box or chest with drawers added. Illustrated is a late-18th-century Hepplewhite design.
☐ ALSO SEE American (17th century) *18*, 19-20, *21-22*
     (18th century) 58
     (19th century) 186-87
   English (17th century) 421, 449, 483
     (18th century) 535
     (19th century) *286*
   French (18th century) 1261-62
   Italian (18th century) *1893*

CHEST OF DRAWERS

CHEST ON CHEST

CHEST ON CHEST. A chest of drawers in two parts, with one set of larger drawers. It is also called a double chest.

CHESTERFIELD. An overstuffed, heavily upholstered couch or sofa. It is usually a large piece of furniture with a continuous back. The scrolled, roll-over arms are the same height as the back.

CHESTNUT. A soft wood with a coarse grain. It resembles oak, and can be used in its place when a quartered effect is not desired. Chestnut is unsuitable for fine details because the grain is coarse and it has marked annual rings. Certain cuts were used in late-18th-century England to imitate satinwood.

CHEVAL GLASS

CHEVAL GLASS OR MIRROR. Literally a "horse mirror," a mirror suspended between horses (see *Horse*). A mirror which is decoratively mounted so as to swing in a frame and large enough to reflect the whole figure. A full-length mirror. It was a French innovation which was introduced into England in the late 17th century. In the 18th century in England it was made in both large and small table models. The cheval mirror is also called a "swing glass" and "psyche."

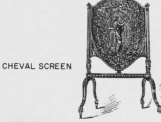

CHEVAL SCREEN

CHEVAL SCREEN. A fire screen which stands on two bracketed feet. A Sheraton design is illustrated.

CHEVRON. French for "rafter." In ornament, a zigzag design or molding. A continuous band of *V*'s. It was frequently used in Norman and Gothic ornament, and also in the 17th century as an inlay motif.

CHIAROSCURO. Italian for "light-dark." The balance of light and shadow in a picture. See *Clare-Obscure* and *Grisaille*.

CHEVRON

CH'IEN LUNG PORCELAIN. The porcelain manufactured in China between 1736 and 1795, during the reign of the Emperor Ch'ien Lung of the Ch'ing Dynasty. In order to satisfy a thriving export trade to Europe, many craftsmen incorporated Western styles and motifs into their wares.
☐ALSO SEE 281, 298-300, 307-08, 349

CHIEN WARE. A type of Chinese stoneware made in Fukien Province during the Sung Dynasty (960-1279). Chien ware consists mainly of tea bowls of varying shapes and sizes, with dark brown, tan, or black glazes; the most typical Chien ware is cone-shaped and of a reddish black color.

CHIFFONNIER

CHIFFONNIER. A French term for a "rag-and-bone man." It was originally a general unit for collecting and containing assorted odds and ends. In the period of Louis XV, it refers to a tall chest with five drawers; however, in 19th-century England, the term is applied to a sideboard with two doors below enclosing shelves. Sometimes there were shelves at the back and top of the sideboard to hold ornaments, decorative serving pieces, etc. A Thomas Hope, early-19th-century English chiffonnier is illustrated.
☐ ALSO SEE 1531

CHIFFONNIÈRE. A sort of sewing table, with a three-sided gallery on top, drawers, and a shelf at the bottom, which was enclosed and used to hold balls of wool. It was a Louis XV innovation.

CHIMERA. A mythical, dragon-like animal, or composite "part human, part animal" used in decoration. The chimera was used for legs or furniture supports in the Renaissance, Empire, and later-19th-century designs.

CHIMERA

CHIMNEY BREAST. The projecting stone or brickwork of a fireplace which is above the fireplace proper and houses the flue. The illustrated 17th-century design is from Bolsover Castle in Derbyshire, England.

CHIMNEY BREAST

CHIMNEY GLASS. A mirror framed in carved wood or glass and installed between the fireplace mantel and the entablature, or upper wall. Introduced in England during the 17th century, chimney glasses were originally hexagonal; later they were designed in three panels, and in America they were made rectangular in shape.

CHIMNEYPIECE. The ornamental structure surrounding the fireplace and the breast above it. A projecting hood, it is sometimes called the mantel. Many beautiful chimneypieces were designed and decorated by artists and architects of 18th-century England. A 16th-century French chimneypiece is illustrated. See *Mantel.*

☐ ALSO SEE *360,* 361, *414, 605,* 635-38, 666-67, *669, 673,* 826, *957, 1079,* 2018

CHIMNEYPIECE

CHINA. The European name given to porcelains imported from the Orient. A hard, translucent porcelain with a large percentage of bone ash. Illustrated is a late-17th-century Chinese vase of the K'ang Hsi period. See *Hard Paste* and *Kaolin.*

CHINA

CHINA CLOSET or CABINET. A display cabinet, usually with glass sides and front, which was used for exhibiting china collections. A popular piece of furniture in the late 17th and early 18th centuries when Oriental china was rare, and avidly collected. The illustrated laquered design is of the William and Mary period.

CHINA CLOSET

CHINESE BRACKET FOOT or CHINESE FOOT. A bracket-type foot with a reverse S-shape curve (cyma recta) on the face of the bracket. It is also called an ogee bracket foot. A support favored by Chippendale in the mid-18th century.

CHINESE BRACKET FOOT

CHINESE CHIPPENDALE. A period in Chippendale's work, in the mid-18th century, when he was greatly influenced by chinoiserie, Chinese motifs, and the work of Sir William Chambers. See *Chambers, Sir William; Chinoiserie; Lacquerwork.*

☐ ALSO SEE 90, 729-33

CHINESE CHIPPENDALE

CHINESE KEY DESIGN. A continuous geometric border design, similar to the Greek key design or meander. This type of design was used by Chippendale in his fretwork and openwork grille doors for bookcases, secretaries, etc.

CHINESE KEY DESIGN

CHINESE ROOM. An 18th-century English fad or craze. A room in some part of the house was decorated "à la Chinoise," with imported Chinese furniture or adaptations such as Chippendale produced in his Chinese Chippendale period. China (or India or Japan) wallpaper or handpainted paper murals would usually cover the walls. Many of these wallpapers were produced in England after Chinese originals. See *Chinese Chippendale* and *Chinoiserie*.

CHINESE WALLPAPER. A wallpaper introduced into Europe in the mid-17th century under the name of "India" or "Japan" paper. It was sold in sets of 25 rolls, each 12' long and 4' wide with a studied dissimilarity of detail from panel to panel. In the mid-18th century, chinoiserie had reached the peak of its popularity, and Chinese papers were very much in vogue. Among the favorite motifs were flowering shrubs, trees, flowers, birds, and butterflies. These were later replaced with exotic landscapes and curious "oriental" figures. The authentic Chinese wallpapers were greatly imitated by French and English paper printers, and often contemporary 18th-century occidental figures are portrayed wandering through lush pseudo-oriental scenes. James Minikin of England produced wallpapers of this type.

CHINOISERIE. Chinese-type or Chinese-like decorative motifs: gay, picturesque, imaginative occidental versions of oriental designs. Particularly popular in the Louis XV period in France and the 18th-century English styles. See *Chinese Chippendale; Formal; Huet, Christophe; Singerie;* and *Venetian Chinoiserie.*

CHINOISERIE

☐ ALSO SEE English 380, 393, 438, 464, 466, 480, 486, 524, 536,
537, *538,* 540, 636, *638,* 663, 678-81, 685, 720, *721,* 724-33,
734-42, *808,* 810-11, 915, 933, *940,* 942, 943, 961
French 1213, 1215, 1217, 1225, *1262, 1307,* 1308, *1312,*
1323, 1337, *1341, 1359,* 1473
German 1646-50, *1653,* 1655, 1687-88
Irish 1784
Italian 1829, *1847-48, 1855,* 1857, *1882, 1887,* 1888-90, 1891
Netherlandish 1945

CHIP CARVING. A simple, low relief form of ornamentation of the 18th and early 19th centuries, on American furniture. The work was accomplished with flat chisels and semicircular gouges. In the early 17th century, chip carving was used to enrich English furniture.

CHIPPENDALE, THOMAS I. An early-18th-century English cabinetmaker, and the creator of many early Georgian pieces. He was father of Thomas II, the most famous of the three Chippendales.

CHIPPENDALE, THOMAS II (1718–1779). The noted Chippendale. An English furniture designer and cabinetmaker. His earliest work was in the refined Georgian style, and in 1754 he published the *Gentleman and Cabinet-Maker's Director.* Chippendale's designs had great beauty, and he created in a variety of styles, including the decorated Queen Anne, Chinese, and Rococo French, as well as the Gothic. He was noted for his chairs, girandoles, mirrors, frames, and assorted beds (canopy, Chinese, dome, Gothic, field, and tent). He also designed many stands, side and serving tables, and teapoys. Henry Copeland, William Ince, Thomas Johnson, Mathias Lock, Robert Manwaring, J. Mayhew, and others followed in the styles originated by Chippendale. A Chippendale Chinese sofa is illustrated.

THOMAS CHIPPENDALE

☐ ALSO SEE *86,* 87-90, 638, 672, 675, 700-05, 729-33, 777,
826, 872, 892, *893,* 986

CHIPPENDALE, THOMAS III (1749-1822). The son of the noted Chippendale. He designed and executed furniture in the Regency style. He worked in partnership with Thomas Haig.

CHODOWEICKI, DANIEL (1726-1801). The most popular Prussian engraver of his day. Chodoweicki's work was used as source material for Höchst porcelain in Berlin and for some products of the Thuringian porcelain factories.

CHRYSELEPHANTINE. Made of ivory and gold. Certain ancient Greek statues were so made, the exposed body, face, and hands made of ivory, and the clothing or drapery of gold.

CHURCH-GOING CHAIR. A light, portable, folding chair of the 16th and 17th centuries. It is similar to today's folding bridge chairs. The chair was made of wood, with a leather or fabric seat. The chair back was often a colonnade motif made up of spiral colonnettes.

CHURCH-GOING CHAIR

CHURRIGUERA, JOSÉ (1665–1725). A Spanish architect who introduced the Baroque style into Spanish architecture. Heroically scaled motifs were applied onto structures rather than planned as funtioning parts of the construction. Columns and pilasters became spiral or baluster-form shafts; voluptuous volutes replaced pediments; and nudes, cherubim, plaster clouds, waterfalls, draperies and such became lost in the mélange of swirls, curves, and fantasy.

CHURRIGUERESQUE. The bold and massive Spanish Baroque style of the 17th century. The period was mainly influenced by the architect Churriguera. The Baroque period in Spain ran concurrently with the Rococo and up through the mid-18th century. There are an exuberance of color and an extravagance of ornament in this Baroque period which also had an effect on the Spanish possessions in the Americas. Examples of this style are: the west façade of the Granada Cathedral, the west façade of the Cathedral of Santiago de Compostela, and the gardens of the Palace of La Granja.

CHUTE

CHUTE. The French for "fall" or "tumble." The chutes were decorative bronze pieces that fitted over the exposed angles and on the legs of wood furniture pieces. The ornate plates were used to protect as well as reinforce these areas. These functional enrichments appear in 18th- and 19th-century French furniture. Many famous craftsmen like Caffieri made these chased and engraved pieces. Sometimes the chutes were finished as ormolu or as bronze-doré. Illustrated is a typical Louis XV commode. See *Sabots*.

CIEL DE LIT. French for a bed tester or canopy. Illustrated is an early French Renaissance bed.

CIPRIANI, GIOVANNI BATTISTA (1727–1785). An Italian painter of the Adam period in 18th-century England. He painted many ceiling and wall panels, as well as medallion inserts for Adam furniture. Cipriani did elegant, decorative, classic pieces and many graceful arabesque panels.

CIEL DE LIT

GIOVANNI BATTISTA CIPRIANI

CIRE PERDUE. French for "lost wax." A method of bronze casting in which a figure is modeled in wax and then coated with clay. The figure is heated, the melted wax runs out through holes left in the clay, and molten metal is poured into the clay shell. The final details are often worked directly on the bronze casting.

☐ ALSO SEE 1750

CISELÉ VELVET

CISTERN

CISELÉ VELVET. A raised, cut velvet which was typical of the Renaissance in Genoa. The pattern was raised up against a flattened background.

CISELEUR. A chiseler; a craftsman who ornaments bronze and other metals by chiseling, one who does chasing. A term applied to finishers of metal mounts and chutes for 18th-century furniture. A Renaissance metal hinge is illustrated.

CISTERN. In furniture, a wine cooler, sarcophagus, or cellarette of the latter part of the 18th century. It was most often used to keep bottles on ice, but sometimes it was used for washing up. A Chippendale cistern is illustrated. In architecture, a rectangular, metal, open-topped container for cold water. See *Cellarette, Sarcophagus,* and *Wine Cooler.*
☐ ALSO SEE *1212, 1292,* 1807, *2146*

CLAP TABLE. An early 18th-century English pier or console table which usually had a pier looking glass set over it. Illustrated is a clap table designed by Thomas Johnson.

CLAPBOARD HOUSE. The typical 17th-century New England house. Clapboarding (see *Clapboard Wall* below) was originally used as a protection for half-timbered houses in late Gothic–early Renaissance England, and was brought over to the New World. The house of Parson Capen at Topsfield, Massachusetts, (1683) is a typical clapboard house.

CLAPBOARD WALL. An exterior wall facing made up of horizontal, slightly overlapping planks. A weatherboarded wall.

CLARE-OBSCURE. The 18th-century Anglicised form of the French "clair-obscur," a method of painting in lights and shades or "chiaroscuro." It is similar to *Grisaille* painting.

CLASSIC. Referring to the architecture, sculpture, arts, and literary arts of the ancient Greeks and Romans. Something with an antique source or an established degree of excellence. 18th- and 19th-century architecture and arts based on Greek and Roman elements; this style usually called Neoclassic or new classic. Illustrated is the Greek Doric order.
☐ ALSO SEE 415, 486-87

CLASSIC REVIVAL. The early-19th-century architectural trend in England and the Continent which stressed the revival of classic forms and motifs. Classic prototypes were reexamined and supplied inspiration for new structures. Examples of the Classic Revival are the Royal Exchange in London, the Palais de Justice in Paris, the Court Theatre in Berlin. Greek columns and porticoes were frequently used. See *Barry, Sir Charles,* and *Neo-Greek* for illustrations.

CLAVATED. Club-shaped. A type of turning used for furniture legs and stretchers on early Renaissance Spanish furniture. A Louis XIII Renaissance chair done in the Spanish style is illustrated.

CLAVICEMBALO. A predecessor of the pianoforte which resembled a dulcimer with a keyboard attached to it.

CLAVICHORD. A 17th-century forerunner of the piano. A stringed instrument that was used in England during the Carolean, William and Mary, and Queen Anne periods.
☐ ALSO SEE 792

HINGE ORNAMENTED BY CISELEUR

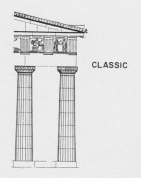

CLAP TABLE

CLASSIC

CLASSIC REVIVAL

CLAVATED

CLERESTORY. A window placed near the top of a wall above an adjacent roof. Clerestory windows in the nave wall of a church are those above the roof of the side aisles. See *Basilica*.

CLERESTORY

CLÉRISSY, PIERRE (1650-1728). The founder of the Moustiers faience industry in 1679. The *Tempesta* style produced between 1680 and 1710, and the *Bérain,* produced between 1710 and 1740, are the principal styles associated with Moustiers during the periods of Clerissy management.

CLIGNANCOURT. A hard-paste porcelain factory established by Pierre Deruelle at Clignancourt, Paris, in 1771. Clignancourt continued to produce fine-quality porcelain until 1798.

CLOCHE. A glass dome fitted over a wood base usually to protect artificial flowers, a clock, or an objet d'art from dust or harm.

CLOCK LAMP. A glass lamp developed about 1730 to provide a way of telling time at night. Oil was stored in a glass container at the top of the lamp, and a wick-holder protruded from one side. The time was told by observing the level of the oil in the glass, which was marked off in hours.

CLODION, CLAUDE MICHEL (1738–1814). A French sculptor who specialized in terra-cotta figures and figurines of satyrs, nymphs, and other decorative and sensual subjects. After the French Revolution, he was able to adapt to the Roman taste, and work on the Colonne de le Grande Armée, and the Arc de Triomphe du Carrousel (1806–1809).
☐ ALSO SEE *1482, 1484,* 1486

CLOISONNÉ. A type of enamelware in which delicate metal partition filaments hold and separate the assorted colored enamels in a pattern. The individual metal partitions are called cloisons. Illustrated is a section of a Japanese copper dish with cloisonné inlay.
☐ ALSO SEE 375, 2064, *2069,* 2070

CLOISONNÉ

CLOSE CHAIR or CLOSE STOOL. An enclosed box or stool equipped with a removable chamber pot. It was in use before the toilet or water closet came into architectural being. Sheraton describes his design in his *Cabinet Dictionary* (1803) as: "made to have the appearance of a small commode, standing upon legs; when it is used the seat part presses down to a proper height by the hand, and afterward it rises by means of lead weights, hung to the seat, by lines passing over the pulleys at each end, all which are enclosed in a case."

CLOTH OF GOLD. A cloth having gold threads or strips of gold woven with other textile yarns.

CLOTH OF SILVER. A decorative fabric having silver threads, silver strips, or threads containing some silver woven with other yarns.

CLOTHESPRESS

CLOTHESPRESS. A chest of drawers, sometimes with a cupboard set above it. The cupboard or cabinet has shelves to hold clothes. Illustrated is a Chippendale design.

CLOVEN FOOT. Decorative foot for a Louis XIV furniture leg. It resembles a deer's cleft hind foot. See *Pied de Biche*.

CLOVEN FOOT

CLUB CHAIR. A large, roomy, upholstered easy chair. It may or may not be skirted, and the type of arms may vary with period or style, from high to low, from thick to thin, from all-upholstered to partially unholstered and partially framed. An oversized bergère.

CLUB FOOT. A flat, round pad ending for a cabriole leg. It was used frequently on early-18th-century English furniture. See *Dutch Foot, Pad Foot*, and *Spoon Foot*.

CLUB FOOT

CLUNY LACE. See *Valenciennes Lace*.

CLUSTERED COLUMN LEG. A furniture leg made up of several grouped or engaged turnings or columns. This type of leg was used by Chippendale and William Ince in mid-18th-century England.

CLUSTERED COLUMN LEG

CLUSTERED COLUMNS. Several columns placed together or having overlapping shafts which form a single support. A Gothic architectural motif.

CLUSTERED COLUMN

CLUTHA GLASS. Glass characterized by a streaky and bubbly effect, worked in unusually shaped vases and bottles. It was developed by James Couper & Sons in Glasgow during the late 18th and early 19th centuries.
☐ ALSO SEE 2090-91

COAL SCUTTLE

COAL SCUTTLE. A box or bucket used as a coal receptacle. Sometimes made of brass and ornamented. See *Pipkins*.

COAT OF ARMS. Originally a lightweight garment, usually embroidered or decorated with heraldic emblems and worn over armor. In more recent terminology, the heraldic emblems of a family or institution. Illustrated is a design by the Adam brothers (mid-18th century) for the English royal family.

COAT OF ARMS

COBB, JOHN. An 18th-century English furniture maker and partner of William Vile. See *Vile, William*.
☐ ALSO SEE 672, 702

COBBLER'S BENCH. A shoemaker's bench with seat, last holder, and compartments for pegs, etc. It was "rustic" and usually made of pine in Colonial America. Reproductions and adaptations are made today and are used as cocktail tables in American-Provincial-type rooms.

COCHIN, CHARLES NICHOLAS (1714–1790). A French designer and engraver who opposed the rococo style and worked in the classic tradition.
☐ ALSO SEE 604, 1340, 1386, 1451

COCK BEADING

COCHOIS, JEAN-BAPTISTE. A French master cabinetmaker (ébéniste) to Louis XVI. He was an inventor of dual purpose and change-about furniture: a chiffonière that converted into a night table, etc.

COCK BEADING or MOLDING. A small convex or half-round projecting molding used around the edges of drawers. See *Single Arch Molding*.

COCKFIGHT CHAIR. A saddle-like chair with a small shelf as the top rail of the chair back. The individual straddles the chair facing the back. The top rail, usually padded, functioned as an armrest. This type of chair was used for reading, writing, and viewing sports events (like cockfighting, etc.) An 18th-century English favorite. See *Fumeuse, Ponteuse, Straddle Chair, Voyelle,* and *Voyeuse.*

COCKFIGHT CHAIR

COCKLESHELL. Also called the escallop or shell ornament. It was used as a carved decorative feature on furniture knees, crestings, and pendants of chairs and other furniture pieces in early-18th-century English, Louis XIV, and Louis XV period designs. See *Rococo* and *Scallop Shell.*

NATURAL SHELL

LOUIS XIV SHELL

LOUIS XIV SHELL

CODEX. A manuscript in the form of a volume with the pages bound together. This replaced the long rolls or scrolls originally used for manuscripts. The codex appears in the early Christian period. Illustrated is a Byzantine enamel from a codex now in the Library of S. Marco in Venice.

CODEX

COFFER. See *Coffered Panel* and *Coffre.*

COFFERED PANEL. In architecture, a sunken panel in the ceiling of a vault or dome, or in the underside of a cornice. The coffer is usually ornamented and decorated. Illustrated is the Pantheon in Rome.

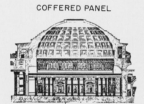

COFFERED PANEL

COFFRE (COFFER). A chest or strongbox used for holding valuables. It also served as a seating unit in Gothic interiors. A French Romanesque example is illustrated.
☐ ALSO SEE 363, *419,* 420

COFFRE

COFFRET. A small chest or coffer, often on its own stand or table.

COFFIN STOOL. A small oak four-legged stool, with stretchers, usually left undecorated. It may have been used originally to hold coffins awaiting interment.

COIFFEUSE. A hairdressing table or makeup table of the Louis XV and Louis XVI periods. See *Poudreuse* and *Table à Coiffer.*

COIN. A corner cupboard.

COIN

COIN GLASS. A drinking glass with a coin embedded in the stem, probably introduced in England about the time of Charles II and fashionable in the 17th and 18th centuries.

COLLAR. An astragal, or molding, which forms a band or ring around a furniture element like a table or chair leg.

COLLAR

COLOGNE STONEWARE. The products of the great stoneware factories in the Rhineland region of Germany. Cologne stoneware was produced as early as the Middle Ages. The typical 14th-century product of the Cologne factories was a gray stoneware jug washed with iron-bearing clay to achieve a brown color. The jugs were often decorated with bearded masks, flowers, oak branches, or figures.
☐ ALSO SEE 1628, 1629

COLONIAL AMERICA. The period in American art and architecture from 1620 up to the Revolution. It is the period of early settlement in America and blending of English, French, and Dutch influences with native provincial interpretations.
☐ ALSO SEE 13-38, 39-64, 65-90

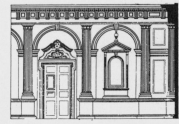

COLONIAL AMERICA

COLONNADE

COLONNETTE

PLACIDO COLUMBANI

SAMUEL COLT

COLONNADE. A row of columns supporting a single entablature. An architectural treatment for a passageway or corridor.

COLONNETTE. A miniature column used in architecture and also as a furniture decoration. In the Sheraton chair back here illustrated, the uprights resemble Corinthian columns. A group or cluster of colonnettes is sometimes used as a support for a pedestal table. A classic motif and a favorite of the Renaissance period.

COLT, SAMUEL (1814-1862). An American inventor and manufacturer of the revolving-breech pistol during the 19th century. □ ALSO SEE 168-70

COLUMBANI, PLACIDO. An 18th-century Italian architectural designer of the Adam period. He worked with the Adam brothers in designing decorative mirror frames, and is especially noted for his chimneypieces. Columbani published *A New Book of Ornaments* in 1775, and *A Variety of Capitals, Friezes, Cornices and Chimney Pieces* in 1776. See *Crunden, John.*

COMB BACK. A Windsor chair back in which the central group of spindles extends above the back proper, and is topped with an additional rail (the cresting rail). The top unit is called the comb piece since it resembles the high, Spanish-type combs that were fashionable in the 18th century. It is also called "three-back" Windsor chair.

COMB BACK

COMFIT GLASS. A small sweetmeat glass of 18th-century origin. In particular, this term applies to a stemmed glass approximately 4 inches high. Comfits were served after drinking or smoking, or at the end of a meal, to sweeten the breath.

COMMEDIA DELL'ARTE. Traditional form of Italian comedy popular with the artists and designers in the 18th century. Jacques Callot, Claude Gillot, and Antoine Watteau used scenes, costumes, and characters from the commedia dell'arte in their works.
□ ALSO SEE 267, 276, 649, 1258, 1660, *1672*, 1676, 1851, *1888*, 1889, *1890*, 1894

COMMERCE TABLE. An 18th-century collapsible or folding X-shaped frame which supported an oval card-table top. It was used to play Commerce, a card game.

COMMODE. A chest of drawers or a cabinet, usually low and squat. In about 1700, in the Louis XIV period, the term "bureau commode" was used to describe a large table with drawers. In the Regency and the Louis XV periods, the commode was often bombé in shape and it is considered the most typical piece of furniture of that time. The finer pieces showed no dividing rail or strip between the upper and lower drawer. The later units often had only two drawers. See illustration for *Chute* for a Louis XV commode. Also see *Cressent, Charles.* A commode is also a night stand, a bedside cabinet or chest.
□ ALSO SEE American (19th century) 107
English (18th century) *700, 729, 857*
(19th century) *932, 959*

COMMODE

French (18th century) 1226, *1227, 1276,* 1277-78, 1287, *1342-43, 1387-88,* 1389, 1407, *1409, 1446, 1448, 1458, 1502*
(19th century) *1528,* 1531, *1609*
German (18th century) *1688-89*
Italian (16th century) 1802
(18th century) *1855-56,* 1858, *1894,* 1895

COMMODE EN TOMBEAU

COMMODE DESSERTE. A French 18th-century sideboard with a center cabinet area and open shelves on either side.

COMMODES EN TOMBEAUX. Early Louis XV chests, usually designed with two small drawers on top, and two full-width drawers below. The units were heavy in appearance and the lowest drawer was only inches off the floor; the legs were that short. "Tombeau" is French for "tombstone" and these designs were massive, squat, and tombstone-like.

COMPANION CHAIR. Three curved upholstered chairs joined together at one point so that they appear to radiate from that central junction. Each chair is large enough to accommodate two persons. It is like a three-part *Tête-à-Tête* or *Siamoise.* The companion chair was popular in the mid and late-19th century.

COMPANY PAINTING. A type of painting made in the 18th and 19th centuries by Indian artists working for British communities in India. Adjusting their technique to the Western taste for subdued coloring and realistic detail, these artists satisfied the colonists' desire for a pictorial record of their experiences in India. The British East India Company sponsored many of the painters. See *Calcutta Painting* and *Lucknow Painting.*
☐ ALSO SEE 1753-57

COMPASS SEAT. An early-18th-century term for a round chair seat. It was also referred to as a pincushion seat or chair.

COMPO. See *Carton-Pierre, Composition Ornament, and Gesso.* A plaster or papier-mâché-like material molded or applied to a ceiling, panel, frame, or piece of furniture to create a bas-relief enrichment. Illustrated is a late-18th-century girandole, probably designed by Hepplewhite circa 1788, and executed on molded plaster.

COMPOSITE ORDER. A variation of the Corinthian order. The capital resembles an Ionic volute placed above rows of Corinthian acanthus leaves. A classic Roman order.

COMPOSITION ORNAMENT. An ornament or enrichment that is made of plaster or plaster-like material. The material is cast in a mold, and then applied to a surface to make a bas-relief decoration that resembles carving. The material and resulting ornament are also called "gesso" and "yeseria." Composition ornament was introduced into England by the Adam brothers for the decoration of panels, ceilings, walls, doors, etc. See *Anaglypta, Carton-Pierre, Gesso, Papier-Mâché,* and *Pargework.*

COMPOTIER. A container for stewed fruits, jellies, and jams.

CONFESSIONAL. An 18th-century large, upholstered French wing chair. In Catholic Church architecture, a small enclosure in which the priest sits to hear the confession.
☐ ALSO SEE *1235,* 1236, 1319

COMPO

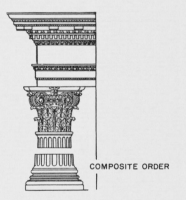

COMPOSITE ORDER

COMPOSITION ORNAMENT

CONFIDANTE. Three seats attached in a single unit. The two end seats are usually smaller, angled, and separated from the prominent center section by arms. A Hepplewhite "centre ottoman" is illustrated.

☐ ALSO SEE *789*

CONFORTABLE. An early French Renaissance all-upholstered chair. A forerunner of the bergère.

☐ ALSO SEE *1553*

CONFIDANTE

CONNECTICUT CHEST. An early American chest, with two rows of double drawers, which stands on four short legs. It was frequently decorated with split spindles, painted black, and sometimes ornamented with three carved panels (see *Aster Carving*). The Connecticut chests were often made of oak, with pine tops, backs, and bottoms.

CONSOLE

CONSOLE. The French term for "bracket." A console is a bracket, usually in an S scroll or curve. It is used architecturally to support a cornice or shelf. In furniture, it is more a decorative device than a functional one. The term often applies to a console table, which is actually a shelf supported against a wall by a bracket, a leg, or a pair of legs.

CONSOLE DESSERTE. A small serving table similar to a sideboard.

CONSOLE LEGS. Scroll legs that are bracket-shaped. They are found in late-18th-century furniture and are also called "bracket feet." Illustrated is a Chippendale wardrobe.

CONSOLE LEGS

CONSOLE MIRROR. A mirror that is set over a console or pier table. Illustrated is a German Empire console mirror and table.

CONSOLE MIRROR

CONSOLE SERVANTE. A serving table with a marble top and a shelf below, of the Louis XVI period. It is similar to the console desserte and commode desserte. A Sheraton design is illustrated.

CONSOLE SERVANTE

CONSOLE TABLE. A shelflike table that is attached to a wall, and supported by a receding front leg or legs, or set on an S-shaped curved or caryatid-type bracket. It was originally popular in 18th-century France and England, and is still in use today in foyers, entries, etc. It is also called a pier table.

☐ ALSO SEE 1238, *1316*, 1319, *1444*, *1892*, *1894*, *1895*

CONSOLE TABLE

CONSTITUTION MIRROR. A very late-18th, early-19th-century rectangular Sheraton-type mirror frame. It was usually gilded and had a row of balls under the cornice and a painted upper panel over the mirror area. In the 19th century the painting was often of the frigate *Constitution* of the War of 1812. It was also called a "tabernacle mirror."

CONTREPARTIE or CONTRE BOULLE. A form of boulle marquetry in which the brass forms the groundwork. The tortoiseshell is set into it, and is therefore the less prominent material. It is the reverse form of the usual boulle work or *Première Partie*.

CONVENTIONALIZATION

CONVOLUTE

CONVENTIONALIZATION. The simplifying or exaggerating of natural forms to make them more acceptable and reproducible in other materials. *A* is a realistic drawing of an acanthus leaf. *B* is a conventionalized form of it.

CONVERSATION CHAIR. This term has been applied to a variety of chairs: the caqueteuse in the 16th century, the roundabout or cockfight chair in the 18th century, and the S-shaped "vis-à-vis" or "dos-à-dos" of the 19th century. Essentially, it is a comfortable chair which is not as low or as deep as an easy or lounge chair.

CONVOLUTE. A scroll or paper-roll shape.

COPELAND, HENRY. An 18th-century cabinetmaker of the Chippendale, and then the Adam, school. With Matthias Lock, he published *A New Book of Ornaments.*

COQUILLAGE. A French rococo shell-like pattern used with birds, flowers, masks, and other carved ornaments to decorate mirrors, frames, clocks, etc. It also appears in Chippendale's French-style furniture as a furniture enrichment.

CORBEIL or CORBEILLE. A sculptured representation of a basket of fruit or flowers.

CORBEL. In architecture, a bracket or shoulder set in a wall to carry a beam. The corbel was also adapted for use on interiors and on furniture, and was popular in Renaissance designs. See *Bracket* and *Console.*

CORBEL

CORBEL

COQUILLAGE

CORBEL TABLE

CORBEL TABLE. A slab of stone or masonry which is supported by a row of corbels.

CORDEN, WILLIAM. One of the artists who contributed to the design of the famous Derby porcelains. Corden designed for Derby in about 1817, and he was one of the first artists to decorate the ware with pictures in the mode of oil paintings, a technique which had been popular for years on japanned iron and *papier-mâché* tea trays. See *Derby Porcelain.*

CORDOVAN LEATHER. The decorated leatherwork made in the technique and style begun in Cordova, Spain, during the Middle Ages. The leather was often stamped, carved, or embossed with gilt arabesques and Moorish patterns.
☐ ALSO SEE 368, 2126, 2127

CORDOVAN TAPESTRY. See *Guadamicil.*

CORINTHIAN ORDER. The most slender, graceful, and elaborate of the classic architectural orders. The Romans made the height of the column equal to ten times the diameter of the shaft. The capital is enriched with rows of acanthus leaves and four volutes.

CORINTHIAN WARE. Pottery produced in the Greek city of Corinth, dating from before 700 B.C. When first produced, it featured geometric, abstract motifs on narrow borders. These evolved into rhythmic curved patterns with bands and stylized geometric designs which were replaced by animal and figure subjects with Oriental motifs, combined with background motifs of rosettes and scaled patterns. From these developed

CORINTHIAN ORDER

CORNER CHAIR

CORINTHIANESQUE

the classic Corinthian decorations which combined abstract and stylized natural figures in black on a buff background. Later, Corinthian ware was given a wash of red ocher, and finally, red figures on black backgrounds were produced.

CORINTHIANESQUE. A design similar to the Corinthian order, but not an exact reproduction. Illustrated is an Italian Renaissance version of a Corinthian-type pilaster.

CORK LACE. Originally, the lace produced in County Cork, Ireland. Today, it has become a generic term referring to all Irish lace. Cork or Irish lace is made from fine linen, muslin, or cambric.

CORNER CHAIR. See *Roundabout Chair.*

CORNER CUPBOARD. A triangular cabinet or chest originally designed by architects as an integral part of a room. In the 18th century it became a mobile piece of furniture. See *Coin* and *Encoignure.*
□ ALSO SEE 59, *1343, 1344, 1409, 1686*

CORNER STILES

CORNER STILES. The corner or end vertical members in a paneled piece of furniture. A late-17th-century cabinet is illustrated.

CORNICE

CORNICE. The projecting top portion of a classic entablature consisting of bed fascia and crown moldings. In Renaissance-type interiors it was used on interior walls directly below the ceiling, without the frieze or architrave moldings. See *Architrave, Fascia,* and *Frieze.* Also, a decorative applied cap to a curtain or drapery arrangement on windows, canopy beds, etc. It is usually made of wood with molding trim, but it may be carved or covered with fabric. It is similar to a valance, lambrequin, or pelmet. In the mid-18th century it was called a "window mantel."

CORNUCOPIA

CORNUCOPIA. The twisting, spiraling "horn of plenty" of mythology. It is often represented with fruits and/or flowers pouring forth. As a decorative motif, it was popular in the Renaissance, Empire, and Victorian periods. Arms and legs of sofas were sometimes cornucopia-shaped in 19th-century furniture.

CORNICE

CORNUCOPIA SOFA. An English Regency sofa (circa 1820), with scrolled arms carved in the form of a cornucopia. The sofa back and legs repeat this motif. The foot was often a lion's paw. The cornucopia sofa also appeared in American Empire furniture.

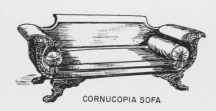

CORNUCOPIA SOFA

COROMANDEL. Also called coromandel ebony, calamander, and Macassar ebony. A hard, dark, brown wood with black stripes. It resembles black rosewood, and was used for banding and veneering in late-18th-century furniture.
□ ALSO SEE Wood *1108,* 1226

COROMANDEL LACQUER. A lacquering technique originally from the Honan province in central China. It was greatly admired and used in the Louis XV period for finishing commodes and cabinets. The background was a reddish-black color which

turned brown with age. The lacquer was very thick and applied in successive layers. It was possible to engrave or incise designs in the thick lacquer. Panels were decorated with figures, houses, landscapes, etc. See *Coromandel Screen*.
☐ ALSO SEE 292, 729

COROMANDEL SCREEN. A Chinese lacquered screen often decorated with an allover pattern in low relief, or executed with a landscape design. These screens were originally introduced into Europe by the East India Company in the middle of the 17th century. The finest were first made in Peking and Soochow.

COSMATI. The marble and mosaic workers of Rome from the 12th to the 14th century. They created pavements, tombs, pulpits, etc., in marble with inlays of mosaic, gilding, colored stones, and glass. By the 14th century, these workers, many of whom were from the same family, were producing sculpture. "Cosmati work" is a generic term for work in colored stone.

COSY CORNER. An upholstered couch that fitted into the corner of a room. Forming a complete right angle, it usually had an upholstered and tufted back, and was a popular piece in the late 19th century. It was similar to the corner ottoman, and was sometimes the main furnishing of a *Turkish Corner*. The mid-20th century, sectional furniture, in a way, fulfills the same purpose: a seating unit for two or more people to sit and talk to one another.

COTELLE, JEAN (1607–1676). Ornamental painter and engraver, a pupil of Guyot and Simon Vouet.

COTTAGE PIANO. An upright piano of the 18th and early 19th centuries. It usually had a fretwork panel in front of and above the keyboard. Behind the fretwork was a pleated silk curtain.

COTTE, ROBERT DE (1656–1735). Cabinetmaker and designer who assumed control of the Gobelins after Mignard. He was first the pupil and later the brother-in-law of Jules-Hardouin Mansart. Cotte directed the construction of the dome of Les Invalides in Paris, built the Hôtel de Ville in Lyons, restored the choir of Notre-Dame de Paris, designed the chapel of the Château de Versailles, the Episcopal Palace at Verdun, and the Benedictine Monastery of Saint-Denis.
☐ ALSO SEE *1396*, 1397

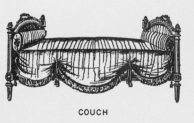

COUCH

COUCH. A lounge chair used for resting, with supports and cushions at one or both ends. It was a French innovation of the early 17th century, and developed into a "daybed." In 18th-century America, couch was synonymous with daybed. In common contemporary usage, a couch is often confused with a sofa or settee.

COUNTER BOULLE. See *Contrepartie*.

COUNTERPANE. A quilt. Usually it is the exposed quilt on top of a bed. The pattern is raised or "quilted."

COUNTRY CHIPPENDALE. A mid-18th-century American provincial version of Chippendale chairs, often made of pine and painted. These were simplified, but were usually very skillfully made.

COUNTRY FRENCH. A heavier, sturdier, more countrified version of the rococo style than the "French provincial" version. The "early-American" look with a French accent.

COURT CUPBOARD. "Court" is French for short. A low cupboard mounted on legs, or a double cupboard, usually heavily carved and massive in appearance. It was originally designed to hold plate, utensils, goblets, etc. In the Tudor period it was a buffet, and probably related to the Italian and French crédence. An oak court cupboard of the Jacobean period (17th century) is illustrated. The panels are decorated with lozenge carvings.
☐ ALSO SEE 420, *421*

COURT CUPBOARD

COURTING CHAIR. An upholstered double chair or settee. It was popular in the Louis XIV period. In the Queen Anne style, the design had an open back effect, and it looked as though two chairs had been joined together with a common seat. It is also called a two-chair back settee. A forerunner of the contemporary "love seat."

COURTING CHAIR

COURTING CHAIR

COURTING MIRROR. A small 18th–19th-century mirror with a simple wood frame with insets of small pieces of glass. The pieces of glass were often painted or decorated. It may originally have been a gift presented by a swain to the girl he was courting.

COVE. A quarter-circle, concave, downward curve from the ceiling to the woodwork of a wall, or from the wall down to the floor. It is also a large concave molding often used in a cornice or under the eaves of a roof.

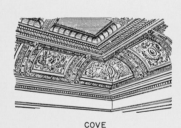

COVE

COVED CUPBOARD. An early American cupboard design with a hoodlike projection on top.

COYPEL, NOËL (1628–1707). A French painter and decorator. As a member of the Gobelins group, he painted furniture panels and designed tapestries. Coypel also worked on the decorations at Versailles.

COZZI, GEMINIANO. A Venetian manufacturer of hard-paste porcelain decorated with gilding and chinoiserie. It was popular late in the 18th and early 19th centuries.
☐ ALSO SEE *1847, 1848,* 1849-51, 1863

CRANBERRY GLASS. The name used to describe a particular form of pink glass that became very popular in England toward the end of the 19th century. It is usually made in the form of fluted vases or bowls with frilled rims.
☐ ALSO SEE 1094, *1095*

CRANDALL FAMILY. Highly inventive American toy manufacturers of the 19th century, originators of nesting blocks and croquet sets.
☐ ALSO SEE 116, *117,* 1138, *1139*

CRANE, WALTER (1845–1915). An English craftsman-designer. A disciple of William Morris and the Arts and Crafts movement. He said, "The true root of all art lies in the handicrafts."
☐ ALSO SEE 210, 213-14, 1078-79, 1142-46, 1159, *1161,* 1170-72, 1728

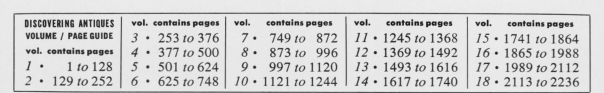

CREDENZA

CRESCENT STRETCHER

CRESTING

CRAPAUD. A low chair with curved back, totally covered in upholstery, produced in France in the 19th century.
☐ ALSO SEE 1535, 1553

CRAQUELURE. The network of fine cracks on the surface of an old painting. It may be caused by shrinkages, movement of paint film, and/or varnish.

CRAZY QUILT. A quilt pattern created by sewing a number of small pieces of colored material together in nonrepeating forms. The finished product is used to make the top of a coverlet or quilt. Each quilt is unique in design and color, and many also have fancy stitchery that enhances the design.

CREAMWARE. Cream-colored earthenware produced during the 18th century in England. The primary factories were Wedgwood in Staffordshire and the Leeds Pottery. Creamware has a rich glaze and was enameled, printed, and ornamented in gold. Creamware was also produced in Germany.
☐ ALSO SEE *756-58*, 759, 783-84, 828, *1018*, 1019, 1705-06

CRÉDENCE. A serving table and sideboard of the French Gothic period which may have evolved from a church piece. It was a chest mounted on a stand, or a display cabinet for plates, or for preparing and carving meats. See *Buffet* and *Desserte*.
☐ ALSO SEE 1802, 1854

CREDENZA. The Italian form of the *Crédence*.

CRÉMAILLÈRE. A swinging crane on a fireplace hearth.

CREMER. An 18th-century, French, Louis XV cabinetmaker who specialized in artificially colored marquetry work.

CREMO. An Italian marble with a creamy white ground and a network of golden veins.

CRESCENT STRETCHER. An arched or hooped stretcher, sometimes used between the legs of 18th-century furniture. It is often used as a reinforcing element on American Windsor chairs.

CRESSENT, CHARLES (1685–1768). A leading French cabinetmaker of the Régence and Louis XV periods. His designs were noted more for their ormolu trim and chased metalwork than for marquetry. Cressent was a student of Boulle, and he designed clocks and wall decorations. He used floral forms, cupids, lovers, garlands, and roses as well as monkeys and grotesques for his metal enrichments. Illustrated is a Louis XV commode attributed to Cressent. Massive gilt bronze mountings were employed.
☐ ALSO SEE 1261-62, 1276-79, 1361, 1367

CREST RAIL. The uppermost or top rail of a chair back. In the 16th and 17th centuries, this element was usually elaborately shaped and carved.

CRESTING. The Renaissance, elaborate carving on the top rail of a chair back or settee. The cresting was often centered on the top rail. The "crown and cherubs" was a favorite English Restoration cresting motif. In architecture, a carved, incised or perforated repeating design along the top of a wall or roof. See *Brattishing*.

CRÉDENCE

CHARLES CRESSENT

CREST RAIL

CRESTING

CRÈVECOURT DISH. An Hispano-Mauresque armorial dish.
☐ ALSO SEE 2112

CREWELWORK. Embroidery done with loosely twisted worsted yarn and a large-eyed needle on unbleached cotton or linen. It was a popular fabric decoration in the 16th and 17th centuries in England. In the Jacobean period it was often used to interpret winding floral designs like the East Indian "tree of life" motif.
☐ ALSO SEE 53, 141, 393, 537

CRICKET. An archaic name for a low wooden footstool. An English and early American design.

CRICKET TABLE. A small, three-legged, polygonal or round-top table of the Jacobean period in England. The straight legs were supported on a triangular frame with high stretchers between the legs.

CRINOLINE STRETCHER. A common device of Chippendale's Windsor chairs. The stretcher is concave in form and separates and reinforces the two front legs. Two short arms extend from the back legs to support the crinoline stretcher. See *Crescent Stretcher*.

CRINOLINE STRETCHER

CRISTALLO GLASS. A delicate Venetian-style glass developed in England in the 16th century. Simpler in design than Venetian and similar in appearance to rock crystal, it was made in a full range of useful and decorative pieces.
☐ ALSO SEE 409-11, 1659-61, 1812, 1813

CROCHET. A kind of needlework done in single, double, or triple loop stitches with a metal or wooden hooked needle.

CROCHET LACE. A delicate fabric crocheted with a fine hook and fine thread into intricate patterns.

CROCKET. A projecting carved ornament used on the side of pinnacles and spires. The ornament is often bud- or leaf-shaped, and appears in Gothic art and architecture. In the 19th-century English Gothic revival furniture, this motif was sometimes carved on architecturally inspired cabinets, bookcases, and thronelike chair posts.

CROCKET

CROMWELLIAN CHAIR. A severe, unadorned chair of the English Commonwealth period (1649–1660). It usually had knob or bobbin turnings, a low back, leather seat and back, and nailhead trim. The illustrated chair is an example of the Commonwealth period.

CROSS RAIL

CROQUET CHAIR. A mid- to late-19th-century woven wicker or rattan barrel chair. The base resembles an inverted woven basket. The arms and back make a continuous line which seems partially to encircle the seated person. The back and seat are usually equipped with button-tufted upholstery. See *Peacock Chair*.

CROMWELLIAN CHAIR

CROSS RAIL OR MEMBER. See *Slat*. A horizontal element which joins two verticals or two sides. In a chair back, the connecting element between the back posts. An Adam armchair is shown.

CROSS STRETCHERS

CROWN GLASS

CROSS STRETCHERS. See *Saltire* and *X-shaped Stretchers.*

CROWN BED. A simple canopy bed of the late-18th and early 19th centuries. The canopy is' suspended over the bed, or extends partially out over the bed from the wall behind. See *Baldaquin Bed.*

CROWN GLASS. An early form of window glass made with a blowpipe. The glass is formed as a flat dish with a button or bull's-eye center. Illustrated is a 16th-century French interior with crown glass set into leaded windows. See *Bull's-Eye.*

CRUIKSHANK, GEORGE (1792-1878). A 19th-century British artist and engraver. He is best known for works illustrating the books of Charles Dickens, characterized by picturesque vitality and a strong element of grotesque humor.
☐ ALSO SEE 951-53, 1145

JOHN CRUNDEN

CRUNDEN, JOHN. An 18th-century English designer (he died in 1828), who created furniture frets, allegorical centers for ceilings, railings, and chimneypieces. In association with Thomas Milton and Placido Columbani, he prepared *A Treasury of New Designs for Chimney Pieces.* Crunden also published *Designs for Ceilings, The Carpenter's Compositions for Chinese Railings, Gates, etc.,* and *Convenient and Ornamental Architecture.*
☐ ALSO SEE 779, 942

CRYSTAL PALACE

CRYSTAL. A clear, transparent quartz which resembles ice. It is usually cut and faceted to sparkle and reflect light. Crystal is often imitated in glass.
☐ ALSO SEE 398, *399, 402,* 403, 412, 499, 544, *545, 547*

CRYSTAL PALACE. Built in London in 1851 as an exhibition hall. It covered an area of 800,000 square feet and was constructed mainly of prefabricated parts. The hall was built by Joseph Paxton, and it was based on ridge and furrow construction used in greenhouses. The entire basis of construction was the 4' sheet of glass (the largest available at the time). It was the first building of its kind and the first of such dimensions constructed of glass, iron, and timber over a framework of cast- and wrought-iron girders accurately bolted together.
☐ ALSO SEE 1906-09, 1913, 1915-16, 1919, 1922

CUBE FOOT

C-SCROLL. An ornamental motif, painted, applied, or carved, which resembles the letter C or various combinations of the letter C. The C's may be inverted, touching back to back, top to bottom, or set askew of each other. This form of ornament is found in Spanish and French Gothic architecture and furniture. The enrichment was used extensively in the Baroque, Rococo, Queen Anne, and Chippendale periods.

C-SCROLL

CUBE FOOT. See *Block Foot.*

CUCCI, DOMENICO. A great French cabinetmaker of the 17th century who designed in the Louis XIV style. He specialized in decorations of gold, bronze, colored stones, ornaments, and figures. Cucci was a rival of Boulle and Caffieri.

CUERDA SECA. Literally, "dry cord," a pottery-glazing technique practiced in Spain from the 11th century. Outlines were painted with manganese and grease to prevent colors from running during firing.
☐ ALSO SEE 2126, 2127, 2175, *2177*

CUP CASTER

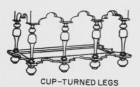

CUP-TURNED LEGS

CUPBOARD

CURRICULE CHAIR

CUL-DE-LAMP

CUP AND COVER TURNING

CUPID'S BOW

CUIVRE. French for "copper."

CUIVRE DORÉ. French for "gilded copper." It is also called pomponne, after the Hôtel de Pomponne, where this plated or gilded ware was originally made.

CUIVRE-JAUNE. French for "brass."

CUL-DE-LAMP. A pendant, either of wood, metal, or stone, used as a bracket for a lamp. These brackets were highly decorated with carving or painting. Illustrated is a 17th-century cul-de-lamp.

CUP AND COVER TURNING. A popular Elizabethan and Jacobean turning used for furniture supports. It resembles a cup topped with a lid or an inverted saucer form. A late-16th-century Elizabethan oak four-poster bed is illustrated.

CUP CASTER. A brass cup with a roller below which fits onto a chair or table leg. A Sheraton book cabinet is illustrated.

CUP-TURNED LEG. The prominent cuplike feature in a turning which was popular in the late 17th and early 18th centuries. It was a development of a Portuguese bulb shape, and was also known as the bell and trumpet leg. In England the cup-turned leg is characteristic of the William and Mary style.

CUPBOARD. A storage cabinet with doors. It may be raised up on high legs, or be set low. The cabinet may have drawers or another cabinet below. The style and design varies with type and use. A 19th-century German design of late Gothic influence is illustrated.

☐ ALSO SEE American (17th century) 20
   (18th century) 59/ (19th century) *187*
   English (16th century) 363-64
      (17th century) 420, *421*
      (19th century) *986, 990, 1010*
   French (17th century) 1238
      (18th century) *1343, 1344, 1409,* 1445
   German (16th century) 1623, *1624*
      (18th century) *1653, 1686*
      (19th century) 1710
   Italian (15th-16th centuries) 1800-02
      (17th century) *1829*
   Netherlandish (16th century) *2132,* 2133-34
      (17th century) *1932,* 1948, *1950, 1952*

CUPID'S BOW. A Chippendale-style top rail of a chair back which is shaped like a bow, with compound curves, and often with spiral volutes on the ends. The cupid's bow with arrows also appeared as a decorative motif in the Louis XV and Louis XVI periods.

CURRICULE CHAIR. A late-18th-century, early-19th-century Sheraton-type chair with a semicircular back and splayed legs which, according to Sheraton, resembles an open carriage of the period.

CURRIER AND IVES PRINTS. American lithographs, produced in the 19th and early 20th centuries. In 1857 Nathaniel Currier

(1813-1888) went into partnership with James Merritt Ives (1824-1895) and, during the fifty years of its existence, the firm produced between seven and eight thousand hand-colored lithographs that faithfully portrayed the life of the times.
□ ALSO SEE *145*, 162-65, 251

CURTIS, LEMUEL (1790-1851). An American clockmaker who developed the girandole clock, a form of the banjo clock decorated with gold leaf.
□ ALSO SEE *109*, 111, 128

CURULE CHAIR

CURULE CHAIR. A 17th-century chair. The arm supports and the back rails are semicircular in shape. The legs are also semicircular. The general appearance is an X created by the two intersecting S curves, or one C resting on an inverted C. A leather strip usually provides the back rest, and the seat is also a piece of leather. The design is based on a classic Roman prototype, the sella curulis of the Roman magistrate. Another version of the curule chair became popular in the early-19th-century Empire and Regency periods. A Sheraton design is illustrated. See *Dante Chair*.
□ ALSO SEE 134, 1503-04, 1532

CURULE CHAIR

CURULE LEGS

CURULE LEGS. X-shaped legs such as were used on classic Greek and Roman folding stools. They became popular again in the Renaissance period, and continued in favor up through the Regency and French Empire periods. A Chippendale design is illustrated. See *Curule Chair*.

CURVILINEAR. Created within curved or arced lines. Some Gothic tracery was curvilinear in concept. A German Rococo console table, here illustrated, shows the curvilinear line quality which was prevalent during the Rococo period.

CURVILINEAR

CUSHION. A shaped, flexible bag of fabric or leather, filled with feathers or other filling materials. A pillow. Illustrated is a Louis XVI sofa with a separate cushion seat. It is added to the upholstered platform and back for extra softness and comfort.
□ ALSO SEE 22, 364, 392-95, 1193

CUSHION

CUSHIONED FRIEZE. A Rennaissance convex or cushion-shaped frieze. Sometimes used on cabinets of the late 17th and early 18th centuries. Illustrated is the top of a chest of the latter part of the 17th century.

CUSPS. The pointed endings of a trefoil or quatrefoil in Gothic architecture. The meeting points are the pendants between the arcs. Chippendale and Sheraton used cusping as a carved decorative trim on some of their chair backs. See *Quatrefoil* and *Trefoil*.

CUSHIONED FRIEZE

CUSSEY, DOMENICO. A French 17th-century cabinetmaker to Richelieu, the chief minister to Louis XIII.

CUSPS

CUT GLASS. Glass decorated with faceted, deeply incised designs. The process evolved from gem cutting and is done in much the same manner. Cut glass first flourished as an art in the Middle East. Glass cutting developed in Europe during the 16th century in Bohemia. After 1730, English cut glass was very popular. In 1780, Ireland began to produce a variety of heavy glass that was more deeply incised and ornate. In about 1825, molded pressed glass was developed in America and was widely used as an inexpensive substitute for cut glass. See *Pressed Glass*.

CYLINDER FRONT

CUVILLIÉS, FRANCOIS DE (1698–1767). A great French furniture maker of the Louis XV period. He was an architect and engraver in the extreme Rococo style and favored the Chinese style in applied decoration.
☐ ALSO SEE 604, *1667*, 1668-70, *1671*, 1686-88, *1689*

CUVILLIÉS THE YOUNGER (Jean-François) (1731–1805). A designer of ornaments and decorations influenced by Germanic styles.

CYLINDER FRONT. A quarter-round front of a desk or secretary which is mounted so that it can be pivoted. Illustrated is a late-18th-century Sheraton desk design.

CYLINDER TOP

CYLINDER TOP. A rolltop cover to a bureau or desk. It differs from the tambour top in that it does not roll up on itself. See *Gouthière, Pierre,* for an illustration of a Louis XVI cylinder secrétaire.

CYMA CURVE. An S-shaped curve.
☐ ALSO SEE 59

CYPRESS CHESTS. Early Renaissance chests made to hold tapestries, robes, and such. Cedar was used because its aroma is repellent to moths. The cypress chest was a prototype of current cedar chests.

DAGOBERT CHAIR

DAIS

DADO. The lower portion of the wall when it is treated differently or separated from the rest of the wall by a molding strip. A wainscot. In classic styles the dado had a base, shaft, and cap molding, and it was often paneled or ornamented.

DADO CAP. The crown or cap molding of a dado. It is also called a *Chair Rail*.

DAGLEY. A 17th-century French craftsman who introduced the secret of Japanese lacquer into France. The technique was used at the Gobelins and called *Vernis de Gobelins*.

DAGOBERT CHAIR. A famous 7th-century folding chair, originally made of gilt bronze supposedly by St. Eloi. The back and arms were added in the 12th century by Abbé Suger. It is one of the very few pieces of furniture remaining from this period.

DAGUERREOTYPE. First photographic process, invented in 1839 by Louis Daguerre. A faint image was produced which had to be viewed from an angle for clarity.
☐ ALSO SEE 1102, 1594

DAIS. A low raised platform usually located at the end or side of a room. Illustrated is a bench on a dais in a 10th-century interior.

DALOU, JULES (1838-1902). A French sculptor whose small terracotta models were cast in bronze in multiple editions.
☐ ALSO SEE *1566*, 1568, *1569*

DAMASCENE WORK (Damascening). See *Damascus Work*.

DAMASCUS WORK. A type of metal inlay work in patterns or arabesques. The design is incised in metal and then inlaid with other metals or wires cut to fit.
☐ ALSO SEE 2011, 2151, *2152*

DAMASK. A firm, glossy, patterned fabric with a Jacquard weave. It was introduced into Europe by Marco Polo, and named for the city of Damascus. It is similar to brocade, but it is flatter and reversible and can be in one or two color designs. On the reverse side, the pattern changes in color or may appear shiny (the pattern is matte on the face side). Damask was originally made of silk but is now woven in cotton, rayon, linen, silk, wool, or a combination of the above fibers.

DAMMOUSE, ALBERT. A French ceramicist and glass designer known for his delicate Art Nouveau vases in *pâte-d'émail*, a porcelainlike substance combining crushed glass with colored oxides.
☐ ALSO SEE *1564*, 1593, 1612

DAN-DAY CHAIR. A form of the Windsor chair produced in Suffolk in the early 19th century. It was named for its maker. Norwegian copies were made of this chair, with slight variations on the design of the underframe.

DANTE CHAIR. An X-shaped chair of the Italian Renaissance period. It was usually heavily carved and upholstered in leather. The X curved up from the floor and became the arms of the chair. Variations of this design appeared in French, Spanish, English, and Teutonic early Renaissance furniture. See *Curule Chair* for another version of the X chair.
☐ ALSO SEE 1802

DARBY AND JOAN CHAIR. A mid-18th-century English chair with a double or triple chair back and a wide seat which would accommodate several persons. A two- or three-chair-back settee named for characters in a poem, "The Joys of Love Never Forgot," published in 1735.

DARLEY, MATHIAS. An 18th-century English architect, designer, engraver, and publisher. Darley engraved plates for Chippendale's *Director* and may have assisted him with his designs. He also published *A Compleat Body of Architecture, Embellished with a Great Variety of Ornaments* and, with George Edwards, *A New Book of Chinese Designs*. See *Fire Irons* for Edwards designs.

DARNICK. An 18th-century coarse damask fabric.

DAUPHINE. A matte finish, silk fabric which was popular in the late Louis XVI period.

DAVENPORT. An early-19th-century small kneehole desk with a lift top writing slope, and drawers at the side. It was named after a Captain Davenport. In contemporary usage it is an overstuffed upholstered sofa with padded arms and back. It was named after a Mr. Davenport of Boston who originally made these sofas. Illustrated is a Sheraton late-18th-century design with a loose pillow back.

DAMASCENE WORK

DAMASK

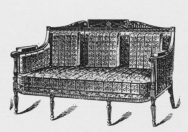
DANTE CHAIR

DARBY AND JOAN CHAIR

MATHIAS DARLEY

DAVENPORT

DAVENPORT POTTERY. The earthenware poduced by John Davenport's factory at Longport, Staffordshire. Situated in the midst of fine clay deposits, the Davenport factory operated from 1793 to 1882, at first producing only earthenware, then manufacturing porcelain and glassware.
☐ ALSO SEE *1028*

DAVID, JACQUES LOUIS (1748–1825). A French painter, considered the "dictator of the Empire style." He was a classic painter, both in technique as well as in subject matter, and was Court painter to Louis XVI. David joined in the French Revolution, was a friend of Robespierre, and was imprisoned for a while. Later, he became court painter to Napoleon I. Among his works are: "Blind Belisarius Asking Alms," "Brutus," "Coronation of Napoleon," "Mme Recamier," "Death of Socrates," and "Rape of the Sabines."
☐ ALSO SEE 142, 931, 1378, 1407, 1452, *1453*, 1493, 1495, 1497, *1502*, 1503-04, *1507*, 1509

DAVILIER. A 17th-century French designer and architect under Louis XIV. He created many interior detail designs.

DAVIS, ALEXANDER JACKSON. An early-19th-century American architect who in 1832 designed "Glen Ellen," the Gothic-type country estate of Robert Gilmor near Baltimore. It was equipped with oriel windows, crenellated towers, gables with crockets and finials, and a highly irregular plan.

DAVIS, JOHN. An early-18th-century American cabinetmaker who worked in Lynn, Massachusetts.

DAYBED

DAYBED. A "studio couch," rest bed, or narrow bed, placed lengthwise along a wall. It may have equally tall head and foot boards, or none at all. The daybed was introduced as a seating unit in the 17th century. It is related to chaise longues and couches. Illustrated is a caned daybed of the second half of the 17th century. The scrollwork on the stretchers and head-rails is typical of the time. See *Studio Couch.*
☐ ALSO SEE American *136*
English *417*, 418, *448*, 449, 482, *533*
French *1236*, 1237, *1318*, 1320, *1493*, *1502*, 1503, 1532

DECANTER. From the French for "to pour from one vessel to another." A crystal, glass, or metal container which holds wine or other liquids. It is a serving piece. A rock crystal decanter of the French Renaissance is shown here.
☐ ALSO SEE 74, *486*, 906-07, 977, 979, *1164*, *1167*, *1578*, *1713*, 1792-93, *2055*

DECANTER

DECEPTION BED. A concealed or partially concealed bed unit in 18th-century American cabinetwork. The term also refers to a bed which converts from a chest, chair, table, etc.

DÉCOR AUX CINQ BOUQUETS. A popular style of decoration typical of Tournai porcelain. *Décor aux cinq bouquets* is a blue and white design of five sprays or sprigs of blossoms, painted in the Chinese-influenced Meissen style. One spray is painted in the center of the plate and four are painted around the rim. The blue of the bouquets is sometimes outlined in gold. The concept of the design, placing a central figure on the center of the plate and corresponding or complementary ones on the rim, was popular during the 18th century and featured subjects such as flying birds or St. George and the Dragon. *Décor aux cinq bouquets* is also called *decor rotunda*.

DECORATED PERIOD. The English Gothic architecture of the 14th century. It is noted for geometric and flowing tracery, enlarged clerestories, and star-shaped, or stellar, vaulting. It is also called the Geometrical, Curvilinear, Middle Pointed, Edwardian, and Later Plantagenet period. Illustrated is a window from the Cloisters at Westminster Abbey, A.D. 1360.

DECORATED PERIOD

DECORATED QUEEN ANNE PERIOD. The English furniture style prevalent about 1710 to 1730, also called the Early Georgian period. It was basically a continuation of the Queen Anne style with cabriole legs, claw-and-ball feet, carved and shaped splats, and more ornate and heavily carved than the previous period.

DECORATED
QUEEN ANNE PERIOD

DÉCOUPAGE. An art form created by cutting and pasting down assorted materials in interesting new patterns and arrangements. It became popular in the 18th century as the "poor man's" method of embellishing wood furniture. The technique was also employed to decorate boxes, screens, trays, etc. Découpage is similar to *Arte Povera, Collage,* and *Montage.*

DELANOIS, LOUIS (1731–1792). A French master cabinetmaker under Louis XV. He was a protégé of Mme Du Barry and designed much of the furniture at Versailles.

DELFT. The name of a city in Holland, and also the name of brilliant blue-colored, heavily glazed pottery produced in Delft. The rich blue designs are on a white field, and they are either scenic or provincial-type patterns. Ceramic tiles are also made in this particular blue and white, and they have been used to face fireplaces and walls and are also used on floors.

☐ ALSO SEE *1935,* 1964
  Majolica 1941, 1943, 1945
  Tiles 1669

DELFT TILES

DEMARCY, GASPARD AND BALTHAZAR. 17th-century French craftsmen who worked in stucco and wood and also did metalwork. Charles Le Brun employed them during the period of Louis XIV.

DEMIDOME. A half dome topping cupboards, bookcases, and other architectural furniture of the early and mid-18th century. The demidome was often interpreted as a shell-shaped niche in Georgian furniture and interiors. Illustrated is the Lord Mayor's stall in St. Paul's Cathedral in London designed by Sir Christopher Wren at the end of the 17th century.

DEMIDOME

DEMILUNE. A half of a circle or half-round plan. A semicircular commode, console, or sideboard. A late-18th-century Sheraton design with tambour doors is illustrated. See *Doe's-Foot Leg* for a Hepplewhite demilune table.

DEMILUNE

DEMI-PATERA. A half-patera or rosette. It is often found in mid- and late-18th-century pier tables, consoles, or demilune commodes. An 18th-century Hepplewhite pier table is shown. See *Demilune.*

DEMI-PATERA

DEMOISELLE. See *Wig Stand.*

DEMILUNE

DEMOISELLE À ATOURNER. A Gothic wig-stand which also served as a dressing table. It was usually a round tabletop on a shaft base with a carved wooden head placed in the center to hold the wig. See *Wig Stand*.

DENTIL. One of a series of small projecting rectangular blocks in a cornice. It appears in Ionic and Corinthian cornices, and was also used as a furniture and interior detail by Adam and Hepplewhite.

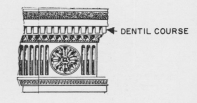
← DENTIL COURSE

DENTIL COURSE. A series of dentils in a row. Illustrated is a design for an Ionic entablature designed by the Adam brothers in the mid-18th century in England.

DERBY PORCELAIN. English porcelain, manufactured in Derby, from before 1750 to the second half of the 19th century. Originally, Derbyware consisted of medallions, figurines, and tableware, creamy white in color and characterized by realistic figures. Later, delicately colored hard-paste ware showing the influence of Meissen designs was produced.
☐ ALSO SEE 563-64, 647-50, 740, 747, 1575

DERBYSHIRE CHAIR

DERBYSHIRE CHAIR. A provincial type of Jacobean chair. The straight upright ends have inward scrolls on top. The top rail and crossrail are often arch-shaped.

DERUTA MAJOLICA. The ware produced in Deruta, Italy, having both polychrome and luster decoration. Of especially high quality in the early 16th century, Deruta pieces are characterized by a silver luster with a hard yellow tone.
☐ ALSO SEE 1805, 1807, 1808, 1863, 2146

DESK

DESK. A writing surface with or without drawers and/or cabinets. See *Bureau, Cylinder Top, Drop Lid or Dropfront, Escritoire, Kneehole Desk, Pedestal Desk, Scritoire, Secrétaire,* and *Secretary*.

DESORNAMENTADO. Spanish for "without ornament." A severe style of architecture and decoration developed by the Spanish Renaissance architect Juan de Herrera under Phillip II in the mid-16th century. Examples of his work are the Escorial near Madrid, and southern portion of the Alcazar in Toledo with its grand staircase enclosed under a barrel vault.

DESSERTE

DESSERTE. A small serving table or sideboard with one or more under shelves, similar to a dumbwaiter. It appears in the Louis XVI period. See *Buffet* and *Crédence*.

DEU-DARN

DEU-DARN. A two tiered *Tri-Darn* or a court cupboard without the dresser.

DIAMOND ORNAMENT. See *Lozenge*. A favorite late-Tudor ornament used to enrich carved chest fronts, bedsteads, cabinets, etc.

DIAMOND ORNAMENT

DIAPER PATTERN. An allover or repeating pattern without definite limits, applied as a decoration to a plain surface. Often the area is latticed and floral, or geometric designs are set into boxes. It is and was used on walls, wallpapers, cabinet enrichments, etc.

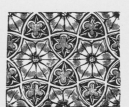
DIAPER PATTERN

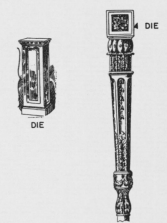

DIE

DIE

DIE. The space between the cap and base of a pedestal. Also, a rectangular block on the top of a leg. Illustrated is a Sheraton furniture leg. See *Patera*.

DINANDERIE. A 15th-century metal alloy of copper, tin, and lead. A forerunner of pewter. It was used to make ornamental figures in Dinant in Belgium. It is also called bell metal.

DIP SEAT. A chair seat which is lower in the center than at the sides. It is also curved (concave) to accommodate the body of the sitter. Illustrated is a mid-18th-century Chippendale chair. See *Dropped or Dipped Seat*.

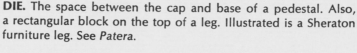

DIP SEAT

DIPTYCH. A small, two-panel, hinged screen, either painted or carved, which may be made of wood, metal, ivory, etc.

DIRECTORY. The "Directoire" period in France (1799–1804). Antique Greek and Roman decorations found even greater favor and were superimposed on the already classic lines of the Louis XVI style. The Directory period led into the Empire. See *French Directoire*.

DISHED

DIPTYCH

DISHED. A term applied to the sunken areas in the top surface of card tables. The depressed areas were used to hold money or candles. A dished-top table has a raised edge or rim which gives the effect that the entire table surface is sunken.

DISK FOOT. A small, flattened ball foot or pad on a cabriole leg in the Queen Anne style.

DISK TURNING. Flat circular turnings used to ornament furniture.

DISTEMPER. An art medium: opaque water color paints, similar to tempera, consisting of pigments, water, and white of egg, size, or emulsion of egg yolk.

DISTRESSED. Said of old pieces of wood furniture which show small scratches or holes, the result of age and use. In present-day furniture, these holes and scratches simulated in paint or spatter. "Fly-specked."

DIRECTORY

DIRECTORY

DIVAN. A long, armless and backless, upholstered settee. The word originally meant a Turkish or Persian court or council, or a room where such gatherings take place. The French adapted this cushion-like seat into the upholstered bench. See *Bench*. In current usage, a divan is a couch.

DOCCIA POTTERY AND PORCELAIN. The wares produced by a factory founded in Doccia, Italy, in 1735. Although gray in color, Doccia porcelain is similar to English hard-paste porcelain. During the 18th century the factory produced tableware, centerpieces, and figurines. Doccia imitations of Oriental porcelain produced in the 19th century are considered collector's items.

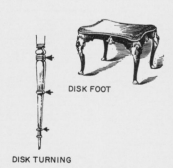

DISK FOOT

DISK TURNING

DOCUMENT BOX or DRAWER. A small vertical drawer in 18th-century English and American secretaries and cabinet desks. It is usually ornamented with colonnettes, and the document drawer is found on either side of the central compartment in the interior of the desk.

DOCUMENTARIES. Fabrics, wallpapers, etc., which are based on, or derived from, authentic period designs.

DOE'S FOOT LEG

DOG'S TOOTH

DOG'S TOOTH

DOUBLET

DOULTON WARE

DOE'S-FOOT LEG. An elongated S-shaped leg typical of the Louis XV period. It originally terminated in a deer's cleft hoof. A Hepplewhite demilune table is illustrated.

DOG GRATE. A fireplace accessory. A movable fire grate.

DOG'S TOOTH. A form of ornamentation used in Early English Gothic architecture. It resembles a row of teeth.

DOME BED. An 18th-century canopied bed with a dome-shaped tester. It is usually heavily draped and swagged, and was also called a "Polish Bed." A Chippendale design is illustrated.

DOMED TOP. See *Hooded Tops*.

DOMINO PAPERS. Marbleized squares of wallpaper, originally produced in Italy in the late 16th and early 17th centuries.

DOREUR. The French word for one who gilds or applies a gilt finish to wood, metal, etc.

DORIC ORDER. The oldest and simplest of the Greek classic orders of architecture. In the Roman version, the column was eight times the diameter of the shaft, and the entablature was two diameters high. See *Classic*.

DORURE. French for "gilding."

DOS-À-DOS. French for "back to back." A seating device which consists of two attached seats facing in opposite directions. In order to converse, the seated persons must turn around in their seats and look over their shoulders. See *Conversation Chair* and *Vis-à-Vis*.

DOSSIER. French for "chair back" or "splat." A 16th-century French armchair or fauteuil (illustrated). Also a high-backed, canopied, wooden bench built into the wainscot of an English Gothic building. It was usually made to hold four, and it served as a seat for dining. In French interiors the term could also refer to the headboard or footboard of a bed.

DOSSIER PLAT. A "flat back." A French term used to describe the back of a chair. A late German Renaissance armchair is shown.

DOUBLE CHAIR. See *Courting Chair*.

DOUBLET. In ornament, the term refers to a pair or two of the same design. Illustrated in a hanging armoire of the early French Renaissance.

DOULTON. English pottery and porcelain, first manufactured in the early 19th century by John Doulton, who specialized in the production of such household objects as jugs and mugs made of salt-glazed stoneware.
☐ ALSO SEE 1091-92, *1093*, 1120

DOME BED

DORIC ORDER

DOSSIER

DOSSIER PLAT

DOUNE FIREARMS. The pistols made in Doune, Scotland, from about 1646. The weapons have characteristic butt-profiles known as lemon-butt and fishtail.
□ ALSO SEE 2095, 2098

DOWER CHEST. See *Cassone, Connecticut Chest,* and *Hope Chest.*

DOWNING, ANDREW JACKSON. A mid-19th-century American landscape architect and "tastemaker" of the period. He came from Newburgh, New York, and published *The Architecture of Country Houses* in 1850. The book had a great impact on the period, and the trend toward "Italian-style" villas. Downing also advocated "Gothic cottages" because they were not only "picturesque, but their floor plans are well suited to our informal world."
□ ALSO SEE 988

DRAGON'S CLAW FOOT

DRAGON'S CLAW FOOT. See *Ball-and-Claw Foot.* An 18th-century furniture leg ending which was a carved representation of a dragon's scaly claw, often grasping a ball or pearl.

DRAGON'S HEAD. The dragon is an oriental motif, and it is often found on heavily carved oriental furniture. It is also the symbol of Wales, and the dragon's head appears as an ornamental carved motif on English Tudor and Jacobean chests. Illustrated is an 18th-century dragon from George Edwards and Mathias Darley's *A New Book of Chinese Designs* (1754).

DRAGON'S HEAD

DRAKE FOOT. An 18th-century English furniture foot with three toes which resembles the contracted claw of a male duck.

DRAPERY. Fabric hangings on either side of a window, or covering a window or door, or an entire wall of windows. The fabric may be shirred, pleated, or pinched, and may be made of natural or man-made fibers. The choice of fabric, color, pattern, texture, and type of treatment depends upon the period of decoration and the general scale of the opening to be draped. The regular vertical falling drapery may be enhanced with swags, jabots, lambrequins, and cornices. Drapery may also refer to the fabric treatment on 16th-, 17th- and 18th-century beds.

DRAUGHT CHAIR

DRAUGHT CHAIR

DRAUGHT CHAIR. An 18th-century-designed upholstered winged chair with or without closed sides, which was constructed to protect one from draughts. It is similar to a *Porter Chair.*

DRAW LEAF TABLE. See *Draw Table.*

DRAW RUNNER. A supporting device for the drop-lid or fall-front surface of a secretary or desk. It is a small strip of wood inserted into a slot immediately below the surface to be supported.

DRAW RUNNER

DRAPERY

DRAPERY

DRAW TABLE. A three-leaved, refectory-like table. The two end leaves rest under the center one. When these two end pieces are drawn out from under the large central table surface, the center leaf falls down into the opening thus created, and the two end leaves make a large, continuous flush surface with the central leaf. It is the forerunner of the telescope dining table. The illustrated example is of late-17th-century England and shows the Dutch influence. It is also called a "draw-leaf table."
□ ALSO SEE *363,* 364, *418,* 420, *1194, 1951*

DRAW TABLE

DRAWING

DRAWING TABLE

DRESSING MIRROR

DRESSOIR DE SALLE À MANGER

DRAWING BOOK CHAIR BACK

DRESSER

DRESSING TABLE

DROP HANDLE

DRAWING. The art of representing images, shapes, patterns, or three-dimensional elements on a two-dimensional surface.

DRAWING BOOK CHAIR BACK. A popular Sheraton design for a chair back which was widely copied by American cabinet-makers from Sheraton's book *The Cabinet-Maker and Upholsterer's Drawing Book.*

DRAWING TABLE. A late-18th-century worktable designed by Sheraton for artists or designers. The top of the table rises on a double horse and is adjustable so that the artist may stand or sit to work. A small flap draws out of the top to hold a "still life" or the small model being painted. The sliders at each end hold drawing instruments and lamps. See *Architect's Table.*

DRESDEN PORCELAIN AND POTTERY. See *Meissen.*

DRESSER. Originally a sideboard or buffet with storage space for plates, etc., or a cabinet with drawers and/or shelves. Illustrated is a Queen Anne oak dresser of the early 18th century.
☐ ALSO SEE 420, *1087*

DRESSER, CHRISTOPHER (1834-1904). An English commercial designer of glass and silver whose work reflects a functionalist aesthetic.
☐ ALSO SEE *1005,* 1006, 1078, 1165, *1166,* 1168-72, 1244, *2090, 2091*

DRESSING MIRROR. A small, standing, portable mirror, or a mirror on a stand, sometimes with drawers, which was set on a table, low chest, or cabinet and used as an adjunct to dressing. Also called a "toilet mirror."

DRESSING TABLE. A kneehole type of table with large and small drawers surrounding the central knee area. A mirror is usually attached to the table surface. In its present form it is based on a 19th-century innovation. For an earlier type of dressing table, see *Poudreuse.*
☐ ALSO SEE American 22
    English 450, *533,* 535, *704,* 842-43, *858, 1128, 1129*
    French 1346, *1388,* 1522, *1531,* 1532, *1610*
    Russian 2067

DRESSOIR DE SALLE À MANGER. French for a dining-room dresser or buffet. A 16th-century, large dresser-top cupboard unit like this French Renaissance piece of the period of François I. See *Buffet, Crédence, Dresser,* and *Welsh Dresser.*

DRINKING TABLE. See *Wine Table.*

DROP FRONT. See *Drop Lid.*

DROP HANDLE. A pendant-like piece of hardware that functions as a drawer pull.

DROP LID. A top or front of a desk hinged to cover an inner compartment of drawers, boxes, pigeonholes, etc. When the front is dropped down, the inner surface of the desk front

DROP LID

makes a flat writing surface flush with the inner compartment. There are usually drawers below the enclosed top area. See *Slope-Front Desk*.

DROP ORNAMENT. A carved, shaped, or pierced ornament which extends below the underframe of a chair or cabinet, but does not extend across the whole width of the underframe. When it extends across the whole length it is called an apron, front, or skirt.

DROP ORNAMENT

DROP-LEAF TABLE. See *Flap Table*.

DROPPED OR DIPPED SEAT. A seat with a concave surface between the two side rails. A depressed center area in a chair seat, also called a "scoop seat." A late-18th-century Sheraton design is illustrated. See *Dip Seat*.

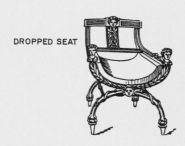

DROPPED SEAT

DRUM TABLE. A round table wih a deep apron, sometimes made with drawers set in all around the apron. The table usually presents a squat, drumlike appearance.

DRUM TABLE

DRUNKARD'S CHAIR. Also called a "lover's chair." A Queen Anne period vogue which lasted through the 18th century. The seats were up to 33" wide, and allowed one person to sprawl comfortably, or two to nestle closely. In current usage it is sometimes referred to as a "chair and a half."

DRUNKARD'S CHAIR

DRY SINKS. 19th-century low kitchen cabinets usually made of pine. They were made to hold a pitcher and washbasin on the top surface, and there was usually closed cabinet space below. The top of the sink was sometimes covered with slate or marble. "Water benches" served the same purpose as the sinks.

DRYPOINT ENGRAVING. The simplest of all etching techniques. It consists of drawing with a hard steel "pencil" on a metal plate. The burr that results from scratching the surface gives the "dry point" its ability to catch the ink, and it prints with a depth which adds sharpness to the design. Not too many impressions or printings can be made from a plate. Drypoint engraving is a form of intaglio engraving.
☐ ALSO SEE *1581*, 1582

DU CERCEAU, JACQUES ANDROUET. A 16th-century French Renaissance architect, draftsman, and furniture designer who studied in Italy under Bramante. In 1550 he published *Recueil Grave de Muebles* which set forth rules of proportion and ornamentation to be used on furniture based on antique forms. Du Cerceau originated the use of long columns, on buffets and cupboards, which rose from the base to the top of the unit. Illustrated is a bench made from a design by Du Cerceau.
☐ ALSO SEE 1192, 1193, 1194, 1202

JACQUES ANDROUET DU CERCEAU

DUAL-PURPOSE UNIT. Something designed to serve more than one purpose, like a convertible couch. See *Library Armchair*, *Library Press Bedstead*, and *Library Steps*. A Sheraton design is illustrated.

DUAL-PURPOSE UNIT

DUBOIS, JACQUES (c. 1693–1763). Cabinetmaker of the French Régence and Louis XV periods. Twisted fishtails or mermaid appendages appear in several of his pieces as terminal ends for his mounts.

DUCHESSE

DÜRER

DUCHESSE BED

DUST RUFFLE

DUBOIS, RENE. An 18th-century French cabinetmaker for Louis XV and Louis XVI.

DUCHESSE. A chaise longue in one piece. It is described by Sheraton as two bergères with a footstool in the middle. A Sheraton design is illustrated.

DUCHESSE BED. A canopy bed without posts. The tester is attached to the wall above the bed, and extends over the bed. The draperies from the tester are pulled back to either side of the bed, and they usually extend down to the floor. It was originally an 18th-century French design.

DUCHESSE BRISÉE. A chaise longue with a separate foot piece.

DUCHESSE LACE. See *Valenciennes Lace.*

DUCK FOOT. A webbed furniture foot of the late-17th- early-18th-centuries. It is found in Flemish and English furniture.

DUGOURC. An 18th-century French designer of the Louis XVI period. He was especially partial to the quiver and arrows as a decorative motif, and he faithfully produced Pompeii-inspired furniture. Dugourc was made the designer of costumes and decorations for the opera in 1784. His masterpiece was the Grand Salon à Coupola at Bagatelle.
☐ ALSO SEE 1530

DULCIMER. A small, stringed musical instrument of antiquity. It is triangular in shape, and the strings are struck with hammers to produce the musical notes.

DUMBWAITER. A three-tiered, tripod, circular table, dating from the 18th century. Sheraton designed many elaborate dumbwaiters with drawers, shelves, and trays. See *Rafraîchissoir.* In the Victorian period, a dumbwaiter was a lift for bringing up food from the basement kitchen to the dining room.
☐ ALSO SEE 1346

DUMMY BOARD FIGURES. Also called "picture board dummies." See *Fireside Figures.*

DUNCAN PHYFE. See *Phyfe, Duncan.*

DÜRER, ALBRECHT (1471-1528). A German Renaissance painter, draftsman, engraver, and designer of woodcuts. His intellectual concern with the arts, together with his keen observation of nature, resulted in superbly lifelike studies of figures, animals, plants, and landscapes.
☐ ALSO SEE 368, 404, 1618, 1619, 1620, 1621, 1631, 1636-40, 1900

DUST RUFFLE. A shirred, pleated, or tailored fabric piece which extends, usually, from under the mattress of a bed down to the floor. It covers the legs of the bed frame, and supposedly sets up a barrier to keep the dust from getting under the bed. Examples of dust ruffles are seen from the Elizabethan period on up to the present. A mid-18th-century Chippendale bedstead is illustrated.

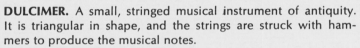

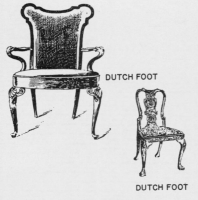

DUTCH FOOT

DUTCH FOOT

DUTCH LEG

DUTCH DRESSER. A hutch cabinet. A two-section unit with a closed cupboard or drawer unit, and open shelves above. See *Welsh Dresser.*

DUTCH FOOT. A pad foot or spoon foot on a cabriole furniture leg. It was especially popular in late-17th-century and early-18th-century furniture. See *Pad Foot.* See *Easy Chair* illustration.

DUTCH LEG. A wood turned leg consisting of rounded forms spaced with flattened oval discs. It usually ends in a squared-off form, and rests on a flat, oval foot.

DUTCH SETTLE. A wooden settle with a hinged tabletop surface behind. When flipped up on to the settle top, the unit becomes a table.

EARPIECE

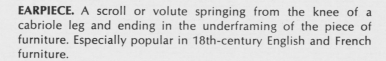

EARPIECE. A scroll or volute springing from the knee of a cabriole leg and ending in the underframing of the piece of furniture. Especially popular in 18th-century English and French furniture.

EARLY AMERICAN. The period in American art, architecture, and furniture from about 1600 to about 1720. The designs are basically Jacobean, Carolean, and William and Mary, but executed simply and provincially in native woods. Dutch influences were strongly felt in areas like New York.
☐ ALSO SEE 13-38, 39-64, 65-90

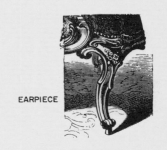

EARLY AMERICAN

EARS. In architecture, moldings or cornices over doors or windows which overlap the uprights of the door or window frame. They were used as a cornice decoration in the 18th century in England and America. In furniture, the extended parts of the top rail beyond the upright supports of the chair back.

EARTHENWARE. Pottery made of coarse clay. It is heavy, soft, porous, and opaque like a common red flowerpot.

EASTLAKE, CHARLES L., JR. (1793–1865). An advocate of the Gothic revival in England during the 19th century. He was an architect and furniture designer who combined Gothic and Japanese ornaments, and, using machine methods, arranged to produce assorted pieces of furniture embellished with heavy hardware, metal, and tile panel inserts, etc. Cherrywood was the principal wood employed. Illustrated is a chair from Eastlake's *Hints on Household Taste.*
☐ ALSO SEE 216, 217, 1077, 1082, 1086

EARS

CHARLES L. EASTLAKE, JR.

EASY CHAIR. A roomy, comfortable, upholstered chair of any style or period, which is made for ease and relaxation. It is usually based on the bergère and wing chair. An 18th-century easy chair is shown.
☐ ALSO SEE *447*, 449, 481, *1234, 1235,* 1236

EASY CHAIR

ÉBÉNISTE. French for "ebony worker." In the early French Renaissance (15th and 16th centuries), furniture was often made of ebony glued onto blackened pearwood for strength and size. The cabinetmakers who worked on these pieces were called "ébénistes" or "joiners and carpenters on ebony." Maître ébéniste" was the official title of the "King's cabinetmaker." Illustrated is a French cabinet of the period of Henri II (mid-16th century). See *Stabre, Laurent.*
☐ ALSO SEE 1192-94, 1223, 1276, 1286, 1288-89, 1317, 1343,
1406, 1456, 1459, 1504, 1529, 1531, 1537

ÉBÉNISTE

EBONY. A tropical, hard, dense, heavy brown-black wood with a fine grain. It was popular in France during the Louis XIV period, and again in the Empire and mid-19th century. True ebony comes from Ceylon, and black ebony is found in North India and the Himalayas.

☐ ALSO SEE *522, 1204, 1225,* 1226, *1289, 1717,* 1829, 1950, 1951

ECHINUS

ECHINUS. An oval-shaped molding. It is part of a classical capital, and it is located between the shaft and the abacus. In furniture ornament, the egg-and-dart, egg-and-tongue, or egg-and-anchor motif carved on the ovolo molding of furniture.

ECKHARDT, ANTHONY GEORGE. An 18th-century English manufacturer of printed fabrics and wallpapers. He had a patent for printing designs on silk, cotton, muslin, calicos, and wallpaper. He worked in association with his brother Frederick, and they employed talented French designers like Boileau, Feuglet, and Joinot. The wallpaper designs were produced with wood blocks or copper plates. Often hand details were added, as well as silver and gold leaf embellishments.

ECLECTICISM. The borrowing and combining of art forms and motifs from assorted past periods and adapting them to contemporary uses. The Victorian 19th century was considered an era of eclecticism. Older patterns and styles were borrowed and adapted to the new mechanized processes of the times. Illustrated is a German mid-19th-century chair which strongly resembles Early Renaissance prototypes.

ECLECTICISM

ÉCOLE DES BEAUX ARTS. The leading French art institute of the 19th century. It tended to give greater unity and consistency to the architecture and art of France, and it had a great influence on maintaining standards of taste, refinement, and correctness of style. It also, unfortunately, negated the advancement of new ideas and styles.

ÉCRAN

ÉCRAN. A fire screen, or a small screen set on a table to shield one from the firelight. A small shade on a candlestick. Illustrated is a design by Antoine Watteau (18th-century France).

ÉCRAN À CHEVAL. A frame with a sliding panel, used as a fire screen. See *Banner Screen, Cheval Screen,* and *Horse Screen.*

ÉCRAN À COULISSE. A French term for a cheval or fire screen.

ÉCRAN À ÉCLISSE. See *Pole Screen.*

ÉCUELLE. A French term for a decorative centerpiece that generally rests on a stand. Écuelles were made of silver and porcelain.

☐ ALSO SEE 1302, *1303,* 1382, 1681, 1903, *2056*

ÉCRAN À CHEVAL

EDOUART, AUGUSTIN (1783-1861). The outstanding maker of silhouettes and hair pictures.

☐ ALSO SEE 869-70, *919,* 922, 1274

EDWARDIAN PERIOD. See *Decorated Period.*

EGG AND DART

EGG AND DART. A molding decoration which resembles a continuous string of egg or ovoid forms separated by dartlike or arrowhead points. "Egg and tongue" and "egg and anchor" moldings are almost identical. See *Echinus*.

EGG FAMILY. Swiss gunsmiths who worked in England. Durs (1748-1831) acquired an international reputation for his military and sporting weapons; his nephew Joseph contributed advances to gun technology, and his cased sets of pistols are considered among the finest examples of firearms craftmanship.
□ ALSO SEE 901, *1044*, 1045-48

"EGG-SHELL" PORCELAIN. A term for porcelain that is semi-transparent, light, and delicate.
□ ALSO SEE 240, *244*, 352, 1543

ÉGLOMISÉ. An art form in which the painting is done on the reverse side of glass, and often embellished with gold leaf.

ÉGOUTTOIR. A piece of French provincial furniture with open rack shelves for drying or storing dishes.

EIGHT-LEGGED TABLE

EGYPTIAN STYLE. Sphinxes and Egyptian heads used as decoration on furniture and in architecture. This style began to appear in Europe after Napoleon's Egyptian campaign in 1798, and interest was furthered by later archeological discoveries. The Egyptian style recurred at intervals throughout the 19th and the first part of the 20th centuries.
□ ALSO SEE 216, *217*, 956, 2067

EIGHT-LEGGED TABLE. An 18th-century English form of the gateleg table. It was usually made of mahogany. See *Gateleg Table* and *Thousand-Leg Table*.

ELGIN MARBLES

ELGIN MARBLES. The pediment and frieze sculptures of the Parthenon brought to the British Museum by Lord Elgin in the early 19th century. Illustrated is one of the carved metopes. While Ambassador from England to Turkey, Lord Elgin, with a group of architects, sculptors, and painters started excavations at the Acropolis in Athens. After much labor, effort, and money was expended he was able to get the now famous marbles to England.

ELIZABETHAN

ELIZABETHAN. Referring to the reign of Elizabeth I of England 1558–1603. Illustrated is the Great Bed of Ware, a state bed. Renaissance motifs are here intermingled with the remnants of the Gothic tradition. See *Chest* for an Elizabethan chest, *Center Table* for an Elizabethan interior, and *Alcove* for an Elizabethan oriel window.
□ ALSO SEE 357-86, 387-412, 430-33, 495

ELLIOTT, JOHN. An 18th-century American cabinetmaker who worked in Philadelphia. He was noted for his wall mirrors and dressing cases.

ÉMAUX DE NIELLURE. A French term for an enameling process like niello. Lines are cut into the metal and then filled with enamel.

EMBLEM. A decorative symbol or device used in heraldry. It appears in carvings, embroideries, and painted panels. Examples are Napoleon's bee and the salamander of François I.

EMBLEM

EMBOSSED

EMBOSSED. Decorated with a raised design produced on a surface by hammering, stamping, or molding.

EMBOSSING

EMBOSSING. In fabrics, a process for pressing a design onto a fabric by passing the fabric through hot engraved rollers. A piece of embossed velvet is shown. See *Cut Pile*.

EMBROIDERY. The art of decorating a fabric with a raised design or pattern. The design is worked out with a needle and thread, either by hand or machine. The design may be of one or more colors, and a great variety of stitches or combinations of stitches may be employed. A 16th-century example of Spanish Renaissance embroidery is illustrated.

☐ ALSO SEE English 54, 367-68, 450, *596*, 597, *698*, *822*, *1080-81*, 1082, 1930
French *1334*, 1480, 1516
Indian 1762-66, 1928
Russian 2017, 2032-35
Spanish 2143
Turkish 2173, *2183*, 2184

EMBROIDERY

EMPAISTIC. Sculpture or structural elements made of, or covered with sheet metal which has been hammered in decorative patterns. It was a forerunner of boulle work. See *Boulle, André Charles*.

EMPIRE

EMPIRE

EMPIRE. The Napoleonic period in France and the great classic revival style of architecture, art, and decoration. The period roughly extends from 1804 to 1820. It is a period which combines the grandeur and martial symbols of Rome with Ancient Egyptian motifs and the elements of Greek architecture. The furniture of the period is massive, architectural in concept, and lavishly trimmed in bronze and brass on rosewood, mahogany, and ebony. Charles Percier and Pierre Fontaine were the great designers of furniture and interiors of the period, and Jacques Louis David was the major art force of the time. The style spread into England where Thomas Hope and Thomas Sheraton became leading exponents of the Empire style. Duncan Phyfe in America developed a style along the lines of the Empire, and in Germany and Austria, the Biedermeier style evolved. See *Biedermeier; David, Jacques Louis; Empire Drape; Fontaine, Pierre François Léonard; Normand, Charles P. T.;* and *Percier, Charles*.

☐ ALSO SEE 133-37, 1474, 1507-11, 1514-37, 1540-58, 1615

EMPIRE BED. A typical bed of the early 19th century in France. It was low and usually set against a wall or in an alcove, with only one major side exposed. Curved sweeping ends form the headboard and footboard. The Empire bed is similar to the boat bed and the gondola bed, and was a forerunner of the American sleigh bed. Illustrated is Napoleon's bed at the Grand Trianon, Versailles.

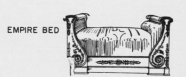

EMPIRE BED

EMPIRE DRAPE. A simple, classic drapery treatment. The fabric is caught at the top hem at equidistant points, and the valleys, formed between these points, fall freely. A formal pattern is created of fairly rigid verticals from the caught points to the floor, alternating with draped billows. It was very popular in the Empire period (early 19th century). Illustrated is a wall treatment in the Royal Palace in Venice in 1834.

EMPIRE DRAPE

EN CAGE BOX. A small box for cosmetics, snuff, sweetmeats, or souvenirs, popular in 18th-century France. The exterior consists of a thin framework of gold bordering miniature paintings under glass.

☐ ALSO SEE *1270, 1271,* 1273

EN CAMAÏEU. A French term for monochrome painted decoration.

☐ ALSO SEE 277, 1267, 1273, *1292,* 1336, 1593

EN CAS or EN CASE. A small table of the Louis XV period similar to a night table (table de chevet). It was usually marble-topped and had a drawer and a cupboard below.

EN CONFESSIONAL. See *Confessional.*

EN TABLEAU. An upholstery technique of the late 18th century. A sharp ridge, outlined in gimp, braid, or cord, defined the straight lines of the sofa or chair. Illustrated is a late Sheraton sofa.

EN TABLEAU

ENAMEL. A colored glaze used to decorate metal or ceramics. After firing, the paint becomes hard and permanent. It is applied to pottery or porcelain after a preliminary glaze. The piece is then fired again to fuse the enamel to the original glaze.

ENAMEL

☐ ALSO SEE 245-48, ·370, 459, 651-55, 800, *911,* 1195-98, *1271, 1272, 1273, 1427, 1428, 1429, 1430,* 1600-03, *1634,* 1736-39, 1752, *1760,* 2024, 2026, 2062-64, *2068,* 2069

ENCARPUS. A fruit or flower festoon used to enhance flat surfaces. It was employed extensively in the Italian Renaissance and in the Louis XV and Louis XVI periods.

ENCARPUS

ENCOIGNURE. A corner cabinet or table, often built in as part of the architecture of the room. See *Coin.*

ENDIVE MARQUETRY. A Queen Anne style of fine flowing-line marquetry similar to seaweed marquetry. The flowing lines resemble the leaves of the endive plant. See *Seaweed Marquetry.*

ENCOIGNURE

ENGINE TURNING. The parallel ridges on pottery made by turning the ware on a lathe after wheel-throwing, a feature of Leeds and Wedgwood ceramics.

☐ ALSO SEE *756, 759, 1271,* 1273, *1428,* 2064

ENGRAVING. A generic term covering many methods of multiplying prints. In general terms, a design is cut in a hard material such as copper, steel, or wood. The artist may incise his design; or he may cut out the areas around it, thus making a raised design. The design is inked, and impressions are taken. Some engraving techniques are: woodcut, linocut, line engraving, drypoint, etching, mezzotint, aquatint, wood engraving, intaglio engraving.

☐ ALSO SEE American (16th-17th centuries) 23-26
    (18th century) *96,* 98
    (18th-19th centuries) 142-44
    (19th century) *147-49*
  Dutch (16th century) 2031
    (17th century) 1959-60, 1979-80
  English (16th-17th centuries) 513-17
    (17th century) *458, 460*
    (18th century) *529, 530, 567, 568,* 814-15

French (17th century) 1206, 1216-17, *1256, 1257, 1258*
   (18th century) 1468-71, *2171, 2172, 2173*
   (19th century) *1514, 1515, 1516, 1517*
German (16th century) *1197*, 1636-40
Italian (16th century) 1873
   (17th century) *1837, 1838*
   (18th century) 1896-1900

ENRICHMENT

ENRICHMENT. A painted or carved repeated design on moldings, such as the guilloche, egg and dart, honeysuckle, chevron, etc. Illustrated is a section of a French Romanesque portal showing a series of "enriched moldings."

ENROULEMENTS DÉCOUPÉS. A French term for slashed or pinked edged scrolls. A decorative carved or painted French motif of the Renaissance period. Illustrated is a panel over a doorway at St. Madou in Rouen (16th century). See *Strapwork*.

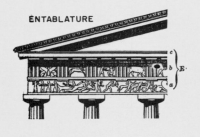

ENTABLATURE

ENTABLATURE. In architecture, the upper portion of a classic order which consists of an architrave, frieze, and cornice. The entablature rests upon the column. See *Classic*, and *Cornice*.

ENTRELAC

ENTRELAC. A Louis XVI decorative carved interlacing motif which is similar to a *Guilloche*.

ENVELOPE TABLE. A square table top with four "envelope flap" hinged sections which, when flipped back, increase the tabletop surface. A late-18th-century design, also found in the Directoire period. It is often used for card table designs, and is similar in concept to the triangular *Handkerchief Table*.

ÉPERGNE

ÉPERGNE. A French word for an ornamental stand with a dish on top. It may have candelabra branches extending out from the stand, below the dish, or it may have a trumpet-like container rising above the dish. The bell-like opening is used as a flower container. The épergne is usually used as a table centerpiece.
☐ ALSO SEE *599*, 602, 663, *985*

ESCUTCHEON

ESCABELLE. An early French Renaissance stool or chair supported on trestles. It is similar to the Italian sgabello.

ESCABELLE

ESCRITOIRE. A French term for a small desk with drawers and compartments. A secretary.
☐ ALSO SEE 1532

ESCUTCHEON. A shield with a heraldic device. In hardware, a decoratively shaped plate for a keyhole, knob, pull, or doorknob backing.

ESPAGNOLETTE. A terminal ornament popular in 16th- and 17th-century French furniture. It is a female bust used as part of a support, or the ending of a volute. In the French Régence period it is a female head with a tall, stiff lace collar or ruff that gives a generally Spanish flavor. The ornate head was a popular decorative motif for wood carvings and bronze mounts.
☐ ALSO SEE *1278*, 1279, 1284

ESCRITOIRE

ESPAGNOLETTE

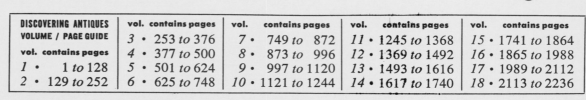

ESTAGNIÉ. A French provincial open hanging shelf unit used to hold pewter utensils. The piece sometimes had a drawer under the shelves.

ESTRADE. The French version of the Spanish estrado, a drawing room. The word also refers to an elevated part of the floor or room, a platform placed at one end. It originally meant a couch or bed area in an alcove. A feature in 17th-century Spanish architecture. See *Alcove.*

ÉTAGÈRE. Hanging or standing open shelves. A light, elegant unit for displaying books, bric-a-brac, etc. A "whatnot" unit. Illustrated is a hanging étagère designed by Chippendale. In the 19th century this same term was applied to worktables with several shelves.

ÉTAGÈRE

ETCHING. A form of intaglio engraving. A copper plate is covered with a resinous ground impervious to acid, and the artist or etcher then draws on this surface with a needle. The plate is bathed in acid, which bites into the scratched lines, engraving the design. The design is inked and impressions are taken. Rembrandt was a famous etcher, and the 17th century was a noteworthy period in the production of etchings.
☐ ALSO SEE Dutch (17th century) 1979, 1980-81
    English (18th century) *717*
       (18th-19th centuries) 949-53
       (19th century) 1057-58
    French (18th century) 1468-71
       (19th century) 1580-84
    Irish (18th century) 1779, *1781*
    Italian (17th century) *1838*
       (18th century) *1896*, 1898-1900
    Spanish (18th-19th centuries) 2157-60

ETIOLLES PORCELAIN. French hard-paste porcelain made after 1768, characterized by neoclassical floral decoration and, more rarely, by figure and landscape subjects.
☐ ALSO SEE 1473, *1474*

ETRUSCAN ORDER

ETRUSCAN ORDER. Also called the "Tuscan order." A Roman variation of the simple Doric order. A heavy, massive column, seven diameters high. See *Diameter* and *Doric Order.*

ETRUSCAN STYLE. French style of furniture and interior decoration, the last phase of Louis XVI neoclassical taste. Inspired by the painting on supposed Etruscan vases, it was characterized by austerity of line and ornament.
☐ ALSO SEE 1502-06, 1550

ETRUSCAN WARE. Vases and urns designed by Josiah Wedgwood in the 1760's, based on the supposed Etruscan finds of archeologists in Italy.
☐ ALSO SEE *782*, 785

EVOLUTE. A continuous wave or Vitruvian scroll. A classic motif used in the 18th century as a decoration on bands, cornices, friezes, etc. See *Vitruvian Scroll.*

EVOLUTE

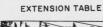

EXTENSION TABLE

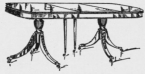

EXTENSION TABLE. A tabletop which separates in the center, and extends outward in both directions. Additional leaves are then added in the open space which has been created. Illustrated is an early-19th-century Duncan Phyfe extension table.

FABERGÉ, PETER CARL (1846-1920). A Russian goldsmith and jeweler, jeweler to the Tsars Alexander III and Nicholas II. He is best known for designing the Fabergé Fantasies, elaborate and expensive cigarette cases, candy boxes, and decorative trinkets, and for his intricate jeweled Easter eggs executed for the Tsars.
☐ ALSO SEE *211*, *248*, 2062, *2063*, 2068-70, 2111

FAÇON de VENISE. A style of glassware produced throughout Europe from the 16th century, based on the elaborate engraved and colored pieces of Venetian design.
☐ ALSO SEE 1659-61, 1663, 1953-56

FAÏENCE. French for "pottery." Terra-cotta. A peasant type of glazed pottery originally made at Faenza, Italy. A glazed bisquit ware. It may be used as a facing for buildings or walls in the form of tiles or blocks. It is also used as a flooring material. See *Terra-Cotta*.
☐ ALSO SEE Belgian and Dutch 243
French 1210-15, 1244, 1246, 1268, 1399-1403, 1597, 1646

FAIRINGS. Small, mass-produced china pieces made in Germany after English designs, sold at English fairs. These 19th-century curios were usually intended to be humorous, representing scenes and misadventures of daily life.
☐ ALSO SEE 1040-43

FAKE. A counterfeit reproduction of an object made to pass as the original. It is usually artificially aged or patinaed.

FALDISTORIUM. A late Italian Renaissance curule chair which was made of wrought iron and brass, and had a leather or velvet seat. See *Curule Chair*.

FALDSTOOL. A folding or portable stool of the Gothic period.

FALL FRONT. See *Drop Lid*. Illustrated is a Queen Anne toilet chest.

FAMILLE NOIRE, VERTE, JAUNE, ROSE, ETC. French names for Chinese pottery having a colored background. Literally it means: black family, green family, yellow family, rose family, etc.
☐ ALSO SEE *312*, 314, 349, *350-51*, 375, *589*

FAN DESIGN. A semicircular, fanlike ornament used in late-18th-century furniture in England and America.

FANBACK CHAIR. A chair or settee with a fanlike motif, either upright or reversed, for the chair back. Originally an 18th-century French design.

FANCY CHAIR. A Sheraton-designed small-scaled, elegant side chair. A late-18th-century favorite.

FANLIGHT. A window set above a door or entranceway. In Georgian buildings, the fanlight is often semicircular in shape, and the panes are separated by bars radiating from the center in a fanlike arrangement.

FARNESE PALACE. Built in Rome in 1534 by Antonio da Sangallo, it is considered to be the grandest palace of the Italian Renaissance period. The "piano nobile" (main level) has alternate triangular and segmented pediment windows.

FAN DESIGN

FANLIGHT

FALL FRONT

FANCY CHAIR

FARNESE PALACE

The upper story, added by Michelangelo, has columns on brackets holding up the triangular pediment. The round-headed windows beneath the pediment are a Michelangelo feature. The crowning cornice is of a magnificent scale, and it was done in the Florentine style. See *Renaissance Revival* for Sir Charles Barry's adaptation of the Farnese Palace in his Reform Club in London.

☐ ALSO SEE 1822

FARTHINGALE CHAIR. A wide-seated chair, without arms, made to accommodate the voluminous skirts (farthingales) of the Elizabethan costume.

☐ ALSO SEE *418*, 419, 497, 1193

FARTHINGALE CHAIR

FASCES. A Roman symbol of power. A bundle of rods enclosing an axe. It appeared most recently as the symbol of the 20th-century Italian Fascists.

FASCIA. The projecting crown molding of a cornice. A molding with a flat vertical plane in section. Also spelled "facia."

FASCES

FASHION PLATE. An illustration of a clothing style.

FAUDESTEUIL

FAUDESTEUIL. A Romanesque bench or seating stool with curved X-shaped supports. This type of stool usually had a leather sling for a seat, and the piece was collapsible. In the Gothic period, the legs are fixed and the chair does not usually fold. Illustrated is a 14th-century French Gothic faudesteuil made of iron with brass finials and a leather strap for a seat. See *Pliant*.

FAUN. A creature from classical myth, half-man, half-goat, a decorative element in the French and Italian Renaissance period. It also appears in the Adam brothers' designs. The faun is sometimes used as a support or as an Atlas.

FAUN

FAUTEUIL. French for "armchair." An upholstered armchair with open sides, and usually with upholstered arm or elbow pads. The chair was popularized in the Louis XIV period; the arms originally were placed directly over the front legs. In the Régence and Louis XV periods, the arms were set farther back, and the legs were shortened. The early Renaissance armchairs were not usually upholstered. See *Caquetoire*.

☐ ALSO SEE 1193

FAUTEUIL À CHÂSSIS. Armchair constructed by a French method devised in the Louis XIV period (also used to make upholstered sofas). A secondary wood framework was covered with fabric, then slipped into the prime wood frame of the piece of furniture. This technique made changes of upholstery relatively simple; the upholsterer merely put a new framed upholstered seat or back into the ornate carved frame. See *Slip Seat*.

FAUTEUIL

FAUTEUIL DE BUREAU. A desk chair of the Régence and Louis XV periods in France. The chair usually had one leg centered in the front, one centered in the back, and one at either side of the seat. The curved sloping back was either caned or upholstered in leather. The fauteuil de bureau, or desk chair, was similar to the English "roundabout" chair of the 18th century.

FAUVE. French for "wild beast." An early-20th-century art movement. It was a noncoherent group of artists who used bright, strong colors, flat patterns, and wild distortions. Henri Matisse, Albert Marquet, André Derain, Maurice de Vlamenck, and Georges Rouault are grouped in this school.

FAVAS. A Louis XVI decoration which resembles a honeycomb.

FAVRILE. A late-19th-century iridescent glass, made by Louis C. Tiffany in a variety of delicate and decorative patterns, many in the Art Nouveau style.

FAY, JEAN BAPTISTE. A famous 18th-century French textile and wallpaper designer. His work captured the spirit and quality of the Louis XVI period.

FECONDITÉ. Decorative motif, a female figure representing fecundity. This image was widely used in French metalwork and pottery of the 16th century.
☐ ALSO SEE *466, 1186*

FEDERAL. An American period of architecture, art, furniture, and decoration from about 1790 to 1820. It is a classic period greatly influenced by the Adam brothers, Hepplewhite, Sheraton, and the English Regency. Duncan Phyfe is the leading American furniture designer of this period.
☐ ALSO SEE *65*, 66-67, 68, 91-114, 115-22, 129-44

FEDERAL ARCHITECTURE. The architecture of America from 1790 to 1820 with considerable emphasis on the style of the Adam brothers of England. Usually the house had a flat or low-pitched roof with a balustrade over the cornice. Generally, the house was a boxlike structure on the outside, and stucco facing replaced the Georgian brick or timber façade. The main rooms sometimes were circular or elliptical in plan.

FERETORY. A portable reliquary from the Middle Ages. The feretory was a chest with a lid that resembled a church roof. Although it was an ancient article of church furniture, the finest examples were designed during the 14th and 15th centuries. These were elaborately carved in high relief, painted, and studded with gold and precious gems.

FERRARA TAPESTRIES. The Renaissance tapestries woven in Ferrara, Italy. The manufacture of these tapestries was begun by Duke Hercules II (1508-1559). He imported Flemish workmen who brought with them the skills and techniques that made Flemish weaving prized throughout Europe.

FERRONERIE VELVET. An antique Venetian velvet with a delicate wrought-iron-like pattern.

FERRULE. Formerly "verrel" from the French "virole," a metal ring holding an object fixed to the end of another. In current usage, a metal cup (usually of brass) placed on the bottom of a wood furniture leg for protection and as a reinforcing agent.

FERRULE

FESTOON

FESTOON. A string or chain of any kind of material suspended between two points to form a curved or inverted arc drop. In architecture, a sculptured garland of leaves, flowers, fruits, etc., suspended between two points. A favorite Renaissance motif. In furniture, usually a carved or painted arced design of leaves, flowers, fruits, etc.

FIDDLEBACK CHAIR

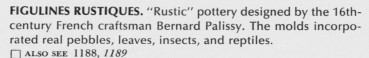

FÊTE GALANTE. A French 18th-century romantic version of a picnic with ladies and their escorts, in rich court apparel, gaily flirting and playing musical instruments and games. This theme appears in murals, tapestries, designs, and painting.

FIDDLEBACK CHAIR. A Queen Anne type, American colonial chair. The back splat is shaped like a fiddle or a vase and the seat is usually made of rush. The chair has cabriole or bandy legs. A similar chair appears in Louis XV period furniture.
☐ ALSO SEE *1775*

FIDDLE BRACE BACK. See *Braced Back*.

FIDDLE-STRING BACK or STICK-BACK. A name sometimes applied to a Windsor chair or any chair which has a back made up of many rods or thin turnings which resemble the strings of a fiddle.

FIELD or FIELDED PANEL. The surface of a panel which is on the same level as the surrounding woodwork and defined or outlined by a sunk bevel or applied molding.

FIELD BED. A small-scaled, arched canopy bed originally intended to be moved from place to place; used in the field by army officers, etc. In 18th-century design the term means a bed with smaller tester and less imposing bedposts. A Chippendale design is illustrated.

FIGULINES RUSTIQUES. "Rustic" pottery designed by the 16th-century French craftsman Bernard Palissy. The molds incorporated real pebbles, leaves, insects, and reptiles.
☐ ALSO SEE 1188, *1189*

FIL DE BOIS. Veneer used in a full, uninterrupted length on a piece of furniture.

FIL D'OR. French for "gold thread." A gilded silver thread originally made in Genoa and used in tapestries from the Middle Ages up to the 18th century.

FILET LACE. A type of lace in which the design is created by embroidering on net with a thread similar to that used in making the net. See *Lace*.

FILIGREE. Decorative openwork. It usually refers to fine, lace-like work done in gold or silver wire.
☐ ALSO SEE 2024, *2183*, 2184

FIN DE SIÈCLE. French for "end of the century." The end of the 19th century and the *Art Nouveau* style.

FINIAL. The terminating ornament on a post, pediment, or intersection. In various antique periods it has resembled a pineapple, urn, knob, or a cluster of foliage.

FIRE DOGS. See *Andirons*.

FIRE IRONS. Hearth accessories: the poker, tongs, and shovel used to tend a fire. Illustrated is a collection of fire irons and bellows from George Edwards and Mathias Darley's 18th-century Chinese-type ornaments.

FIELD BED

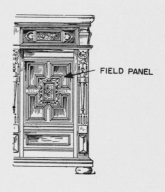

FIELD PANEL

FIN DE SIÈCLE

FINIAL

FIRE DOGS

FIRE IRONS

FIRE SCREEN. An ornamental screen set in front of an open fireplace to keep the sparks from shooting or flying into the room or to provide protection from intense heat. The screen shown served the latter purpose.

FIREBACKS

FIREBACKS. Metal liners or screens, often quite decorative, which were placed behind a fire in a fireplace. They served to reflect the heat back into the room and also to protect the masonry. These pieces, which were popular in the 17th and 18th centuries, were usually made of cast iron.

FIRE SCREEN

FIRESIDE FIGURES. Fire screens made of wood and/or canvas, representing contemporary figures in just under life size. Often these figures were female and dressed in exotic, oriental-type costumes. The fireside figures were also called "picture board dummies" and were popular in the late 17th century.
☐ ALSO SEE *418*, 421, 446

FIRING. The heating of clay in a kiln to harden it. A term used in pottery making.

FISH TAIL. A carved detail which resembles a fish's tail which sometimes appeared on the top rail of spindled or banister-back chairs of 18th- and 19th-century American design.

FLAG

FITMENTS. An English expression for units (bookcases, cabinets, etc.) designed and built to fit the walls of a room. Illustrated is a mid-19th-century chimneypiece with built-in bookcases, cabinets, etc. The doors are perforated brass; the units are carved walnut with colored marble decorations.

FITMENTS

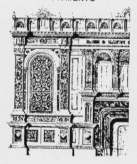

FITTINGS. Metal hardware, mounts, escutcheons, etc.

FITTINGS

FLABELLA. An ecclesiastical fan used from early Christian times to keep flies from the altar.

FLAG. A long grass which is twisted and woven into provincial-type seats. See *Rush*.

FLAMBEAU

FLAMBEAU. A flame or flaming torch used as a decorative motif. Popular in the 18th and early 19th centuries in England and France.

FLAMBEAU

FLAMBOYANT. French for "flaming." The late Gothic style in French architecture (14th and 15th centuries). The window tracery was designed in conventionalized flamelike forms, reversed curved lines. See *Tracery*.

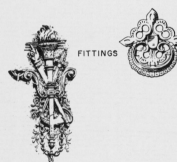

FLAME CARVING. A finial carved in a swirling, spiral effect to simulate a flame. It was used to decorate urns in the late 17th and early 18th centuries.

FLAMBOYANT

FLAME CARVING

FLÂNEUSE. From the French "flâner" which means "to lounge." A garden-type lounge chair with a footrest, it is similar to the current deck chair. The flâneuse usually had a caned seat, back, and footrest.

FLAP TABLE

FLATTED

FLEMISH CHAIR

FLEMISH CHAIR AND FOOT

FLEMISH FOOT

FLEMISH SCROLL

FLAP STRAPPING. See *Strapwork.*

FLAP TABLE. An early-17th-century table with a fixed center slab and two side flaps which can be lowered by folding back the legs which support them. These legs fold back under the central table surface. The flap table is a form of gateleg or eight-legged table. An American Jacobean thousand-leg table is illustrated.
☐ ALSO SEE 60

FLARE. An outward spread, as in a chair seat which is wider at the front than at the back. Illustrated is an early-19th-century Sheraton design.

FLATTED. A term used to describe painted furniture, such as was popular in the Louis XV and Louis XVI periods.

FLAXMAN, JOHN (1755-1826). An English sculptor and draftsman. From 1771 until 1787, while working as a designer for the Wedgwood pottery manufactory, he produced many excellent plaques, cameos, and medallions.
☐ ALSO SEE 852, 931, *960*, 961, *962*, 963, *964*, 1077, 1111

FLEMISH. Referring to Flanders, the old name for the area now covered by Belgium, Holland, and parts of northern France.

FLEMISH CHAIR. A high-backed chair, with or without arms. The splat was a panel of cane, upholstery, laths, or balusters surmounted with an elaborate carved cresting. The legs had straight backs with bold curves in front, and they were supported by scroll feet. The stretcher consisted of two concave curves joined by a convex curve in the center. It was made in late-17th-century England. See *Flemish Scroll.*

FLEMISH EAR. A late French Renaissance and baroque furniture foot. It is similar to the Flemish scroll foot, except the design (the S or C) is inverted. The Flemish ear appears on some furniture of the Louis XIV period. See *Flemish Foot* and *Flemish Scroll.*

FLEMISH FOOT. A scroll-like ending to an S or C curved leg. This particular foot was popular in 17th-century styles in Flanders, England, and France.

FLEMISH SCROLL. An S or C curved ornamental form in which a scroll is broken by an angle. It was used in Flemish Renaissance furniture and also in the English Carolean and William and Mary styles.

FLEMISH SILVER. Flemish silverwork of high artistic quality, produced in Flanders as early as the 15th century.

FLEUR DE LIS or FLEUR DE LYS. A decorative, conventionalized iris flower which has symbolized royalty and the French Bourbon kings.

FLEURETTE. French for "small flower." A small flower motif carved on Louis XVI furniture and accessories.

FLEURETTED TREILLAGE. Anglicized French for "beflowered trellis." The beflowered trellis or latticework was a popular decorative motif in carved and painted form in French and German rococo and Louis XV furniture and accessories. Illustrated is the back of a sofa designed by François Peyrotte.

FLARE

FLEMISH

FLUER DE LIS

FLUERETTE

FLUERETTED TREILLAGE

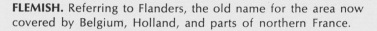

FLINT-LOCK. A gun or pistol lock of the 17th and 18th centuries. A piece of flint in the hammer, struck sharply against steel, produced small sparks of incandescent steel. These sparks ignited the charge.

FLOCKING. A technique for applying flock. Originally, the finely powdered wool was scattered over the entire surface to be decorated, but the particles adhered only to the tacky surface, or that part of the surface which was treated with glue. The rest of the flock, which did not stick to the fabric, leather, canvas, or paper, was blown or brushed off. This technique was developed during the Middle Ages, and was first applied to paper during the 17th century. Paper subjected to this treatment was called "velvet paper." The design was painted, stenciled or printed on the paper with a slow drying adhesive or varnish. When powdered color was sprinkled on in place of flock, the paper was called a "counterfeit flock." In 1634, Jérôme Lanyer was granted a patent for flocking.

FLOORCLOTH. An early-18th-century rug made of heavy linen or canvas which was heavily sized and coated and then painted or ornamented. It was similar to *Wachstuch-tapete.*

FLOREATED

FLOREATED. A term used to describe Gothic tracery and ornaments, which used floral and leaf motifs in flowing, rhythmic lines.

FLOWER STAND. See *Jardinière.* A stand for holding a plant or pot of flowers. Adam designed flower stands with sloping legs, rams' heads, and garland enrichments. A Chippendale design is illustrated.

FLOWER STAND　　　FLOWER STAND

FLUTING. Continuous parallel hollows or channels, usually cut perpendicularly, as in a column, pilaster shaft, or furniture leg. It is like narrow concave moldings used in parallel lines. Spiral fluting is sometimes used on columns and furniture supports. Short flutings are often used on friezes as a form of ornamentation.

FLUTING

FLY BRACKET. A bracket, similar to a fly rail, used to support a drop-leaf on a *Pembroke* or library table. The bracket sometimes had shaped or diagonally cut ends. See *Loper.*

FLY RAIL. The folding bracket support for the flap or drop leaf of a table.

FOILS. The small arcs which make up Gothic tracery. The foils are separated by the cusps. See *Multifoil.*

FOILS

FOLD OVER. A desk or table with a "desk leaf" which folds over the upper surface. It was used in the late 18th century in France and England, and particularly by Sheraton.

FOLDING FURNITURE. Collapsible furniture which can fold into a compact unit like a folding stool, folding chair, table, bed, etc. This principle was employed by the ancient Egyptians, Greeks, and Romans, and has continued in use and popularity up to our current bridge sets. In the mid- and late 18th century, Shearer, Hepplewhite, and Sheraton designed many folding and convertible pieces of furniture (i.e., library steps).

FOLDING FURNITURE

FOLDING TABLE

FOLDING TABLE. An early English Renaissance multilegged table. It often had from twelve to as many as twenty legs, and the entire table could be folded to about one-third of its full size. It was the forerunner of the gateleg table, and worked on the same principle of expansion. Illustrated is a later 17th-century example (Stuart or Restoration period).

FOLIAGE. In decoration or ornament, plant and leaf forms carved, painted, or otherwise decoratively interpreted. A carved 13th-century frieze (from Notre-Dame) is illustrated.

FOLLY. A pseudoclassic or Gothic ruin specially so built to create a view or a charming effect in a garden or park. This was popular in 18th-century France. The Chippendale frame shown illustrates the classic "folly" as a decorative carved design.

FOLWELL, JOHN. An American cabinetmaker who worked in Philadelphia in the late 19th century. His designs were greatly influenced by Chippendale styles.

FONDEUR. French for "metal caster." One who makes metal mounts, hardware, furniture embellishments, and accessories.

FONDI D'ORO. The Italian term for a technique of decorating glass with gold foil; a gold-foil design being incised on formed glass and encased by a second layer of glass. The technique, known to the ancient world, was also used by 18th-century German glassmakers. See *Zwischengoldglas.*

FONTAINE, PIERRE FRANÇOIS LÉONARD (1762–1853). A French architect-designer who, with *Charles Percier,* created the architectural and interior style known as the Empire for Napoleon at the start of the 19th century. Together they designed interiors and furniture for Malmaison, St.-Cloud, the Tuileries, and the Louvre. Their creed was: "simple lines, pure contours, correct shapes replacing . . . the curving and the irregular." See *Empire.*
☐ ALSO SEE 956, 1351, *1422,* 1504, 1509, 1510, *1511,* 1520, 1530, 1550

FONTAINEBLEAU. A French Renaissance château begun in the reign of François I in the early 16th century. The rooms that were created at this time had Italian Renaissance style paneling with classic order details and Vitruvian motifs. Raphael-type arabesques made of modeled plaster and fresco paintings were also used. Additions were made to the château, and variations in periods and styles of decoration are clearly discernible. The Renaissance peristyle of the château is illustrated.
☐ ALSO SEE 1179, *1182-83,* 1200, 1242, *1396,* 1397

FOOTBOARD. A supporting wooden piece at the lower end of the bed which connects with the two side rails. It can be an important decorative feature, carved and ornamented, or simply a horizontal rail, depending upon the style or period of the bed. In the contemporary Hollywood bed, the footboard is completely omitted.

FOOTRAIL. The lower supporting stretcher between two legs of a chair or table. An early-18th-century English chair is used to illustrate the footrail.

FOOTSTOOL. Originally an accompanying step for high throne seats and currently used as a stool or bench. A small, low hassock.

FOLIAGE

FONDEUR

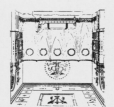
PIERRE FRANÇOIS LÉONARD FONTAINE

FONTAINEBLEAU

FOLLY

FOOTRAIL

FOOTBOARD

FOOTSTOOL

FORGED

FORGED

FORGED. A term applied to metals which have been heated and then hammered or beaten into a shape.

FORM. A long, backless bench or seat of the Jacobean period, often furnished with loose pillows.

FORMAL. Regular, symmetrical, traditional in effect. Usually describes an arrangement or placement of furniture or decoration which is stately and carefully balanced. Not haphazard or whimsical. Illustrated is a late-18th-century Sheraton elevation with a chinoiserie influence.

FORTY, JEAN FRANÇOIS. An 18th-century French designer, engraver, and metal carver. He published eight volumes on design, and created some of the most beautiful metal accessories and furniture mounts of the Louis XVI period.

FORTY WINK CHAIR. See *Wing Chair.*

FOUR-POSTER BEDSTEAD. A bed with two posts in front and two in the back, or posts rising from carved or paneled foot and head boards. It sometimes was made to support a tester and drapery, or a fabic canopy. Designs vary with the changing periods and styles.

FRACTUR (or fraktur) PAINTING. Decorative birth and marriage certificates of the 18th- and 19th-century Pennsylvania Dutch.

FRAGONARD, JEAN-HONORÉ (1732–1806). A French painter and designer of the Louis XV and Louis XVI periods. He decorated many dainty boudoirs with murals and other wall decorations. Among his charming paintings are "The Swing" and "Progress of Love," which was originally created for Mme Du Barry's home. (She rejected the painting.)
☐ ALSO SEE 1469, *1470*

FRAILERO. A Spanish Renaissance monk's chair, usually made of walnut, with plain legs and a broad front stretcher. Decorative nailheads secured the leather seat to the two side rails and the back panel between the two uprights. These were usually capped with finials. The arms were wide and simple. The frailero was probably the most typical chair of the Spanish Renaissance. See *Mission.*

FRAME. The skeleton or basic structure of a piece of furniture which will later be filled in with webbing, stuffing, muslin, upholstery, etc. The unfinished, raw basic wood framework. Illustrated is the frame of a Louis XV type of wing chair.

FRAME. A surrounding case or structure for the protection and enhancement of drawings, paintings, mirrors, etc. It can be carved of wood, trimmed with moldings, or embellished with gesso composition.
☐ ALSO SEE American *86*, 90
English 394, 395, 421, 483, 503, 524-26, *574*, 575, 673-74
French 1228, 1282-84
German 1655
Italian 1798, 1830, *1831, 1892, 1894, 1895*

FORMAL

FOUR-POSTER BEDSTEAD

FRAME

FRAME

DISCOVERING ANTIQUES VOLUME / PAGE GUIDE	vol.	contains pages	vol.	contains pages	vol.	contains pages	vol.	contains pages
vol. • contains pages	*3* •	253 *to* 376	*7* •	749 *to* 872	*11* •	1245 *to* 1368	*15* •	1741 *to* 1864
	4 •	377 *to* 500	*8* •	873 *to* 996	*12* •	1369 *to* 1492	*16* •	1865 *to* 1988
1 • 1 *to* 128	*5* •	501 *to* 624	*9* •	997 *to* 1120	*13* •	1493 *to* 1616	*17* •	1989 *to* 2112
2 • 129 *to* 252	*6* •	625 *to* 748	*10* •	1121 *to* 1244	*14* •	1617 *to* 1740	*18* •	2113 *to* 2236

FRANÇOIS I

FRANÇOIS I (1494–1547). King of France from 1515 in the early French Renaissance period. He was a great patron of the building arts and the châteaux at Chambord, Blois, and Fontainebleau were built during his reign. In his time, the flamboyant Gothic motifs were combined with the advancing Italian Renaissance style.

☐ ALSO SEE 368, 370, *1177*, 1178-80, 1186, 1192, 1193, 1242, 2119, 2120

FRANKENTHAL PORCELAIN. A hard-paste porcelain produced in Frankenthal, Germany, from 1755 until the end of the 18th century. Frankenthal products included a large variety of tableware and ornamental pieces that reflected the influence of both Meissen and Sèvres styles. The porcelain was a creamy white color, with a thin opaque glaze that readily absorbed enamel colors.

FRANKLIN STOVE

FRANKLIN STOVE. Originally called a "Pennsylvania stove." A combination stove and fireplace invented by Benjamin Franklin in the mid-18th century. It burned wood that was set on andirons, and it had a decorative front. Illustrated is an "improved" 19th-century version, the open-grate coal stove.

FREESTANDING COLUMN

FREESTANDING COLUMN. A column with clear or open space all around it. In Sheraton sofas and settees it was usually a vase-shaped extension of the front corner legs. A Sheraton type Regency chair is illustrated.

FRENCH BED

FRENCH BED. An early-19th-century Empire bed with high rolling S-scrolled head and foot boards. Elegant versions were made of rosewood, had carved legs (dolphin- or cornucopia-shaped), and were splendidly embellished with ormolu designs or medallions. See *Sleigh Bed.*

FRENCH BRACKET FOOT

FRENCH BRACKET FOOT. A bracket foot with a concave curve down the mitred edge which gives the foot a splayed effect. It is almost always combined with a valanced skirt or apron. Both the inner and outer edges of the leg are curved, giving the appearance of a stunted cabriole leg. It is also called "French foot," and was popular in 18th-century English and American furniture.

FRENCH BURL. A Persian walnut wood with an interesting curly grain favored for inserts in cabinetwork.

FRENCH CHAIR

FRENCH CHAIR. A general name for upholstered chairs used in England in the mid-18th century. It did not apply to a particular style or decoration but to the general type of rococo chair like the bergère. A Chippendale design is illustrated.

FRENCH DIRECTOIRE

FRENCH DIRECTOIRE. The period in France from 1789 to 1804. It followed the Louis XVI period and was a transitional style leading into the French Empire style. It was essentially a continuation of the classic tradition of the Louis XVI style with the addition of Revolutionary motifs: symbols of liberty, triumphal arches, liberty caps, spirit levels, pikes, oak boughs, clasped hands. Egyptian motifs were also introduced as well as martial Roman elements like spearheads, drums serving as stools, etc. The Directoire was the transition from the Greek styles of Louis XVI to the Egyptian and Roman qualities of the Empire.

☐ ALSO SEE 1493-1506, 1529, 1615, 1616

FRENCH
EARLY RENAISSANCE

FRENCH EARLY RENAISSANCE. The period from approximately 1484 to 1547, covering the reigns of Charles VIII, Louis XII, and François I. It was a transitional period which blended outgoing Gothic structural forms with the incoming Italian Renaissance architectural details and ornaments. For examples see *Château de Chambord, Château de Gaillon, François I,* and *Viart, Charles.*

FRENCH FOOT. See *French Bracket Foot.*

FRENCH HEADING. The gathering of a drapery or valance into regularly spaced folds. The folds are usually stitched in place to give a more set appearance.

FRENCH LATE RENAISSANCE. The period from approximately 1589 to 1643, covering the reigns of Henri IV and Louis XIII. The Italian Renaissance continued to dominate the architecture and decorations of the period, along with Dutch and Flemish influences. In the interiors, wall paneling became a more important wall finish, and "formality" appeared to be the keynote.
☐ ALSO SEE 1178, 1191, 1193, 1251, 1254

FRENCH
LATE RENAISSANCE

FRENCH
LATE RENAISSANCE

FRENCH LEG. A scrolled leg, often carved and ornamented, which was used in 17th- and early-18th-century furniture designs.

FRENCH LEG

FRENCH MIDDLE RENAISSANCE. The reigns of Henri II, François II, Charles IX, and Henri III, covering the years 1547 to 1589. Catherine de Medici dominated the period, and local variations were added to the dominant use of Italian ornament and Renaissance architectural details. The Gothic forms were gradually eliminated. Illustrated is a walnut dresser of the period.

FRENCH MIDDLE RENAISSANCE

FRENCH POLISH. A high, glossy finish on wood which is obtained by adding several layers of shellac to the wood surface.
☐ ALSO SEE 372, 494

FRENCH PROVINCIAL. The term is usually associated with simplified furniture of the Louis XV or rococo style. However, plain, simple furniture was made in the provinces in all times and styles, and usually of walnut, oak, or fruitwood. Provincial furniture is simpler in line than the prevailing high fashion and rarely veneered or decorated with marquetry or ornate carving.

FRENCH PROVINCIAL

FRENCH RÉGENCE or REGENCY. The transitional period (1700 to 1730) between the grandiose formality of the Louis XIV baroque period and the frivolous, asymetrical quality of the Louis XV rococo period. Philippe, Duc d'Orléans, was Regent of France. Flat curved paneling was used for ornament with curves at the corners. Foliage and ribbon ornament was used for embellishment, and curved or cabriole legs began to replace the straight ones. Slight curves, like a crossbow, appeared on the upper parts of cabinets and bookcases. The bombé commode made its appearance at this time, and ebony was

FRENCH RÉGENCE

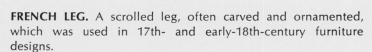

FRENCH WINDOWS

FRESCO

replaced as the favored wood by polished walnut, mahogany, and rosewood veneers. Illustrated is a great clock of the period made of bois de rose and bois de violette marquetry with bronze doré trim.
☐ ALSO SEE 1259-73, 1276-84, 1367, 1438, 1668

FRENCH WHORL FOOT. A furniture foot that swirled or curled forward and often rested on a shoe. It most often appeared as the termination of a cabriole leg in the Régence and Louis XV periods.

FRENCH WINDOWS. A pair of multipaned doorlike windows which extend down to the floor, and, like hinged doors, are used for access to, or egress from, a room. They usually lead out onto a terrace, a balcony or other platform; or into a garden. A Louis XV interior with French windows is illustrated.

FRESCO. The Italian for "fresh." A wall painting in a water-color-like medium (tempera) on wet plaster. The cartoon (full-sized sketch) is applied to the plaster surface. The damp plaster is painted with pigments mixed with water or lime water. The color dries lighter and becomes integrated into the wall or ceiling itself. Frescos were made in Italy in the 14th century, and perfected in the 16th century. Raphael's decoration in the Stanza of the Vatican is a fine fresco. Illustrated is the ceiling fresco by Raphael in the Farnesina in Rome.

FRESQUERA. A Spanish latticework or spindle decorated hanging food cupboard. The openwork on part of the cupboard door was for ventilation.

FRET. A border motif or geometric band of Greek origin. It is made up of interlacing and interlocking lines and forms. It is also called "Chinese key" pattern or "meander."

FRETWORK. Ornamental woodwork cut to represent small interlacing fillets or trellis work. It is usually made in a complicated, repeating, geometric pattern. A favored technique of Chippendale in his Chinese period (mid-18th century).
☐ ALSO SEE *155*, 156

FRETWORK MIRROR. See *Silhouette Mirror*.

FRIAR'S CHAIR. See *Frailero*.

FRIESIAN. Name of a simple technique for carving with a chisel, usually used to create basic geometric forms. A popular technique in Colonial American woodwork. Also called "Frisian."

FRIESLAND. A province in the Netherlands noted for its carved furniture in the baroque style in the 17th century.

FRIESLAND CUPBOARD. A 17th-century cupboard originating in Friesland (the Netherlands). The cupboard is characterized by heavy architectural ornament, such as wide cornices and highly carved moldings and panels. The cupboard is thought to be the forerunner of the Dutch Kas.

FRIEZE. In architecture, the central portion of the classic architectural entablature. It is located above the architrave and below the cornice. It usually has a flat surface which is em-

FRET

FRETWORK

FRIESIAN

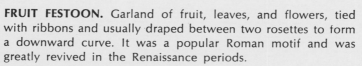

FRIEZE

bellished with decorative sculpture or carving. A frieze is also a painted or sculptured horizontal motif. Illustrated is the frieze and Corinthian order of the monument of Lysicrates at Athens. In furniture, the underframing of a table between the top surface and the legs. See *Apron*.

☐ ALSO SEE 361, 364, 789, *1216, 1726,* 1730, 1802

FRIEZE DRAWER

FRIEZE DRAWER. The top drawer of a chest which extends forward over the main body of the chest. It is usually sup-ported by columns or pilasters. An Empire or Biedermeier early-19th-century (illustrated) design.

FRIEZE RAIL. In a door made up of three horizontal rows of panels, the horizontal rail between the middle and top set of panels. Illustrated is a doorway designed by Inigo Jones (early 17th century). See also *Picture Molding or Rail*.

FRIEZE RAIL

FRISIAN. See *Friesian*.

FRITHSTOOL. In Gothic churches, a seat or chair carved of stone and set near the altar. It was the last and most sacred refuge for persons who sought the sanctuary of the church. "The seat of peace."

FROTHINGHAM, BENJAMIN (1734-1790). An American furni-ture designer who worked in Massachusetts. Frothingham was known for his designs in the Chippendale manner.

☐ ALSO SEE 128

FRUIT FESTOON. Garland of fruit, leaves, and flowers, tied with ribbons and usually draped between two rosettes to form a downward curve. It was a popular Roman motif and was greatly revived in the Renaissance periods.

FRUIT FESTOON

FRUITWOOD. Wood from fruit-bearing trees like cherry, apple pear, etc., largely used in provincial-type furniture. It was an 18th-century favorite which is having a renaissance currently in provincial and country-style tables, chairs, commodes, chests, etc.

FULDA PORCELAIN. The porcelain produced in Fulda, Germany, during the 18th century. Along with the Meissen products, it is considered the finest German porcelain, prized for its delicacy and careful workmanship.

FULHAM POTTERY. The English pioneer stoneware and earth-enware produced at Fulham in the late 17th century by John Dwight and the Eler brothers; also, artistic pottery made after 1864 by C.J.C. Bailey.

☐ ALSO SEE 489-92, *1090-91,* 1093

FUMED OAK

FUMED OAK. A furniture finish of the late 19th and early 20th centuries. The oak wood was stained by ammonia fumes, and the graining became more pronounced and deeper in color. Much of the mission-style furniture was produced in fumed oak as well as late English Victorian pieces.

FUMEUSE. A smoking chair. An 18th-century variation on the voyeuse. The broad crest rail on the narrow, shaped back of the chair often had compartments to hold tobacco, pipes, flints, etc., and the person straddled the chair, facing the chair back and the equipped rail. See *Cockfight Chair*.

FURSTENBERG PORCELAIN. A hard-paste porcelain produced in Furstenberg, Germany, during the 18th and the early 19th centuries. The best Furstenburg products are well-executed rococo figurines and portrait medallions. Late 18th-century pieces display a notable interest in antiquity.

FUSTIC. A light yellow wood from the West Indies. In the 17th and 18th centuries it was used for marquetry and inlay work.

GADROON

GADROON. From the French "godron." A series of elongated egg or ovoid forms in a parallel series or band. It is similar to a bead molding in that it projects above the surface it ornaments. When this type of decoration is used around a circular object, the oval form of ornament is called "splayed gadroon." See *Nulling*.

GAINE. A square post or pedestal which narrows and tapers toward the bottom. The gaine may be supported by human or animal feet. It is used as a decorative support or ornament, and is often topped with a head or bust. Illustrated is a Sheraton bookcase design of the early 19th century in the Regency style. Note the use of gaines for free columns to support the frieze, and on the front ends of the base.

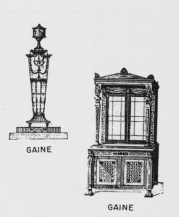

GAINE

GAINE

GALLE, EMILE (1846-1904). The most outstanding artist and technician among French glassmakers of the late 19th century. Gallé created some of his most original work in opaque colored glass in a wide variety of techniques. All his pieces are signed and many are of superb quality.

☐ ALSO SEE 1110, 1587-89, *1590*, *1592*, 1602, 1607-08, *1609*, 1616, 1732, 1736

GALLERIES

GALLERY

GALLERIES. The metal rods and supports at the back of sideboards of the late 18th century in England. They are also the raised metal or carved rims around tabletops or servers.

GALLERY. In architecture, a wide corridor walled in on one side only, and usually located on the upper story. The upper story of seats in a public hall or auditorium. The balcony of a theatre. In furniture, the miniature metal or wood railing along the edge of a shelf or tabletop, as in gallery-top tables.

GALLIPOT. A small ceramic apothecary vessel.

GALLOON or GALON. A narrow, closely woven braid used for trimming draperies and upholstery. It was frequently used in the early 18th century to finish off rough upholstery work. A lace or embroidered band with a scalloped edge on two sides is also called a galloon.

GAME TABLES. Tables devised for particular card games, chess, etc. It is also called a card table, or by the specific name of the game to be played like "bridge table." A Sheraton chess table is illustrated.

☐ ALSO SEE *58*, 60, 420, *761-62*, 763-64, *765*, 1010, *1127*, *1286*, *1690*, 1747

GALLERY

GAME TABLE

GARDE DU VIN. A Hepplewhite term for a "cellarette." See *Cellarette*.

GARDE-MANGER. A french term for a food cupboard; a larder or cupboard.

GARDEN CARPET. A type of Persian carpet, popular from the 16th to the 18th centuries, which represents a garden. The carpet is divided into compartments, each representing sections of a garden filled with trees, birds, and animals.
☐ ALSO SEE 1998, *1999*, 2005-09

GARDEN SEAT. An oriental or Chinese outdoor seat made in the shape of a small keg, barrel, or drum. Originally these pieces were carved of stone, and then they were produced in porcelain. Still later they were made with a lattice-like wooden center part but with a solid top and bottom.

GARDE-ROBE. In furniture, a wardrobe or armoire. In architecture, a privy in a medieval castle. Illustrated is a 16th-century Flemish armoire or garde-robe.

GARGOYLE. In Gothic architecture, a rainspout which often was decoratively carved as a fantastic human or animal head, and ornamentally placed along the top of a parapet or roof. The term is from the Old French for "throat."

GARLAND. A wreath or circlet of leaves, flowers, and/or fruit with ribbon ties. It is used as a carved or painted decoration on furniture and in architecture.

GARNITURE. Any motif used for enriching a surface or area. The embellishing or decorating may be painted, carved, inlaid, applied, etc.
☐ ALSO SEE 433, *1665*, 1840

GATCH. An oriental term for decorative elements made in molded plaster. See *Anaglypta* and *Carton-Pierre*.

GATELEG TABLE. A drop-leaf table with oval or rounded ends. The leaves are supported by single or double wing legs or gates. It was introduced in mid-17th-century Jacobean furniture and was popular in Colonial America. See *Eight-Legged Table, Folding Table,* and *Thousand-Leg Table*.
☐ ALSO SEE 22, *58*, 420, *447*, 450, 572

GAUDY DUTCH WARE. The early 19th-century English pottery from Staffordshire marketed chiefly among the Pennsylvania Germans. The pottery was brightly and extensively painted.

GAUDREAUX. An 18th-century French furniture maker in the Louis XV style. His pieces were often designed by the Slodtz brothers, and lavishly embellished with gilt bronze trim. Oval medallions with gilt bronze bas-reliefs on blue enamel grounds were sometimes used for ornamenting Gaudreaux's furniture.
☐ ALSO SEE *1277*, 1279, 1343, *1344*, 1361

GARDE DU VIN

GARGOYLE

GARGOYLE

GARDE-ROBE

GARNITURE

GATELEG TABLE

GEORGIAN

GENRE PAINTING. A painting representing ordinary people in ordinary situations. The execution of the genre painting is suited to the choice of subject matter: the field of vision is confined, the scale is small, and the figures are related in realistic proportions. In European painting, the genre style was brought to a high state of development by the Dutch in the 17th century.

GEORGIAN. The period of the reigns of the Georges in England (1714 to the Regency, approximately 1811). The golden period of furniture design and architecture: Adam brothers, Chippendale, Shearer, Hepplewhite, Sheraton, etc. An early Georgian chair of the first part of the 18th century is illustrated. It has the typical pierced urn splat, cabriole legs with shell carvings on the knees, and ball-and-claw feet. Usually broken down into three separate periods: Early Georgian, 1714–1750; Middle Georgian, 1750–1770; and Late Georgian, 1770–1810.

☐ ALSO SEE 553-57, 560-69, 572-85, 588-606, 625-43, 646-69, 672-705, 708-21, 724-42, 749-53, 756-79, 782-95, 798-811, 814-43, 846-54, 873-901, 904-912

GESSO

GESSO. A dense and brilliant white ground with a high degree of absorbency (gypsum or chalk). It is used as a ground for tempera painting. The panels to be painted are treated with several coats of gesso and size. Also, a plaster-like composition which is molded to form a raised or bas-relief applied ornament on walls, furniture, frames, moldings, etc. This ornament is often painted and gilded. See *Anaglypta, Carton-Pierre,* and *Composition Ornament.*

☐ ALSO SEE 483, 532, *534*, 536, 1857, 2042

GHIBERTI, LORENZO (1378–1455). An Italian goldsmith and sculptor who is probably best known for the bronze doors of the Baptistry in Florence. The doors consist of twenty-eight high reliefs (the figures are in gilt against a neutral background) enclosed in Gothic frames. The subject matter was based on parts of the New Testament. He later (1423) made another set of doors with ten scenes from the Old Testament, which were much finer in handling and draftsmanship. Michelangelo called these later doors "the doors to paradise."

GRINLING GIBBONS

GIBBONS, GRINLING (1648–1721). An English master woodcarver and sculptor. He worked in close association with Sir Christopher Wren, the noted architect, and he created many famous carved trophy panels and mantels. Gibbons did much of the sculptured embellishment for the choir in St. Paul's Cathedral, as well as the dimensional foliage and festoons of the stalls. He worked mainly in limewoods, used oak for church panels and moldings, and occasionally cedar for architraves. Medallion portraits were sometimes carved of pearwood or boxwood. Gibbons sculptured realistically in high relief, with deep undercuts, and his motifs included fruit, vegetables, game, fish, leaves, and flowers created into swags, festoons, draperies, and frames.

☐ ALSO SEE *442*, 443, 469, 470, 483, 501-05, 524, 529, 531, 1959

JAMES GIBBS

JAMES GIBBS

GIBBS, JAMES (1683–1754). An English architect and furniture designer in the tradition of Sir Christopher Wren. He created, in the first part of the 18th century, many interior architectural features such as mantels as well as furniture. Gibbs is probably most known for St. Martin's-in-the-Fields in London (1721–1726), which is here illustrated. The portico is Greek in feeling, while the steeple is in the style of Wren.

☐ ALSO SEE 67, 777, *805*

GIGLIO

GIGLIO. An Italian word for a decorative element similar to a fleur de lis. It is usually associated with Florence, Italy.

GILDED or GILT FURNITURE. Furniture finished by gilding, an early-17th-century finish which was adopted in England during the early Queen Anne period and also in France. William Kent was a leading designer of English gilt furniture. Illustrated is a Louis XV carved gilt console table. See *Gilding*.

GILDED LEATHER. A popular treatment for leather tapestries from the 16th through the 18th centuries. The leather was sized, then covered with gold or silver leaf. Areas of the leather were then colored in lacquer. Sometimes the surface was tooled or embossed with chisels or patterned punches called "irons." Tiny roses, rosettes, squares, circles, arabesques, and heraldic motifs were popular designs. The Dutch, during the 17th century, often used colored grounds, and bronzed or gilded fruits and cherubs in bold relief. The English favored chinoiserie motifs. See *Cordovan Leather, Guadamicil*, and *Moroccan (Maroquin) Tapestries*.

GILDING. The art of ornamenting furniture, accessories, and architectural details with gold leaf or gold dust. Illustrated is a mid-18th-century gilded frame (English).

☐ ALSO SEE Armour 430, *431, 432*, 434, 1664, *1665*, 1840
Bronze 1816, *1817, 1820*
Furniture 155, 481-83, *532, 534*, 536, 1320, 1530, 1607-08, *1610, 1828*, 1829, *1831*, 1854, *1855, 1856*, 1857, *1891*, 1892, 2065-66
Lacquer *289, 291-92*, 293
Papier Mâché 1007, 1008, 1009, 1010
Porcelain *264, 274*, 275, 277, 650, *809*, 811, *882, 883*, 884, *886, 945*, 947, *1292, 1293, 1295, 1321*, 1322-23, *1324, 1472*, 1474, *1475, 1476*, 1706, 1851

GILES, JAMES (1718-1780). An independent London craftsman of the 18th century. He is well known for his rich gilding and enameling of glass and for his decoration of Worcester porcelain.

☐ ALSO SEE *711, 905, 906*, 907

GILLINGHAM, JAMES. A Philadelphia cabinetmaker of the mid-18th century.

☐ ALSO SEE 128

GILLOT, CLAUDE (1673–1722). A French painter and designer of fauns, satyrs, and grotesques during the period of Louis XIV. He was the master (teacher) of Watteau.

☐ ALSO SEE 488, 1299

GILLOW, RICHARD and ROBERT. Furniture makers in the first half of the 18th century in England. Much of the furniture and cabinetwork produced by the Gillows was exported to the West Indies.

GILDED FURNITURE

GILDING

CLAUDE GILLOT

GILLRAY, JAMES (1757-1815). A British engraver and social and political caricaturist. His political engravings of the 1790's mercilessly lampooned British royalty.
☐ ALSO SEE *642*, 818, *819, 820, 916, 949, 950, 951*, 952-53, 996, *1496*

GIMP or GUIMPE. Originally a woven silk braid of assorted designs. A binding material used on the outer edges of upholstered furniture to cover fabric joins or upholstery tacks, or as an enrichment. Gimp is also used as a trim on draperies, bedspreads, etc.

GIRANDOLE. A multibranched wall sconce to hold candles, which is often mirrored. A late-17th- and 18th-century accessory and lighting device. When lit, it seemed to have the sparkle and shimmer of fireworks. In the 19th century, the term described a circular mirror, often convex, with or without a candle sconce. In American designs, the mirror was often capped with an eagle. In the mid-19th century, a girandole was a Bohemian glass, prism-hung candlestick, often used in pairs on mantels. See *Applique* and *Bull's-Eye Mirror*. It also refers to any branched candlestick.
☐ ALSO SEE *109*, 111, *128, 604, 675*, 790

GIRANDOLE

GLASTONBURY CHAIR. A 16th-century ecclesiastic chair with X-shaped legs and sloping arms and back.
☐ ALSO SEE 364

GLASTONBURY CHAIR

GLAZE. In pottery, a thin coating of glass fired on pottery to give it a glossy appearance. A glaze may also be employed to color the pottery.

GLAZED DOOR. A door made up of panes of glass framed in wood molding strips. It is similar to a French door. In furniture, cabinet, secretary, bookcase, etc., doors which are made of glass panes held together in a decorative framework of wood strips. A Chippendale mahogany bookcase is shown.

GLAZED DOOR

GLASTONBURY CHAIR

GLAZING BARS. The wood or metal strips which form the framework around individual panes of glass in a window.

GLOBE STAND. A favored 18th-century accessory. It was usually a carved tripod made to hold a rotating globe of the world. Smaller stands were made to stand on tables or desks, and larger units were made to stand on the floor.

GLOBE STAND

GLAZING BAR

GOBELINS. A tapestry factory started in Paris in the 16th century by a family of dyers named Gobelin. Louis XIV, in 1662, purchased the factory, and Charles Le Brun was made chief designer and director of the art-producing plant which now turned out textiles, metalwork, silverwork, wood carvings, frescoes, as well as tapestries. It was during this period that the Savonnerie rug factory was combined with the Gobelins. Among the famous artists and artisans who worked at the Manufacture Nationale des Gobelins are the following: Marc de Coomans, François Delaplanche, Laurent Guyot, Guillaume Dumée, Antoine Caron, Simon Vouet, Michel Corneille, Eustache Le Sueur, Nicolas Poussin, Philippe de Champagne, Louis and Charles Le Brun, Antoine and Charles Coypel, Pierre Mignard, Jean-François de Troy, Louis de Boulogne, François Desportes, several members of the Audran family, and the Anguiers.
☐ ALSO SEE 1206, *1218*, 1219-22, *1232*, 1242, 1244, 1307, 1331, 1374-78, 1389, 1492, 1971, 1972

GOBELINS

JOHN GODDARD

GODDARD, JOHN (1724–1785). An American designer and cabinetmaker in Newport, Rhode Island. He produced, in association with his son-in-law John Townsend, a particular type of blockfront desk, secretary, and cabinet, usually with ogee bracket feet and shell ornaments. See *Blockfront.*
☐ ALSO SEE 94, 128

GODROON. See *Gadroon.*

GOLD LEAF. Also called mosaic gold or Dutch gold. Originally, it was made in Germany, and was an amalgam of tin and copper. The bright, shiny, thin sheet is laid over the surface which has been made tacky by a shellac, adhesive, or gold size. The sheet adheres to the sized surface. See *Gilding.*

GONDOLA BED. A 19th-century Empire-style bed with foot and head boards which appear to scroll or "roll over" like the ends of a gondola. Illustrated is a French Empire design. See *Boat Bed* and *Sleigh Bed.*

GONDOLA BED

GONDOLA CHAIR. A low chair for a writing desk, or a sofa whose back curves downward to form the arms. The sweeping, curving line resembles an 18th-century gondola.
☐ ALSO SEE 1505, *1506, 1529,* 1550

GOODISON, BENJAMIN. An 18th-century furniture maker to the English royalty from 1727 to 1767.

GOOSENECK. A double curved pediment popularly used in 18th-century English and American furniture. It is also referred to as "broken arch" or "swan neck."

GOOSENECK

GOSTELOWE, JONATHAN (1744–1806). An American cabinetmaker who worked in Philadelphia, Pennsylvania, in the Chippendale style. He produced many fine mahogany pieces.
☐ ALSO SEE 90, 128

GOTHIC PERIOD

GOTHIC PERIOD. The period from approximately 1150 to 1500 in Europe. It is the only European architectural style not based on classical forms, and it is an outstanding period of ecclesiastic architecture and art. This period was named by the Italians who preferred Greek and Roman architecture, and assumed that only German barbarians (the Goths) could admire such a style. The Gothic period is also referred to as the "Middle Ages."
☐ ALSO SEE English 415
    Flemish 2121-22
    French 1200
    German 1619, 1622-25
    Italian (16th century) 1802
    Netherlandish (16th century) 2133
    Spanish (16th century) 2125, 2131-32

GOTHIC REVIVAL. See *Romantic Epoch.* The renewed interest in Gothic architecture and art forms during the early 19th century in England and on the Continent. John Britton's *The Architectural Antiquities and Cathedrals of Britain* and Sir Walter Scott's novels helped foster this interest in the medieval period. Augustus Welby Pugin was the great architect and advocate of the Gothic revival in England. He erected 65

GOTHIC REVIVAL

"Gothic-type" churches and decorated the interior and exterior of the Houses of Parliament, London, which was influential in popularizing this revival. Pugin was followed by Sir Gilbert Scott and Philip Hardwick, whose Hall of Lincoln's Inn is illustrated.

☐ ALSO SEE American 160, 218
English 557, 636, 730-32, 750-53, 935, 938, 943, 961, 969, 986-90, 997-1001, 1013, 1026, *1050*, 1165, 1173, *1912*, 1913, *1915*, 1919, *1924*
French *1534*, 1536, *1551*, 1552
German 1701-02
Irish 1770

JEAN GOUJON

GOUACHE. An opaque watercolor paint like poster paint. It dries much lighter than it appears when wet. Gouache is an art medium, as well as a technique for making studies for oil paintings. It was a popular painting technique in the 18th century. "Tempera" is the Italian term for gouache.

☐ ALSO SEE *1585*, *1741*, *1742*, 1755-56

PIERRE GOUTHIÈRE

GOUJON, JEAN (1510–1566). A French architect and sculptor. He did reliefs in the Louvre, including some on the exterior and some figures, and the caryatids of the gallery "Salle des Caryatides." He created elongated, elegant figures, somewhat influenced by classic forms. Attributed to him is "Diana the Huntress," made for the courtyard of the Château of Diane de Poitiers. Illustrated is a bas-relief by Goujon for the Hôtel Carnavalet in Paris. See *Bas-Relief* for panels designed by Goujon for the Fountain of the Innocents in Paris.

GOUT CHAIR. An 18th-century chair devised for sufferers from the gout. The footstool could be pulled out from below the seat, so that the affected leg could rest on it in an extended, straight-out position. When not in use, the trundle-like footrest could be pushed back into the seat-rail.

GOUT CHAIR

GOUTHIÈRE, PIERRE (1740–1806). A notable French designer of exquisite ormolu mounts for Louis XVI period furniture. He also created mountings of great refinement and delicacy for vases of jasper, Sèvres, and oriental porcelains, as well as designs for clocks and candelabras. Illustrated is a cylinder secrétaire of the Louis XVI period with ormolu mountings by Gouthière. See *Bureau Plat*.

☐ ALSO SEE *1360*, 1362, 1459, 1518-19

GOUTY STOOL

GOUTY STOOL. A leg rest with an adjustable top for the support of gout-afflicted legs. An 18th-century English design.

GOVERNOR WINTHROP DESK. A typical fall-front desk of Colonial America (c. 1750). It was concurrent with Chippendale's designs in England. The piece has two to four graduated drawers running the width of the desk with "batwing" or "willow" brasses. The desk usually was supported by bracket feet. The interior of the desk was an arrangement of arcaded pigeonholes, with a single or double tier of small drawers beneath. The assorted governors called Winthrop, and there were several, actually lived in the 17th century, so the name is confusing.

GOVERNOR WINTHROP DESK

GOYA Y LUCIENTES, FRANCISCO JOSÉ DE (1746-1828). A famous Spanish artist and engraver. His large production of paintings, engravings, and drawings relate to almost all aspects

of late 18th and early 19th century Spanish life—a period of political and social unrest.
☐ ALSO SEE 1582, 2112, *2143*, 2157-60

GRAFFITO WARE

GRADIN. See *Table à Gradin.*

GRAFFITO WARE. Heavy pottery decorated with a primitively scratched or scribed design. See *Sgraffito.*

GRAINED FURNITURE. Late-19th-century cheap furniture, dark in color, which was painted and artificially grained to simulate oak wood. See *Graining.*

GRAND MIROIR À LA PSYCHÉ. Also called a "psyche." A tall Empire pier mirror which stood on the floor and could be tilted forward or back. A German Empire version with candle brackets is illustrated. See *Pier Glasses.*
☐ ALSO SEE 1522, 1532

GRAND MIROIR
À LA PSYCHÉ

GRANDFATHER CHAIR

GRANDFATHER CHAIR. A large, roomy, upholstered chair developed from the 17th-century wing chair. It was particularly popular in the Queen Anne period.

GRANDFATHER (long case) CLOCK. A floor-standing clock with a wood case which consists of a hood, a waist, and a base. The pendulum and the weights are protected inside the clock which usually stands over six feet high. It was introduced into England after the Restoration, and became extremely popular during the 18th century.
☐ ALSO SEE 108-09, 520-22, 615, *767*, 768, *881, 978*, 1974-75, *1977*

GRANDMOTHER CLOCK. A smaller-scaled and more refined version of the grandfather clock. See *Grandfather (long case) Clock.*

GRAPHIC ARTS. The arts of drawing, engraving, etching, block-printing, etc.

GRANDFATHER CLOCK

GREAT EXHIBITION (1851). An international exhibition held in London and organized by the Society of Arts. The British exhibits were distinguished by their robustness and showiness, the culmination of a great commercial era.
☐ ALSO SEE 157, 988, 1005, 1013, 1076, 1110, 1188, 1723, 1794, 1905-30, 2048

GREAT MONAD or OVUM MUNDI. A circle with a horizontal S shape dividing it into two equal areas which represent the union of the basic principles: the material or feminine, and the spiritual or masculine.

GRECIAN SOFA. Another name for an Empire-style couch. Illustrated is an early-19th-century Sheraton design. The head part is higher and rolls over, as does the lower or foot end. See *Récamier.*

GRECIAN SOFA

GRECO-ROMAN

GRECO-ROMAN. The classic style from about 200 B.C. to A.D. 200. It is Romanized Greek forms such as were unearthed in Pompeii and Herculaneum, and it is the basis of the 18th-century classic style of the Adam brothers and the Louis XVI period.

GREEK REVIVAL

GREEK ARCHITECTURE

GREEK KEY

GREEK ARCHITECTURE. See *Classic.*

GREEK KEY. A fret design. A continuous band decoration of interlacing, hooked squares.

GREEK REVIVAL. A renewed interest in Greek art and architecture in the 18th and 19th centuries. It affected the Directoire, English Regency, and Empire styles.

GRENDEY, GILES (1693–1780). An English furniture maker and exporter of simple, domestic-type Georgian furniture, much of which was japanned.

GRICC, GUISEPPE, also known as **GRICCI, JOSEPH** or **JOSE.** The chief modeler of *Capo di Monte* porcelain. In 1760, Gricc became the director of the Real Fábrica de la China located at the Buen Retiro Palace in Madrid. He created the Porcelain Room in the Aranjuez Palace near Madrid for Charles III.
☐ ALSO SEE 373, *1886,* 1888-89, *1890,* 2112, *2142,* 2153, 2155-66

GRIFFIN. A decorative device. A monster with the body of a lion and the head and wings of an eagle. In antiquity, the griffin was associated with fire, and thus often appears on friezes with candelabras. In heraldry, the griffin represents wisdom and watchfulness and was popular in Gothic architecture. The Adam brothers and later Empire style used the griffin as a decorative motif.

GRILLE. A metal, usually brass, lattice or trellis used in place of glass on cabinet doors, etc. Adam and Hepplewhite made extensive use of this textural material. Often rosettes and other ornaments were added on the intersections of the crisscrossing wires or rods. A late-18th-century Sheraton design is illustrated.

GRIS TRIANON. A soft, grayish, off-white color used for late-18th-century French painted furniture. See *Blanc de Plomb.*

GRISAILLE. A monochromatic painting in neutral grays or beiges only, which gives the effect of a sculptured relief panel. It was popular as a trompe l'oeil painting technique for overdoors or overmantels in the Louis XVI period. Piat Joseph Sauvage was an outstanding painter of the time in that technique. The grisaille may also serve as a first stage for an oil painting, or it may serve as a model for an engraver. Adam, Sheraton, and Hepplewhite used grisaille medallions and plaques to decorate and enhance their furniture. Angelica Kauffmann and Giovanni Battista Cipriani also painted in this style.
☐ ALSO SEE 38, *1196,* 1198, *2053, 2055*

GROS POINT. A coarse tapestry effect produced by using cross-stitching on net, canvas, or coarse linen. The embroidery threads are usually woolen and there are approximately twelve stitches to the lineal inch.
☐ ALSO SEE 482, 537-39

GROSGRAIN. Ribbed or rep silk. The cords are close together and are rounder than those of faille. It is used for draperies and ribbon decorations.

GROTESQUES (GROTTESQUES). Decorations in antiquity like sphinxes, masks, or fantastic monsters which combined human with plant and animal forms in a free manner: winged females,

GRIFFIN

GRILLE

GRILLE

GRISAILLE

GROTESQUE

GUADAMICIL

GUÉRIDON

GUILLOCHE

GUILLOCHE

GUINEA HOLES

GUNSTON HALL

mermaids, etc. These classic ornaments were rediscovered in grottos, hence the name. Raphael was one of the first Renaissance artists to make use of these motifs.

☐ ALSO SEE 1308, *1309*

GUADAMICIL. A leather "tapestry" or decorated hanging. The technique was introduced into Europe in the 11th century by the Arabs from Morocco. It was first produced in Guadamicileria, Spain, in the 16th century. In the 17th and 18th centuries. leather tapestries were produced in France, the Netherlands, England, Germany, and Italy under such names as Cordovan or Moroccan (Maroquin) tapestries. Illustrated is an early-17th-century Spanish chair of carved walnut with embossed leather covering. See *Gilded Leather*.

GUÉRIDON. A small ornamental stand or pedestal. A little round table popular in the late Queen Anne period and adopted from France, where it appeared during the reign of Louis XIII. In the Chippendale design shown, it is also used as a candlestand. See *Torchère*.

☐ ALSO SEE 524, 672, 1226, *1235, 1529*, 1531, *1607, 1651*

GUÉRIDON À CRÉMAILLIÈRE. A small round table or candle-holder of the Louis XVI period. Its main feature was that it could be adjusted to various heights by means of a toothed (crémaillière) support which set into three supporting feet. The table usually was made of mahogany and had a marble top and a gilt brass gallery.

GUERITE. The French word for "sentry box." A high-backed, hooded armchair which enveloped the seated person and also kept out the draughts. In the 18th century it was interpreted in wicker, and the design became a popular piece of garden furniture. Today this piece of wicker furniture is seen on the beaches of French and Italian resorts.

GUILLOCHE. A geometric classic band or border pattern of overlapping or interlacing circular forms. The circles are sometimes filled with ornamental designs. It was much used in Renaissance and Victorian Renaissance furniture and architecture.

GUIMARD, HECTOR (1867–1942). A French architect and furniture designer. Greatly influenced by Victor Horta, he became the French interpreter of the art nouveau style. One of his most noted pieces in this style is the entrance gate to the Métro stations in Paris. The cast iron has been shaped into elegant, twisted, curving, flowerlike forms. In 1938, Guimard moved to New York. See *Horta, (Baron) Victor*.

☐ ALSO SEE 1586-87, 1601, 1608-09, *1610*

GUIMPE. See *Gimp*.

GUINEA HOLES or POCKETS. Dished or scooped-out areas in a gaming table to hold money or chips. It was an 18th-century English device. See *Dished*.

GUNSTON HALL. Built in 1755, near Mount Vernon, for George Mason. The one-and-a-half-story building has a steep gabled roof with dormers and pairs of tall chimneys at either end. There is a central hall with two rooms on either side of it. William Buckland was brought from England to create and supervise the magnificent woodwork for this house. The Chippendale dining room was the first in the Colonies done in the "Chinese style." The drawing room is Palladian in concept. See *Buckland, William.*

H STRETCHER. A reinforcing element for chair, table, and case furniture legs. A wooden piece, or turning, connects each front leg with the leg immediately behind it. A crosspiece from one of these connecting pieces to the other forms an H. A Chinese Chippendale chair is illustrated.

H STRETCHER

HABILLÉE. An art appliqué form in which actual pieces of fabric, lace, etc., are pasted onto a picture. These textures and materials are used to represent clothing, drapery, upholstery, etc.

HADLEY CHEST. An early American (c. 1700), New England chest on four legs. The chest had one, two, or three drawers, and would vary in height (according to the number of drawers) from 32" to 46". These units were decorated with simple incised carvings, and stained red, mulberry, or black. The owner's initials were often carved on the central panel. The top, body of drawers, and back were usually made of pinewood.

HAIG, THOMAS. An 18th-century English cabinetmaker, and partner of Thomas Chippendale II.

HALF TIMBER

HALF TIMBER. A form of Gothic house construction in which the heavy beams and posts form the visible skeleton on the interior as well as the exterior of the structure. The areas between the heavy wood construction were filled with wattle and daub, plaster, stone or brick. Illustrated is a 15th-century dwelling in Rouen.

HALF TURNING. See *Split Spindle.*

HALFPENNY, WILLIAM. An 18th-century English carpenter and architect who helped popularize the Chinese trend in architecture and decoration. In collaboration with his son, he published many books during the early part of the 18th century, including *The Modern Builder's Assistant* and *New Design for Chinese Temples, Triumphal Arches, Garden Seats, Railings, etc.* A pig-tailed Chinese mandarin, with umbrella, often was crowded into his ceilings, over chimneypieces, etc.

WILLIAM HALFPENNY

HALL CHAIRS. 18th-century English formal chairs, usually with decorative backs, originated by Manwaring, and also designed by Chippendale and Sheraton. A late-18th-century Sheraton design is illustrated. See *Light Chair* and *Side Chair.*

HALL CLOCK. See *Grandfather (long case) Clock.* A Sheraton-type case clock of the late 18th century is illustrated.

HALL CLOCK

HALLET, WILLIAM (1707–1781). A cabinetmaker under George II.

HALLMARK. The mark or stamp of official approval of quality that usually appears on metalwork.

☐ ALSO SEE *36,* 56, *84,* 98, 388, 399, 401, *435,* 484, 601-02, 715, *961,* 1167, 1199-1200. *1286,* 1288, 1302, 1626, 1784-86, 1902, 1939, 2025-26, 2068, 2079, 2083, 2128-31

HALL CHAIR

HAMPTON COURT PALACE. A classic example of the domestic architecture of the Tudor period. It was built for Cardinal Wolsey, and the original structure, begun in 1514, was of mellow red brickwork in a diaper pattern with battlement parapets. The brickwork chimneys, the hammer-beam roof, oriel window, terra-cotta busts of the Roman emperors by Giovanni da Maiano, and the many courts are noteworthy details. Sir Christopher Wren redid the Eastern portion in the 17th century in the Renaissance style. Illustrated is the gateway of the west front.

☐ ALSO SEE 429, *475*, 476-77, 480-82, 503, 1123, 2121

HAMPTON COURT PALACE

HANDKERCHIEF TABLE. A small American corner table. The handkerchief table had three legs, a triangular top, and a triangular drop leaf supported by a swing leg when opened. The table derives its name from its resemblance to a folded handkerchief.

HANDLES. Knobs or pulls used on furniture. In the Jacobean period in England wood turnings and wrought iron were favored. Brass handles were introduced into England during the William and Mary period. In France, mounts and handles were chased and engraved and made of ormolu, and were often works of art. The ring hanging from the lion's mouth was one of Sheraton's favorite handle designs (see *Hardware*).

HANDLE

HANDLE

HANGING SHELVES. Wall-attached units used for the display of books, plates, and china collections. These shelves were very popular in the late 17th and through the 18th century in France and England. Chippendale designed Chinese or Gothic types (see illustration). In the 19th-century Victorian period, many hanging "whatnots" or "knickknack" shelves were the vogue.

HANGING SHELVES

HANGINGS. Draperies on tester beds or window curtains and draperies. The term may also refer to wall tapestries or arras. The fabric embellishment may be made of damask, brocade, cotton, linen, wool, leather, etc. A 16th-century wall hanging from the Palace of Fontainebleau is illustrated. See *Arras, Guadamicil, Tapestry,* and *Wachstuch-Tapete.*

HARD PASTE. True porcelain made of kaolin or China clay.

HARDOUIN-MANSART, JULES (1646–1708). French architect who took over from Louis Le Vau the work on Versailles after 1679. He is credited with creating the Hall of Mirrors. His other works include the dome and chapel of Les Invalides, the Place Vendôme and Place des Victoires, the Grand Trianon, and Marly.

HANGING

HARDWARE. In cabinetry, metal handles, pulls, escutcheons, hinges, decorative push plates, etc. They are also called mounts.

HARICOT. French for "kidney bean." A crescent- or bean-shaped small Louis XV table with cabriole legs and small drawers set into the curved apron.

HARLEQUIN TABLE. A gadgety, complicated dressing-writing table, of the end of the 18th century. It was designed with hidden compartments, pigeonholes, small drawers, etc. Shera-

HARDWARE

HARLEQUIN TABLE

ton and Shearer both designed these pieces. See *Rachet* illustration for a lever system devised by Sheraton to raise the various surfaces and compartments.

HARPSICHORD. A piano-type instrument which preceded the pianoforte of the 18th century. The strings are plucked by means of quills which are attached to levers. It works on the same principle as the spinet and virginal.
☐ ALSO SEE *451*, 452-53, 791-95

HARRATEEN. An 18th-century woven curtain material.

HARRISON, PETER (1716–1775). Harrison is considered the first American architect in that he prepared sketches for others to build from. His best known works are in Newport, Rhode Island, and he made it the center of architectural art in colonial New England. Among his designs are: Redwood Library at Newport (liberally based on plates from Palladio's work, Kent's *Designs of Inigo Jones,* and Langley's *Treasury of Design*), King's Chapel, Boston (with assistance from James Gibbs's *Book of Architecture*), and his masterpiece, the Synagogue of the Congregation Jeshuat Israel (known as Touro Synagogue) which was begun in 1759 and is the oldest synagogue in the United States. See *Touro Synagogue*. Harrison was probably the American master of the British version of the Renaissance.

HARVARD CHAIR. An early American (17th-century) version of a Gothic-type three-cornered chair made of wood turnings.

HARVEST TABLE. A long, narrow, drop-leaf table. The legs may be straight or turned, and the flaps have either squared ends, or they are gently rounded. The design is usually associated with 18th-century American furniture.

HASP

HASP. In a hinge lock, the hinged part which swings over the pin. In Spanish Gothic chests, the hasp was usually an ornate piece of metalwork.

HAUSMALEREI. Homemade and amateurish German pottery. The pieces were partially fired, then decorated and returned to the kiln for glazing and further firing. See *Firing*.

HAUT BOY. See *High Boy*.

HAUT RELIEF: In sculpture and ornament, high relief as opposed to bas-relief. See *High Relief*.

HAUT RELIEF

HEART AND CROWN. A pierced motif carved on the cresting of a baluster chair of the late 17th century in England.

HEART-SHAPED CHAIR BACK. A typical 18th-century Hepplewhite shield chair back which resembles a heart.

HEART-SHAPED
CHAIR BACK

HELLENISTIC. Greek art under Alexander in the third century B.C. It is a realistic and emotional form of art with the Roman influence interpreting the Greek forms.

HENRI II and III. The rulers of France during the 16th century whose reigns form part of the mid-French-Renaissance period. The period was noteworthy for its carvings and interlaced strapwork.
☐ ALSO SEE 368, 1178, 1180-83, *1190*, 1193, 1199, 1202, 1242, 2121

HENRY II AND III

GEORGE HEPPLEWHITE

HEPPLEWHITE, GEORGE. An 18th-century English furniture designer who worked in the classic style. In 1788, he published *Cabinet-Maker and Upholsterers Guide*. His work was characterized by lightness of construction, elegant curvilinear forms, and perfection of workmanship. Hepplewhite used heart-shaped and shield chair backs carved with wheat ears, fern leaves, honeysuckle, swags, and Prince of Wales feathers. He designed japanned furniture with fruit and flowers on a black ground, as well as satinwood and inlaid pieces. Hepplewhite favored the spade foot for his delicately grooved and fluted chair legs.

☐ ALSO SEE 105-06, 133, 765, 839-43, 2067

HERCULANEUM. A historic Roman city which was excavated about the middle of the 18th century, and became a source of inspiration for the classic designers of the 18th century in France and England. The influence of Herculaneum is found in the architecture and interior designs of the Adam brothers in England and is the basis of the Louis XVI style in France. Herculaneum also refers to an antique Roman-type chair designed by Sheraton in the late 18th century. Also shown is a bronze stand excavated at Herculaneum. See *Pompeii*.

HERCULANEUM

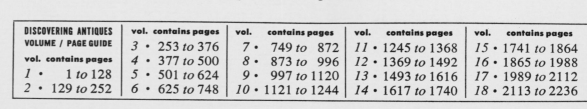

HERCULANEUM

HEX SIGN. A Pennsylvania Dutch motif for good luck, or to ward off evil spirits. It is usually a variation on a circle with a six-pointed star or another geometric motif enclosed in the circle. The design was painted on barns and houses, and used decoratively on chests, furniture, etc. The hex was, and still is, usually painted in bright, pure colors.

HICKS, EDWARD (1780-1849). An American naïve painter whose most famous work is *The Peaceful Kingdom*, which exists in about one hundred versions. These paintings illustrate a prophecy from the Book of Isaiah, showing the lion lying down with the lamb, and are often embellished with scriptural texts. Many of Hicks' paintings were inn signs, taken from popular prints.

☐ ALSO SEE *92*, 175, *176*

HIGH DADDY. An 18th-century American tall chest unit of six or more graduated drawers.

HIGH RELIEF. Sculpture the figures of which are carved out from the background to the extent of at least half their total mass, so that they appear almost detached or full round. See *Haut Relief*.

HIGH RELIEF

HIGHBOY. A tall chest of four or five drawers, on legs, with a cornice or pediment crown. It was originally mounted on a dressing table. The design was introduced from Holland into England during the William and Mary period, and was popular in America through the 18th century. Illustrated is a mid-18th-century flat-top New England highboy. The name may be derived from the French "hautbois" (high wood).

☐ ALSO SEE 58-60, 88-89, 380

HIGHBOY

HILLIARD, NICHOLAS (c. 1547-1619). An English miniature painter, limner, and goldsmith to Queen Elizabeth I. He created highly stylized portraits, emphasizing linear design and

HISPANO MAURESQUE

pattern, and he was much sought after for his ability to portray the sense of poetry and symbolism which were embodied in the spirit of the Elizabethan Age. The majority of his works are inscribed in gold against a blue oval background.

☐ ALSO SEE 369, 381-86, 459

HISPANO MAURESQUE. Spanish art influenced by Moorish designs. It was a part of the Gothic or Medieval period in Spain, and lasted for several hundred years. The Gothic Cathedral of Toledo (1227–1493) is typical of the Moorish craftsman's influence on Spanish architecture: horseshoe arches, pierced stonework, tracery, and rich surface decoration.

☐ ALSO SEE 1029, 2123-27

HISTORIATED

HISTORIATED. Ornamented with figures, animals, etc., which are representational or symbolic. Historiated initials were a popular expression in medieval manuscripts.

☐ ALSO SEE 1809

HITCHCOCK, LAMBERT (1795–1852). An American designer working in Connecticut. He was the designer of the "Hitchcock chair," which was derived from the Sheraton "pillow back" or oval-turned top rail chair. The chair usually was painted black, and had a rush or cane seat, turned, splayed front legs, and gold stenciled fruit and flower decoration of the wide top rail.

☐ ALSO SEE *154*, 155-56

LAMBERT HITCHCOCK

HOCHRELIEF. German for "high relief."

HÖCHST PORCELAIN. A hard-paste porcelain made in Höchst, Germany, during the late 18th century. The factory produced detailed and brightly enameled rococo figurines and tableware.

HOCK LEG. Also called "broken cabriole leg." The curve is broken below the "knee" on the inner side. The sides of the "knees" are sometimes ornamented with carved spiral scrolls called "ears." See *Cabriole Leg*.

HOCK LEG

HOFFMAN, JOSEPH (1870–1956). An Austrian decorator and architect who was the taste and pace setter for Austrian decor in the first three decades of the 20th century. The Palais Stoclet in Brussels (1905–1911) is probably his masterpiece, and in it one can see his subtle compositions which are based on simple geometric forms (rectangles and squares) with delicately handled trims.

☐ ALSO SEE 248, 1593, *1726*, 1727-30

HOGARTH, WILLIAM (1697–1764). A noted painter and illustrator of the life in 18th-century England. He did many series of famous etchings. Illustrated is "Temple Bar."

☐ ALSO SEE 59, 61-62, 572, *573*, *595*, *596*, *599*, 601, *625*, 627, *629*, 818, *910*, 925, 949, 2159-60

WILLIAM HOGARTH

HOGARTH CHAIR. A decorated Queen Anne chair with heavy "knees" and modified cabriole legs. The hoop back is usually hollow-crested and it has a pierced splat.

HOGARTH CHAIR

HOKUSAI, KATSUSHIKA (1760-1849). A Japanese painter and woodblock-print artist. Hokusai was one of the last great representatives of *ukiyo-e,* the popular genre style of Japanese prints. Although he is regarded chiefly as a landscape artist, famous for his *Thirty-Six Views of Fuji,* Hokusai also produced bird and flower prints, as well as prints of figures. Besides woodblock prints, his abundant and varied output includes paintings, sketches, illustrated books, and textile designs.

☐ ALSO SEE 333, 344, 346, 375

HOLLAND, HENRY (1740-1806). An English architect-decorator.

☐ ALSO SEE 720, 779, 913, 917, 930-33, 941, 995

HOM. The Assyrian "tree of life" pattern.

HONEYSUCKLE

HONEYSUCKLE

HONEYSUCKLE. A Greek decoration resembling a conventionalized fanlike arrangement of petals. It is also called "anthemion." It appears on Renaissance furniture as a carved enrichment, and Hepplewhite used it for a chair back design. Adam created a "swag" of honeysuckles to decorate panels, girandoles, furniture, etc.

HOOD

HOOD. In furniture, the case enclosing the dial and works of a grandfather or long case clock. Also see *Hooded Tops.* In architecture, a sheltering overhang.

HOODED TOPS. The rounded tops of cabinets, especially those of the early Queen Anne period (early 18th century in England). They are also called domed, curved, rounded, or semicircular tops.

HOOF FOOT. See *Cloven Foot, Does'-Foot Leg,* and *Pied de Biche.* Illustrated is a Queen Anne marquetry chair with hoof feet.

HOODED TOP

HOOF FOOT

HOOKED RUG. A pile-surfaced rug made of threads or strips of cloth pushed through a canvas backing. Another kind of hooked rug is that made of braided strips of wool or other strips of cloth. The braid is shaped around and sewn together in an oval or circular shape. Color and patterns are unlimited.

HOOPBACK CHAIR. A chair, the uprights and top rail of whose back form a continuous curve or hoop. It appears in the Queen Anne period, and was also prominent in the Hepplewhite period.

HOOPBACK CHAIR

HOPE, THOMAS (1770–1831). The leading furniture designer in the Empire style in England, which is correctly termed the English Regency period. His book of furniture designs, *Household Furniture and Interior Decorations,* published in 1807, had great influence and moderated the extravagant pseudoclassical style of the time. See *Regency (English).*

☐ ALSO SEE 134, *931,* 933, 956, 959, 962

THOMAS HOPE

HOPE CHEST. See *Cassone* and *Cedar Chest.*

HORSE. A simple support for a trestle table. It may be an inverted V or a shaped piece as illustrated in this Tudor period table (early 16th century).

HORSE

HORSE SCREEN. An English term for a "cheval screen." A fire screen with two bracketed feet. A Chippendale design is illustrated. See *Cheval Screen.*

HORSEHAIR. A furniture covering woven from the hair of a horse's tail and mane. Hepplewhite used it as an upholstery material, and it was most prominent in the Victorian period. It is stiff, sturdy, and generally quite dark in color.

HORSE SCREEN

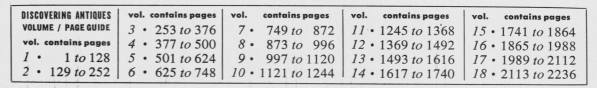

HORSESHOE TABLE. A horseshoe-shaped table, about 30" wide, and popular in the late 18th century. See *Hunt Table* and *Wine Table*.

HORTA, (BARON) VICTOR (1861–1947). A Belgian architect who created in the Art Nouveau style. Two of his most noted works are the home of Baron von Eetveldes (1895) and the "Maison du Peuple" (1896). The interior architecture, in both structures, is significant for the irregularly shaped rooms which open freely onto one another at different levels. The iron balustrades are typically Art Nouveau in their twisted, plantlike elements, as is the curving sweep of mosaic floors, plaster walls, etc. His later works are more traditional.

☐ ALSO SEE 225-29, 245-46, 1601

HOUDON, JEAN-ANTOINE (1741–1828). A great French realist sculptor who made portrait busts of many aristocrats, artists, and philosophers of Europe, as well as American statesmen. Among his noted works are: "Voltaire" (illustrated), "Franklin," "Molière," "Diderot," and "Washington."

☐ ALSO SEE 131, *132*, 1484-85

JEAN-ANTOINE HOUDON

HOURGLASS BASE. A typically Regency base for stools, benches, and sometimes chairs. The base is made up of two curved elements, one set on top of the other to create a rounded X shape. Examples of this base can be seen in earlier 18th-century stools and chairs by Chippendale, Adam, and Sheraton.

HOURGLASS BASE

HOUSEWRIGHT. An 18th-century American term for builders of homes and public buildings. These craftsmen were not architects in the recognized sense of the word. The term was originally used by Richard Munday, who in the early 18th century was one of the foremost builders in Newport, Rhode Island (Trinity Church and Old Colony House).

HUCHIERS-MENUISIERS. The French term for furniture makers of the early French Renaissance period. Literally the term means "hutch carpenters." Illustrated is a crédence of the late 16th century (period of Henri II).

HUCHIERS-MENUISIERS

HUDSON RIVER SCHOOL (1825–1870). A 19th-century American school of romantic landscape painters who glorified nature in their paintings. Washington Allston and Thomas Cole were major artists of the group, as were Frederick Edwin Church and Albert Bierstadt.

HUET, CHRISTOPHE. French artist during the reign of Louis XV. He created many chinoiserie-rococo designs: mandarins, pagodas, parasols, monkeys (singeries), ladders, and fantastic foliage.

☐ ALSO SEE *1312, 1337, 1341*

HUET, JEAN-BAPTISTE (1745–1811). A French designer of toiles de Jouy for Christophe-Philippe Oberkampf, and wallpapers for Réveillon. His designs were full of grace, charm, animation, and a touch of humor. After the French Revolution, he created architectural and geometric backgrounds against which were set medallions, classic figures, and arabesques. These early designs were usually printed by a cylinder printing machine.

☐ ALSO SEE *1306*, 1308, 1481

HUNT TABLE. A popular 18th-century English table, with a horseshoe-shaped top surface. The table often had drop leaves at the two ends of the horseshoe. A swinging decanter stand (which followed the inner edge) was sometimes added.

HUNTING CHAIR. An 18th-century Sheraton chair design with a special wood strip or footrest in front.

HURD, JACOB (1702-1758). A prominent American silversmith from Boston.
☐ ALSO SEE 62-63, *64*, 127

HURRICANE LAMP. A tall, glass cylinder shade set over a candlestick to protect the flame. It was introduced in the late 17th century and used through the 18th century. In current decorating, hurricane lamps are often used in pairs trimmed with prisms, and flame-shaped bulbs have replaced the candles. It is similar to the 19th-century *Girandole* or *Lustre*.

HUSK ORNAMENT

HUSK ORNAMENT. A decorative representation of the husks of oats when ripe. The spreading of the husk into two halves makes it possible to create a chainlike pattern by having husk drooping from husk. This motif was very popular in England in the Adam and Sheraton periods. It was used as an inlay design, as a composition ornament of walls and ceilings in painted decoration, and also by Wedgwood on his jasper pottery. A section of an Adam mantel is illustrated. See *Bell-flower Ornament*.

HUTCH

HUTCH or HUCHE. "Huche" is Old French for "bin" or "chest." Originally a Gothic chest. In current usage, a hutch is a cabinet or cupboard placed over a buffet unit. The cupboard part may be left completely open, or have doors on two sides with an open shelving area in the middle. See *Ménagère*.

HYDRIA

HUYGENS. A 17th-century Hollander who was brought to France during the reign of Louis XIV by Charles Le Brun. He was a furniture designer especially noted for his lacquerwork.
☐ ALSO SEE 518-20, 1973-74, 1977

HYDRIA. A Greek three-handled water jar.

HYPOSTYLE. A covered hall, the roof of which rests on pillars or columns. The two central rows may be higher than those at the sides. This accomplishes what the clerestory does: allows more light into the interior. Illustrated is the early Egyptian Hypostyle Hall of Karnak.

HYPOSTYLE

ICON. An image or portrait depicting a sacred figure. The worship of painted images is first mentioned in the 5th century, and the earliest surviving icons, found in the monastery of Saint Catherine on Mount Sinai, are from the 6th century. Icons were important in early Christian, Greek, and Russian churches.
☐ ALSO SEE 2033-35

ICONOCLASTIC MOVEMENT. In the early 8th century, sculptural representations of humans or animals were prohibited by the Eastern Emperor Leo III. He feared that the statues might foster paganism and idolatry. The resultant typically Byzantine and near-Eastern decoration was dependent upon floral and geometric patterns in rich color and texture.

ICONOCLASTIC MOVEMENT

ICONOSTASIS. A three-doored partition which screened off the apse with the altar in the sanctuary. This was typical of most Byzantine church plans. This screen was often decorated with many tiers of icons (religious portraits). The iconostasis was a characteristic of Russian churches of the 15th and 16th centuries. This screen differs from the retable in that the latter served as a background to the services while the iconostasis shielded the people from viewing the rites which were conducted behind the screen. See *Retable*.
☐ ALSO SEE 2034, *2038,* 2041, 2065

IDEOGRAPH. The illustration of an idea, word, or object. See *Rebus*.

IKKWAN. A great Japanese carver of *netsuke* of the mid-19th century.
☐ ALSO SEE *317,* 318, 375

ILLUMINATION

ILLUMINATION. The medieval art of hand-decorating manuscripts with scrolls, arabesques, foliage, etc., in rich color and gold and silver. Religious manuscripts were often greatly enriched with colored illumination. See *Historiated*.

ILLUSIONISM. See *Trompe l'Oeil*.

IMARI WARE. A term used loosely to describe a variety of Japanese porcelain styles brought to Europe from the Arita region of Hizan Province by Dutch traders in the late 17th and early 18th centuries. The porcelain is characterized by soft shades of green, blue, yellow, and orange-red, with typical Japanese design.
☐ ALSO SEE 322, *324-25,* 351, 375

IMBRICATE. To place in overlapping tiers or to give a fish-scale-like appearance. A technique used for tile roofs and also on columns, walls, etc.

IMBRICATE

IMPASTO. An oil painting technique developed by Titian. Thin layers of opaque pigment and oil glazes are used to create a depth of color. When so many layers are applied as make the paint appear thick or lumpy, and the brush strokes are clearly evident, the painting is said to be "heavily impasted."

IMPRESSIONISM. One of the first of the modern art movements in the 19th century. The aim was to achieve greater naturalism by analysis of tone and color, and the rendering of light on surfaces. Paint was often dabbed on in bright colors, even in the shadows. There was a lack of firm outline. Major Impressionists were: Claude Monet, Camille Pissaro, and Alfred Sisley.
☐ ALSO SEE 1580-84

INCE, WILLIAM. An 18th-century English cabinetmaker, and follower of Chippendale. With Thomas Mayhew, he published *The Universal System of Household Furniture,* from 1762–1763. It contained designs for lanthorns, sideboard tables, bookcases, beds, etc. Ince used fretwork, combined with Chinese and Gothic motifs, and chair backs carved with ribbons and scrolls and patterned with brass nails. See *Mayhew, Thomas*.
☐ ALSO SEE *635,* 638, 675, 732, 733, 752, 765

INCISED. The opposite of relief carving. The pattern is produced by cutting or etching into the material. The design is engraved below the surface. See *Intaglio*.

WILLIAM INCE

INCISED LACQUER. Several coats of lacquer are applied to create a certain thickness. A design is then cut or carved into this thickness. This form of decoration was used on Chinese-style lacquered furniture and screens.

INDIA PAPERS. (Also called Japan papers.) Chinese papers that were imported into Europe in the mid-17th century by means of the Dutch, French, and English East India companies; hence the name "India papers." See *Chinese Wallpaper*.

INDIENNE FABRICS. The French interpretation of India print cottons made during the late 17th and the 18th centuries. See *Toiles d'Indy*.

INDITIA. An altar cloth, often elaborately embroidered.
☐ ALSO SEE *2034*, 2035

INGRAIN. A reversible, flat woven wool, or wool and cotton, carpet made on a Jacquard loom. The ground color on one side becomes the top or design color on the reverse side. Ingrain is also a woven, multicolored fabric with a flat weave. The threads are dyed before they are woven.

INLAY. A technique in which a design is cut out of the surface to be decorated and then filled in with other contrasting materials cut to fit exactly into these openings. The contrast of color or materials creates the decoration. The inserts may be of wood veneer, metals, shells, ivory, etc. Illustrated is a Hepplewhite tabletop. See *Boulle Work, Certosina, Intarsia or Tarsia,* and *Marquetry*.

INLAY

☐ ALSO SEE Bronzes 1816, *1817*
Firearms 897, *899*, *1526*, 1527
Furniture 137, 293, 362-64, *418*, 420, 481, *702*, 789, 825-26, 956, *1087-88*, 1106-07, *1129*, *1203-04*, *1224-28*, 1225, 1345-46, 1381-82, *1457*, 1459, *1502-03*, 1504, 1552, 1622, 1624-25, 1652, *1655*, *1745-47*, 1746-48, *1800*, 1801-04, 1829, *1894*, 1948, 1951, *2162*
Ivory 336, *337*
Jade *300*, 1751

INLAY, IMITATION. A painted decoration or decalcomania which simulates inlay work, but is recognizable by its smooth, uninterrupted surface.

INSET PILASTER

INRO. A Japanese lacquered seal-case hung from the kimono girdle and held by a *netsuke* at the end of two cords.
☐ ALSO SEE 315, *317-18*, 319, 335, 375

INSET PILASTER. A flat half column set against a flush surface, usually at the front corners of a chest, cabinet, or other case piece. Illustrated is a late 16th-century chest.

INSET PILASTER

INTAGLIO. Designs cut out of a surface, leaving a relief in reverse. The finished design is below the plane which has been worked upon.

INTAGLIO ENGRAVING. Distinguished from other metal plate engraving techniques by the printing process used. The ink

DISCOVERING ANTIQUES VOLUME / PAGE GUIDE	vol.	contains pages	vol.	contains pages	vol.	contains pages	vol.	contains pages
vol. • contains pages	*3* •	253 *to* 376	*7* •	749 *to* 872	*11* •	1245 *to* 1368	*15* •	1741 *to* 1864
	4 •	377 *to* 500	*8* •	873 *to* 996	*12* •	1369 *to* 1492	*16* •	1865 *to* 1988
1 •	1 *to* 128	*5* •	501 *to* 624	*9* •	997 *to* 1120	*13* •	1493 *to* 1616	*17* •	1989 *to* 2112
2 •	129 *to* 252	*6* •	625 *to* 748	*10* •	1121 *to* 1244	*14* •	1617 *to* 1740	*18* •	2113 *to* 2236

lies in the engraved furrows, rather than on the smooth surface. A piece of paper is dampened and laid on the plate, and both are rolled through a mangle-like heavy press. The damp paper is forced into the furrows, and picks up the ink. When the paper is dry, the engraved inked lines stand up in relief. See *Aquatint, Drypoint Engraving, Etching, Line Engraving,* and *Mezzotint.*
☐ ALSO SEE 544-47, 1636, *2089*

INTAILLE. French for "intaglio."

INTARSIA

INTARSIA or TARSIA. Incised work which is inlaid with contrasting materials. A type of mosaic. It was used by the Italian designers in the early Renaissance period who used shell, bone, and ivory inserts. Illustrated is intarsia work from a stall in Santa Maria Novella in Florence. See *Certosina, Inlay, Intarsio,* and *Nonsuch Furniture.*
☐ ALSO SEE 364, *365,* 1622, 1625

INTARSIATURA. Italian for "marquetry."

INTARSIO. Pictures executed in wood veneers and inlays. A highly sophisticated form of inlay.

INTERLACED CHAIR BACKS. An interlaced strap or ribbon-back chair similar in character to fretwork. It was used in late-18th-century French furniture, and in the Chippendale and Hepplewhite styles.

INTERLACED CHAIR BACK

INTERRUPTED ARCH. An arched pediment top for cabinets and chests of the 18th century. The apex or top central segment of the arch is missing. See *Broken Pediment.*

INTONACO. The final layer of wet plaster upon which the fresco artist actually works. The final coat is applied to just that area which the painter will be able to cover before the plaster dries. See *Arricciato* and *Fresco.*

INTERRUPTED ARCH

INVERTED CUP. A detail in the wood-turned shaped legs of the William and Mary period in England. The turning module resembles an inverted cup.

IONIC ORDER. A classical order of architecture and decoration. The spiral-shaped volute or scroll is characteristic of the capital. The Romans proportioned the columns at 9 diameters high. For an illustration of the Ionic capital, architrave, frieze, and cornice see *Zoophorus.*

IONIC ORDER

INVERTED CUP

IRIDESCENT GLASS. Shimmering Art Nouveau glassware, including Louis Tiffany's Favrile ware; also produced in Austria by Ludwig Lobmeyr and the Lötz factory.
☐ ALSO SEE 221, 224, 1716, 1732, *1733, 1734*

IRISH CHIPPENDALE. Mahogany furniture made in Ireland in the mid-18th century, and based on Chippendale drawings. The furniture lacked the refinement and lightness of the original Chippendale pieces. Lion masks and paw feet are often found on Irish Chippendale furniture.

ISABELLINA. The Spanish term for the Gothic phase of minute, detailed, patterned design. The Renaissance phase was termed "plateresco." "Manuelino" is the Portuguese counterpart of "Isabellina."

ISINGLASS. Thin, translucent sheets of mica which were used for fenestration in the 18th- and 19th-century homes.

ISABELLINA

IVORY

ISNIK POTTERY. Turkish under-glazed pottery known for very high quality in the 16th century. Most characteristic are large dishes, often with foliate rims, covered with floral arabesques. Tiles from Isnik were widely used to decorate mosques.
□ ALSO SEE 1575, *2174*, 2175-77

ISTORIATO. See *Historiated.*

IUVARA (or IVARA), FILIPPO (1676?-1736). Italian architect, born in Messina, chief architect to the House of Savoy. He designed the central portion of the Royal Palace, La Granja, near Segovia in Spain.
□ ALSO SEE *1822*, 1826, *1880*, 1881, 1883, 1891, *2140-41*

IVORY. The tusks of elephants, which has been and is still used for decorative inlay work and carving. It is a rare material but has been imitated in plastics. Illustrated is a 15th-century French 9½"-tall statue.
□ ALSO SEE Carved 246, 269-71, *297, 315, 316, 317, 318,* 319, 335-37,
398, *402, 566,* 567-69, 1336, *1685,* 1752, 1816, *1923, 2064*
Inlay 448, *732,* 1109, 1354, *1357,* 1625, 1745-48, 1800
Miniatures 838, 1756

IVY

IVY. A decorative leaf design. The leaf is the symbol of friendship, and was also sacred to Bacchus, and therefore appears on many ancient vases. The ivy leaf is usually broad, five-lobed, and appears at the end of long shoots in lancelike forms.

JABOT. A ruffle or frill. The cascading side pieces of a swag.

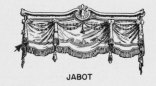

JABOT

JACKFIELD POTTERY. The English earthenware from Jackfield, Shropshire, introduced in 1713, characterized by a brilliant black glaze.
□ ALSO SEE 570, *571*

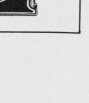

JACOB, FRANÇOIS HONORÉ GEORGES. A French cabinetmaker of the Louis XVI and Directoire periods. He also made and designed furniture for Napoleon.

JACOB, GEORGES. The father of the equally famous François Honoré Georges Jacob. A noted cabinetmaker of the Louis XVI period.
□ ALSO SEE 931-32, *1502,* 1503-06, 1509, *1529,* 1530,
1550, 1552, *1553*

JACOB-DESMALTER

JACOB-DESMALTER, FRANÇOIS-HONORÉ. An important cabinetmaker of the early 19th-century French Empire period. He executed designs created by Charles Percier. Illustrated is a piece of furniture of the type made by Jacob-Desmalter in mahogany embellished with bronze and gilt.
□ ALSO SEE 1504, *1519,* 1521-22, *1528,* 1531, 1551-52, *1553*

JACOBEAN

JACOBEAN. The period (1603–1649) in English architecture and art which extends over the reigns of James I and Charles I. It is a term which covers the merging of English Tudor designs and motifs with the Renaissance in England.
□ ALSO SEE 387-95, 398-421, 424-38, 458-61

JACOBEAN ORNAMENT

JACOBEAN ORNAMENT. Bands of molding applied to furniture in geometric patterns to create a paneled effect. This was a popular decoration on Jacobean furniture made in England in the 17th century. A table (c. 1630) is illustrated.

JACQUARD. In carpeting, the pattern control on the Wilton loom. It was invented by Joseph-Marie Jacquard in Brussels, Belgium, and adapted to the Wilton loom in 1825.

JACQUARD, JOSEPH-MARIE (1752–1834). The Frenchman who, in 1801, created the Jacquard loom, which revolutionized the production of figured woven textiles. The loom made it possible to produce certain multicolored designs inexpensively. In 1825, the loom was adapted for the carpet industry.
☐ ALSO SEE 140, *141*, 1033, *1035*, 1083-84, 1481, *1909*, *1926*, 1927, *1929*, 2092-94

JACQUARD WEAVE. A weave with intricate, multicolored patterns. It is produced on the type of loom created by Joseph-Marie Jacquard in the early 19th century. Damasks, tapestries, and brocades are all Jacquard weaves.

JACQUEMART AND BENARD. French wallpaper manufacturers from 1791 to 1840. They were the successors to Réveillon.

JALEE. In India, the decorated pierced marble or stone work such as was used in the Taj Mahal. Illustrated is an open-work stone window arch.

JALEE

JAPANNING. An 18th-century finishing process. Furniture and metalwork were enameled with colored shellac, and the decoration was in relief and painted in color and gilt. The technique was an imitation of the brilliant lacquered colors of the Japanese work which was imported by the Dutch into Europe during the 17th century. See *Lacquer* and *Martin Brothers*.
☐ ALSO SEE *57*, 58, 371-72, *448*, 449, 482-83, 524, *533*, 536, 720, 729, *732*, 763, 1007-10, 1336, 1857, *1894*, 1895

JARDINIÈRE. A plant container or stand made of wood, metal, or porcelain. The jardinière reached the height of elegance during the latter part of the 18th century in France and England. A Chippendale design is illustrated.
☐ ALSO SEE *1266*, 1325, 1531, *1675*

JARDINIÈRE

JARDINIÈRE VELVET. A silk velvet of several depths of uncut loops set against a damask or silk background. It is usually a multicolored pattern resembling a flower arrangement against a light satin background. The velvet was originally produced in Genoa.

JASPER WARE. An 18th-century type of hard bisquit ware (pottery) introduced by Wedgwood in England.
☐ ALSO SEE 636, *637*, *824*, 825-26, *827*, 828, 1382, 1704,1706, 2055

JEFFERSON, THOMAS (1743–1826). The third President of the United States, and a great political philosopher. He was interested in architecture, and besides designing his own home, Monticello, he was active in the planning of Washington, D.C. Jefferson was much impressed by Roman architecture, and he designed the Capitol in Richmond, Virginia (1785–1792) based on the Maison Carrée at Nîmes (see *Maison Carrée*). The rotunda of the University of Virginia in Charlottesville, Virginia (1822–1826), was planned by Jefferson in association with Benjamin Henry Latrobe.
☐ ALSO SEE *67*, 68, 90, *93*, 94-95, 130-32

THOMAS JEFFERSON: MONTICELLO

JET. A dense variety of lignite or anthracite found in coal formations. Jet is a soft black mineral that cuts well without splitting and can be highly polished.
☐ ALSO SEE 459, *461*, 1010, 1025-26, 1404, *1405*

JEWELING. Any small, ornamental feature carved on furniture or a building, either above or below the surface, to resemble a polished or cut jewel, Illustrated is an ornamental detail from a 16th-century English building.

JEWELING

JIGSAW DETAIL. A cutout or fretwork design made with a jigsaw. It was used for the enhancement of buildings of the mid and late 19th century. The bargework was often made with a jigsaw. The "gingerbread" or "steamboat Gothic," late Victorian period was jigsaw work in its most aggravated form.

JIGSAW MIRROR

JIGSAW MIRROR. A type of mirror that was popular in the 18th and 19th centuries in America and England. The earlier examples were hand cut, and had detailed scrolls, while 19th-century pieces were cut on a jigsaw, one of the first of the power-operated tools. Shown here is a Queen Anne type of mirror of the early 18th century.

JOHNSON, THOMAS. A mid-18th-century English carver of fanciful and eccentric girandoles, sconces, etc. He was a contemporary of Chippendale, and used a mixture of Gothic, Chinese, and Louis XV rococo styles.
□ ALSO SEE 672-74, *675, 730,* 732, 733

THOMAS JOHNSON

JOINT STOOL. A 17th- and 18th-century simple stool made of turnings, and joined together. An oak stool of the Jacobean period (17th century) is shown.

JOINT STOOL

JONES, INIGO (1572–1653). A famous English Renaissance architect who introduced the classic Palladian style into England. Besides designing assorted public buildings, and the Queen's House, Greenwich, he created fanciful and imaginative masques and balls for royalty. Jones has been called the English Palladio. Illustrated is the Banquet Hall at Whitehall. See *Palladio, Andrea.*
□ ALSO SEE 415-17, 442, 443, 554-55, 776, 1837, 1838

INIGO JONES

JONES, WILLIAM. An 18th-century English architect. In 1739, he published *The Gentleman's or Builder's Companion* with plates of chimneypieces, slab tables, pier glasses, tabernacle frames, ceilings, etc.

JUDGE'S CHAIR. An 18th-century high-back chair. The upholstered back is raised up from the seat, and curved to cradle the head and shoulders. The upholstered arms curve around at the same level as the bottom of the chair back. The arm stumps and back chair rails are exposed. The legs are squarish, and bracket out at the seat. Box stretchers connect the four legs.

JUGTOWN POTTERY. The early-American utilitarian pottery from Steeds, North Carolina, a mid-18th-century settlement of Staffordshire colonists.
□ ALSO SEE 47

JUGENDSTIL. German for "youth style." The period contemporary with the Art Nouveau of France (1895–1912).
□ ALSO SEE 245, 1716, 1726-30

JUVARA, FILIPPO. See *Iuvara (or Ivara), Filippo.*